An Introduction to Public Administration

An Introduction to Public Administration

Politics, Policy, and Bureaucracy

James W. Davis, Jr.

THE FREE PRESS
A Division of Macmillan Publishing Co., Inc.
New York

COLLIER MACMILLAN PUBLISHERS
London

353
D262i

The Free Press
A Division of Macmillan Publishing Co., Inc.
866 Third Avenue, New York, N.Y. 10022

Collier-Macmillan Canada Ltd.

Library of Congress Catalog Card Number: 73–16906

Printed in the United States of America

printing number

1   2   3   4   5   6   7   8   9   10

Library of Congress Cataloging in Publication Data

Davis, James Warren
    Politics, policy, and bureaucracy: an introduction to public administration.

    Includes bibliographical references.
    1. United States--Executive departments.
2. United States--Politics and government.
I. Title.
JK421.D38   353   73-16906
ISBN 0-02-907080-5

84-7784

Copyright Acknowledgement

The Powers of the Purse: Appropriations Politics in Congress, Richard I. Fenno, Jr., pp. 411, 412, 413. Copyright © 1966, by Little, Brown and Company (Inc.). Reprinted by permission.

Contents

Preface

Since this textbook has been written with students in mind, some instructors may not view it altogether favorably. Yet the students, who must read and understand the book, seem the proper audience to satisfy. I have tried to include material most likely to be at once useful and interesting to the largest number of students. I have tried primarily, though not exclusively, to focus on public administration as an *activity* rather than as a *discipline* or academic field.

The book deals largely with the national government. Although some instructors may question this apparently narrow focus, it rests on my experience in the classroom. Students read about the national government and national politics and commonly express more interest in this area than in state or local politics. If they have had any course in political science, it was probably American Government or American Politics. Similarly, their instructor is apt to be interested in national politics, and current illustrations of textbook topics will be found readily at the national level. Of course, for many topics—from organizational behavior to bureaucratic politics—there should be no dearth of state or local illustrations. Within limits, bureaucracies are bureaucracies.

To some readers the book will appear repetitive, but a text is a teaching and learning device, and one way to teach or learn is to repeat. I did not think it sufficient to have just one chapter on Congress and the bureaucracy; the role of Congress is further discussed in chapters on budgeting and on reorganization and, indeed, in another chapter focused on the President and the bureaucracy. Common bureaucratic goals such as growth and autonomy are brought up in several contexts, as are the general subjects of bureaucratic politics and agency conflict and competition. The aim is to develop a set of problems and questions that students will recall almost automatically in a variety of bureaucratic situations.

The book begins with some attention to the meaning of public administration and its context. The second chapter briefly describes the political and governmental context, including some material essential for the student with very little background in American government and emphasizing that public administration does not go on in a vacuum. Another chapter summarizes the policy process.

Part II focuses on executive branch organizations. It begins with a detailed review of the structure of the executive branch and the variety of its organizations and goes on to look at executive branch personnel. One chapter considers individual behavior in formal organizations, and another discusses the structural and operating characteristics of executive branch organizations.

Part III turns to bureaucratic politics. After focusing on politics inside bureaucratic organizations, attention turns to the relations between executive branch organizations and other participants in the policy-making/political process. Particular attention is paid to the relations between executive branch organizations and the President, the Congress, and the various interest groups active in American politics. What affects the relations between these institutions? Under what conditions may the President or Congress influence the behavior of bureaucrats and bureaucratic agencies? Under what conditions will administrative agencies be able to retain their autonomy? These are obviously political questions, but they are also questions that any student of public administration must be concerned with.

Part IV discusses various activities that go on within many if not all government organizations—program planning, budgeting, reorganization, and program evaluation. In a sense these can be viewed as administrative or management activities, but they obviously have policy impact and political implications. An epilogue draws on the growing future literature to suggest the possible course of the future bureaucracy.

Throughout the book, tabular data has been kept to a

minimum. As such things as budget and personnel data (and even organization titles) quickly get out of date, students should supplement the text by reference to such sources of current data as the *Budget of the United States,* the *Statistical Abstract,* the *U.S. Government Organization Manual,* agency annual reports, and so on. In addition, the text contains no extended case studies of administrative events. Given the number of cases now in print and the number of brief paperbacks readily available, it seems sensible to keep the text short and let the instructor and student supplement it as appropriate.

The brief selected bibliography includes books and articles that are especially useful or provocative, and a number of such items are also included in the footnotes. In addition, remember that the current press provides frequent illustrations of many topics discussed in the book. Three daily newspapers that are good sources of executive branch news are the *New York Times, The Washington Post,* and the *Wall Street Journal.* The latter includes much news on public policies and government agencies. A number of the magazines and journals that students may find useful include *Public Administration Review, The Public Interest, Public Policy, National Journal, Business Week, Policy Sciences,* and the *Washington Monthly.* In addition, professional political science journals (the *American Political Science Review,* for example) occasionally have articles bearing on one aspect or another of public administration.

In addition to reading widely the student should become actively involved in the subject of politics and administration by constantly asking questions. When you learn of an organization or official taking a particular position or proposing a particular course of action, ask why. What are the assumptions on which the behavior or proposal is based? What are the goals? What are the possible consequences, and what are the likely problems? Where are support and opposition likely to come from? To gain support or reduce opposition, what steps are possible? This last question illustrates an important mental habit—thinking in terms of alternatives or choices. How else could things be done? What else could be proposed or might be? What other solutions might work or at least be acceptable? How else could resources be allocated? How else can an organization be put together? To answer such questions, the student of administration needs to be able to see, foresee, and analyze problems. He needs wide familiarity with American politics and the social sciences, and he needs to be willing and able to do research. Most important he needs imagination. In the end the student of public administration must be part management or administrative analyst, part policy analyst, and part political analyst.

Like the author of any book, I have a number of debts, some of which need to be made explicit. I owe first the numerous writers and teachers who have given me ideas. I owe a great deal to students who have listened to and challenged me as I talked about the subjects in the book over the course of the last few years. I certainly owe thanks to The Free Press for putting up with many delays in the completion of the manuscript. And finally, I owe a great deal to Jean, Warren, and Clare. They let me write and tolerate cheerfully my reading and my writing.

James W. Davis, Jr.
ST. LOUIS

PART I A PRELIMINARY SURVEY

The three chapters of Part I constitute an introduction, provide some context for understanding public administration, and may for some students provide a review of familiar material. Chapter 1 provides a basic orientation and considers the meaning of public administration and public policy. Chapter 2 discusses very briefly the American political system. Chapter 3 considers the formation of public policy. Although I did not include a chapter on the socioeconomic context of American public administration, it is worth emphasizing that to understand public administration and public policy in any country, one must know something of its population and economy and indeed something of its history.

1 Approaching Public Administration

This is a book about public administration, but it emphasizes politics—bureaucratic politics and policy politics. Although intended for students of political science and American politics in public administration courses, it does not assume that most students will have a career in the civil service. Rather they will go into business, be doctors and lawyers and engineers, and follow numerous other careers. Such students do not need to know the details of management, but they will find it useful to know how bureaucracies operate and what they do. Every citizen today has direct contact with some organizations of the federal government—the Internal Revenue Service, the Social Security Administration, the Postal Service—and is affected by the work of many more—the Food and Drug Administration, the Federal Trade Commission, the National Highway Traffic Safety Administration, and the Environmental Protection Agency, to name only a few. In a sense we live in an administered world; government by bureaucracy is both a cliché and a reality. If the reader of this book is enabled to offer sensible explanations for what happens in bureaucratic organizations and perhaps make plausible forecasts, about how things will work and what can go wrong, then the book will have done its job.

A Definition of Public Administration

What is public administration? When you study public administration, what do you study?[1] For a start, public administration can be best identified with the executive branch of government. Political scientists interested in public administration have focused their research and writing on organizations and people in the executive branch of the government. Students who take graduate degrees in public administration commonly go to work in executive-branch organizations, the "civil service" or "the bureaucracy." Public administration has also been associated with a particular discipline or field of study—political science. Although many political scientists may think of public administration as a branch of political science, it may be more accurate today to view it as an independent field of professional study and activity to which and in which some political scientists contribute, along with economists, sociologists, statisticians, and indeed engineers. This broad interdisciplinary conception of public administration should make it patent that this book represents only the political-science part of public administration, not the part that would be written by an economist or someone from a business school.

Public administration, both as a subject of study and as a professional activity, contains a number of more or less separate fields. Traditional texts in the field include discussions of finance, personnel, and organization. Today one might add operations research, systems analysis, and policy planning. But the core of public administration is politics and public policy. Indeed public administration can be defined as the formulation, implementation, evaluation, and modification of public policy.

Why study public administration? There are a number of reasons. In my view it behooves the student interested in public policy to learn something about the organizations that in some measure develop it and in almost every case administer it. (We

---

1. On these subjects see James C. Charlesworth (ed.), *Theory and Practice of Public Administration: Scope, Objectives, and Methods* (Philadelphia: *The Annals* of the American Academy of Political and Social Science, 1968); Herbert Kaufman, "Emerging Conflicts in the Doctrine of Public Administration," *American Political Science Review*, 1956, 50 pp. 1057–1073; Dwight Waldo, *The Administrative State*, (New York: Ronald Press, 1948); Dwight Waldo, *The Study of Public Administration* (New York: Doubleday, 1955).

shall see as we go along that administration involves interpretation which means that to some degree administrators inevitably make policy.) Anyone interested in social change (or resistance to it) probably ought to be interested in the executive branch of the government.[2] And most generally anyone who wants to pretend to a thorough understanding of American politics and policy making must have some acquaintance with the bureaucracy. Finally, of course, some students may be considering government employment and for this reason find a course in public administration useful.

The Executive Branch: An Overview

Although most readers of this book probably have some understanding of what the executive branch includes or means, some discussion may be useful. The executive branch and the President are not synonymous. The executive branch contains the President but consists also of all the organizations—departments, agencies, administrations, bureaus, services, and commissions—that are in form supervised by the President.[3] "In form" is a term used here purposely. The executive branch is large, complex, and diffuse. It is millions of people and a multitude of organizations, and many of the men and organizations have substantial support in the political system quite apart from the President. We will inquire later into such relationships in detail. Here it suffices to emphasize that the President can be ignored and frustrated by personnel and organizations that on paper are clearly part of the executive branch. In the organization charts of the executive branch the President appears on top, but in practice this is often far from the case. Rather, the

---

2. The political columnist Richard Rovere has written: "During most of this century, most advocates of social change of any broad and consequential kind have felt that the federal government, and especially its executive branch, is the only really effective agency of change." In the same vein the sociologist Peter Blau has observed: "In the large and complex society of today the implementation of new social policies requires bureaucratic machinery." But it is also worth noting here that any particular bureaucratic organization may grow rigid and resist any change it views as detrimental to the organization's own best interest.

3. The student is strongly advised to find as soon as possible the current edition of the U.S. Government Organization Manual and leaf through it. States also have official manuals that provide useful organization overviews.

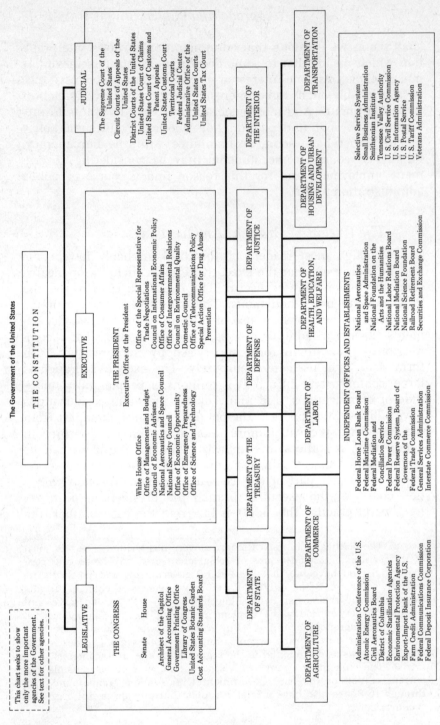

The Government of the United States

THE CONSTITUTION

LEGISLATIVE · EXECUTIVE · JUDICIAL

This chart seeks to show only the more important agencies of the Government. See text for other agencies.

LEGISLATIVE

THE CONGRESS

Senate   House

Architect of the Capitol
General Accounting Office
Government Printing Office
Library of Congress
United States Botanic Garden
Cost Accounting Standards Board

EXECUTIVE

THE PRESIDENT

Executive Office of the President

White House Office
Office of Management and Budget
Council of Economic Advisers
National Aeronautics and Space Council
National Security Council
Office of Economic Opportunity
Office of Emergency Preparedness
Office of Science and Technology

Office of the Special Representative for Trade Negotiations
Council on International Economic Policy
Office of Consumer Affairs
Office of Intergovernmental Relations
Council on Environmental Quality
Domestic Council
Office of Telecommunications Policy
Special Action Office for Drug Abuse Prevention

JUDICIAL

The Supreme Court of the United States
Circuit Courts of Appeals of the United States
District Courts of the United States
United States Court of Claims
United States Court of Customs and Patent Appeals
United States Customs Court
Territorial Courts
Federal Judicial Center
Administrative Office of the United States Courts
United States Tax Court

DEPARTMENT OF AGRICULTURE
DEPARTMENT OF COMMERCE
DEPARTMENT OF STATE
DEPARTMENT OF THE TREASURY
DEPARTMENT OF LABOR
DEPARTMENT OF DEFENSE
DEPARTMENT OF JUSTICE
DEPARTMENT OF HEALTH, EDUCATION, AND WELFARE
DEPARTMENT OF HOUSING AND URBAN DEVELOPMENT
DEPARTMENT OF THE INTERIOR
DEPARTMENT OF TRANSPORTATION

INDEPENDENT OFFICES AND ESTABLISHMENTS

Administration Conference of the U.S.
Atomic Energy Commission
Civil Aeronautics Board
District of Columbia
Economic Stabilization Agencies
Environmental Protection Agency
Export-Import Bank of the U.S.
Farm Credit Administration
Federal Communications Commission
Federal Deposit Insurance Corporation

Federal Home Loan Bank Board
Federal Maritime Commission
Federal Mediation and Conciliation Service
Federal Power Commission
Federal Reserve System, Board of Governors of the
Federal Trade Commission
General Services Administration
Interstate Commerce Commission

National Aeronautics and Space Administration
National Foundation on the Arts and the Humanities
National Labor Relations Board
National Mediation Board
National Science Foundation
Railroad Retirement Board
Securities and Exchange Commission

Selective Service System
Small Business Administration
Smithsonian Institute
Tennessee Valley Authority
U. S. Civil Service Commission
U. S. Information Agency
U. S. Postal Service
U. S. Tariff Commission
Veterans Administration

Source: U. S. Government Organization Manual, 1972/73

executive branch is a complex and confusing collection of organizations supervised only more or less closely, with varying degrees of success, by the President.

The organizations of the executive branch (for example, the Defense Department, the Department of Agriculture, the Social Security Administration) are often spoken of individually as bureaucracies (their employees are of course bureaucrats), and the executive branch as a whole may be referred to as "the bureaucracy."[4] Immediately you should understand that the word *bureaucracy* has a host of meanings. To a sociologist or other professional student of formal organizations, the term may be applied to a form of organization exhibiting particular characteristics (see Chapter 7). Some of the organizations in Washington might fit and others not. To a political candidate (politician) on the campaign platform, bureaucracy is likely to be a fighting term used to refer to organizations in far-off Washington who do not understand state needs or the local situation. In this usage, bureaucrats are unknown, uninformed men who likely could not make a living in private business.

Neither the technical or political uses should be understood here, but rather the use that simply means both the executive branch as a whole and particular organizations within it. In a somewhat more limited use, "the bureaucracy" may refer to the career government as opposed to the presidential government, which comes and goes.

It would be hard to overemphasize the importance of the men and organizations in the executive branch and the activities they carry out. (I do not mean to imply that all these activities are carried out as effectively as possible or that everything that goes on within the bureaucracy is important.) One can begin to appreciate the magnitude and importance of the executive branch by reviewing the recent development of the American national government. In 1940 there were barely one million civilian employees in the executive branch; in 1972 there were more than 2½ million. (The population of the country had grown from less than 132,000,000 to over 200,000,000.) As recently as 1960, budget outlays were below $100 billion a year. For 1974 the President proposed budget outlays of about $269 billion a year, and the trend is clearly upward. Organizations and pro-

---

4. Perhaps the single most useful work on bureaucracy is Anthony Downs, *Inside Bureaucracy* (Boston: Little, Brown and Co., 1967).

grams that only a few years ago were not thought of, exist today
in abundance. Obvious examples include the Atomic Energy
Commission, the National Aeronautics and Space Administration, the Environmental Protection Agency, and the National
Science Foundation. Older agencies find themselves playing new
or expanded roles. Obvious examples include the Federal Trade
Commission (expanded consumer-protection activity) and the
Office of Education (expanded role in providing financial aid
to state and local educational systems).

Several reasons for the expansion of government activity
(and the increased number and size of government organizations) can be suggested. More is demanded of the government
today than ever before—in social welfare, in environmental
protection, in economic regulation and manipulation, in national
security. In response government organizations have been created and often enlarged. Certainly budgets have grown, and were
it not for grants to the states and contracts with private companies the executive branch would likely be much larger than it
is. The development—indeed, the explosion—of technology has
led to whole new areas of government activity. The financial
difficulties of state and local governments have led to increased
activity at the national level. To all these reasons might be added
the consideration that government officials often want their own
organizations to grow.

The organizations of the executive branch are most obviously important because they implement or execute the policies
and programs of the government. To any particular person, most
of this activity is invisible and may seem of little consequence
except that it adds to taxes. Yet taken as a whole the impact of
executive branch activity on everything from individual lives to
international affairs is enormous. Executive branch personnel
(in different organizations, obviously) approve social security
claims, arrest and prosecute persons accused of having violated
federal laws, award research grants to scientists, manage national parks and other public lands, predict the direction of the
economy over the course of the next 12 months and longer, and
decide whether, when, and how to collect intelligence about foreign countries. Public employees normally possess what many
writers refer to as administrative discretion in carrying out
their tasks. In essence this means that executive agencies operate under more or less general guidance from Congress and the
President. Interpretation of general laws, development of detailed

regulations, and actions in particular cases are all matters of government agency activity. Within agencies decisions are made about where to concentrate effort, what contingencies to prepare for, how to allocate resources. Such decisions are not particularly visible and not particularly glamorous, but they are not unimportant.

Congress has, in effect, coped with its workload by delegating many jobs to agencies in the executive branch. Administrative agencies today devise rules to implement legislation left very general by Congressmen, who know they are not equipped and do not have the time to legislate details. In addition the judicial role of administrative agencies has been expanded by Congress. When the courts cannot cope with their work-load, Congress has two obvious alternatives. One is to increase the number of courts, and this step has been taken. Another is to give administrative agencies judicial authority to hear certain types of cases, and this step has also been taken. Part of the job of the independent regulatory agencies (and other agencies as well) is to hold hearings and make judgments.

Too often, even apparently knowledgeable observers seem to think that passage of a law by Congress is what really matters, or indeed is all that matters. By and large, nothing could be further from the truth. If one takes the development of regulations, the interpretation and enforcement of particular laws, and the treatment of particular persons to be important, it is clear that the activities of administrative agencies cannot be ignored. Administrative activity is clearly part of the policy process. To be sure, an administrative decision may not have the visibility or symbolic impact of a Congressional vote, but it may have substantial effects all the same. In everything from civil rights to environmental protection to aid to education, passage of a law may be not an end, but only a beginning. Perhaps it is appropriate to recall the words that Winston Churchill used in a very different context: Passage of a law by Congress is only the end of the beginning. Whether the law is in fact being implemented or enforced (by no means a sure thing) and how, is in large measure up to the executive branch organizations concerned.

To fully appreciate the importance of executive branch organizations you must also realize that executive branch organizations are frequently heavily involved in the planning and development of their own programs. To be sure, the popular image of American government is otherwise. The common view is that legislation authorizing or establishing programs comes from Congress and is simply implemented by executive agencies. Another view of policy-making is that the President proposes, the Congress reviews and authorizes, and after Presidential approval executive agencies implement. But a third view is that much program legislation is initiated by the agencies themselves, is reviewed by Presidential staff, goes to Congress where it is considered and acted on, and then after approval by the President goes back to be implemented by the agency that initiated it. In fact, all these versions may have some truth in them; who plays what role may depend on everything from the issue involved, to the relative strength of different parties, to the age of an administration, to the personnel in the relevant bureaucracies. But the policy impact of administrative agencies is obvious.

The importance of the bureaucracy can be emphasized another way, if we simply ask what is included in program initiation and program implementation. The answer is that program initiation includes such activities as data collection and analysis (this might be called search or intelligence activity) problem formulation, program design, legislative bill drafting, and program selling or lobbying. Program implementation may include such activities as organization creation or reorganization, resource acquisition and allocation, staffing and training, rule development and enforcement, and public education. These terms make even clearer the breadth and significance of executive branch activity. But the point must be qualified. Not all of the many different organizations in the executive branch perform the several functions that have been described equally actively or well. While it is convenient to speak of the executive branch or of the bureaucracy, it is important to remember that it is made up of many very different organizations.

Problems confronted by the government today can often be managed only with information and techniques possessed by men in the executive branch, not by men in Congress or on the bench. The executive branch is the home of the expert, the specialist, the professional. In the executive branch there are numbers of men who can bring knowledge to bear on problems and program design.

Another factor has enhanced the importance and influence of at least some executive branch organizations: the frequent need, particularly in national security matters, for secrecy and for speedy decision and action. Neither Congress nor the Courts are

well fitted for secret or quick operations. Congress by design is
a deliberate body; it is characterized by intermittent sessions,
open committee hearings, and open debate. None of these is consistent with either secrecy or speed. As the need for both has
become more common in governmental matters, the consequence
of executive branch organizations has grown. But to these observations may be added another. Just because secrecy does affect
power relations secrets may be kept in circumstances where the
need to do so is doubtful or debatable. National security demands some secrecy, but executive secrecy under the umbrella of
national security may be used to prevent political embarrassment
or simply weaken the Congress vis-a-vis the administration.

Public Policy Considered

What is public policy? The answer is not so obvious as the
question; in fact, there are many answers. A policy may represent
a goal or objective; it may represent a statement of intent. Policy
may mean guidelines and directives. Policy may mean nothing
more than precedent and common practice. It is a frequently
used word—public policy, foreign policy, domestic policy, social
policy, agency policy, transportation policy—but the precise
meaning must be taken from the context.

A number of other words may be associated with the word
policy. One such is *program*. I am not sure that it has an agreed-
upon definition, but I think of a program as being located in
an organization and having funds appropriated for it and manpower associated with it. A program seems at once more concrete and more specific than a policy.

The federal government has several programs that assist
veterans and several that assist farmers. By skimming through
the U.S. Government Budget or the Budget in Brief, the student
will quickly see the great variety of programs that the government supports. Perhaps it will be useful to think of policies
(that is, goals) as being met or not met through the development and implementation of specific programs (viewed here as
means). *Project* is another policy-related word; I use the word
to refer to parts of a program—as a single irrigation project
may be part of a widespread program of desert reclamation.
And still another word is *mission*—used particularly when speaking of what an organization does. Thus one may speak of the
mission of the Department of Labor, the mission of the Social

Security Administration, the mission of the National Park Service, and so on. Mission means in this sense both the *raison d'être* of the organization and its policies. To some extent these words are used interchangeably, and, moreover, these words can be connected to others. Policies and programs represent choices, decisions—and they are also outputs, products, services.

Several observations can be made about public policies. First, policies have a variety of costs. Probably the most obvious are the money costs. The budget records the direct money costs of the policies and programs of the government, though it may not record the costs clearly. Indeed, the administration or an agency may on occasion have an interest in trying to conceal the true cost of a program. Still it is possible by going through the Budget of the United States to get some notion of program cost, and it is possible to find out how much money goes to which organizations and major policy areas. But programs have costs in addition to money. A health-care program requires medical manpower; schools require teachers; a large army diverts men from the civilian economy. A space program attracts engineers from other occupations and may attract students into engineering and away from other careers. In short, any program has manpower requirements, and there are also material requirements. Agencies need space, transport, and supplies to carry out their mission.

In addition to money and other economic costs, policies may have a variety of political and other social costs. Policies may attract, maintain, or repel support. If a program is politically costly it may mean that executives cannot be recruited or retained, that Congress will be in opposition, that group support is lost, that votes will be in short supply. It is hard for the government to do anything without spending money and incurring some political costs—no matter what is done. The problem, of course, is to maintain enough support, which is perfectly consistent with incurring some costs. In addition to strictly political cost, programs may have other social costs. Policies that resulted in maintaining high rates of illiteracy or high rates of mortality would be viewed as socially costly. So might a law enforcement program that reduced individual freedom or invaded individual privacy.

In brief, policies have several kinds of costs associated with them, and a policy-maker's job involves making a choice from among costly alternatives. Presumably it would be sensible to hunt for the least costly alternatives, but data on cost is hard to come by. Even if it is possible to find out what a program cost in the past, the cost of an untried program is another matter. Moreover, common sense suggests that those who favor a program will understate its cost while those who oppose it may overstate its cost.

To these cost difficulties another must be added. It is by no means the case that the least costly alternative on the money dimension is also the least costly alternative on the political dimension. Closing army bases or veterans hospitals may be economically sensible and politically suicidal. What is politically sensible may be costly in terms of dollars and perhaps impossible in terms of resources. In the field of health, for example, policies that might make great political sense may be impossible, given a supply of medical manpower that is fixed in the near term. The problem then is one of balancing a variety of costs, and the final outcome may not mean a least costly solution on any dimension.

The choice problem in public policy or the development of programs is both eased and complicated because policies and programs have benefits as well as costs. Assessing these, to say nothing of giving them a dollar value, has stumped many an analyst. On one dimension children are educated, the sick are cured, the criminals are kept off the streets and perhaps rehabilitated, roads are built, and so on. And in addition to such direct consequences a program may have political benefits: support from groups is obtained, Congressmen choose to cooperate rather than obstruct, votes are gained in elections, cabinet members may remain with an administration, the editorials in the press are favorable. In addition, overseas allies may be gained and the economy may be stimulated. There is no necessary relationship between program effectiveness and political benefits. Appearances are important, and it is certainly possible for an ineffective program to bring support and an effective program not to. Given the conflicting demands of various interests in the population, it is well nigh impossible to benefit or satisfy everybody. The problem is to gain enough support.

Final choice of policy or problem involves of course some balancing of costs and benefits. There may be analysis, but there is also likely to be negotiation, bargaining, reliance on routines, expert judgment, and arbitrary choice. As there is much to consider, commonly there is simplification, reaction, feedback, and modification. On occasion there may be miscalculation. There may be unanticipated and/or unintended costs or benefits. And the consequences that were expected from a program may not occur. Policy makers may not only or always "muddle through," but they do so frequently.[5]

One can approach an understanding of public policy from a somewhat different direction. Assume or rather simply observe that the resources available to a government are limited. Further, observe that there are multiple and on occasion conflicting demands placed on a government. To make the situation vivid, assume finite resources and infinite needs or demands. And then assume the need (desire) to maintain support and remain in office. The question then is: What may be done in order to remain in office? Resources may be expanded somewhat, but raising taxes has its own costs. Resources can also be expanded through borrowing, but debts are not free. There may be attempts to use available resources more efficiently, but demands may still outstrip resources. What then? The existence of a problem may be denied, or its severity may be deprecated. Voluntary action may be advocated or a pilot program started. A commission or task force may be appointed to study the problem. Expenditures may be delayed. Symbols, images, and public relations may be called on to give an impression of effective action (benefits) while not much is done; and careful empirical assessment of results may not take place.

The reader may by now be wondering what all this has to do with the bureaucracy. There are several links. The most obvious of course is that administrators, civil servants, bureaucrats, are responsible for carrying out programs, which means that in the end they are the ones both delivering benefits and administering costly and unpopular programs. They are also involved in the initial and continuing assessment of costs and benefits; they are among the decision-makers. It is worth noting that agencies are likely to be sensitive to the costs and benefits that will accrue to them if particular decisions are made and particular programs carried out. In assessment and in administration, administrative agencies are not neutral, a fact which gains in significance the harder it is objectively to measure either the costs or benefits of a program.

---

5. The phrase is from Charles Lindblom, "The Science of Muddling Through," *Public Administration Review*, 19, Spring 1959, pp. 79–88.

Conclusion

Some basic points about the Executive Branch and the making of public policy can be put down here. You may want to keep them in mind as you go through the course. You may want to see if they fit your experience. You may want to challenge them.

The President shares power over the executive branch.

Executive branch organizations are more or less independent of the President. Some are virtually autonomous.

Executive branch organizations not only implement but also develop or take part in the development of policy.

Passing a law is just the beginning; implementation is critical.

Policies have a variety of costs and benefits that different people will assess differently.

Decision-makers try to minimize their costs and maintain sufficient support while balancing limited resources with unlimited demands.

2 The Governmental and Political Context

To begin to understand public administration and policy development in the United States one must have some broad awareness of American government and politics.[1] To convey this understanding in a chapter or indeed a single book is impossible. The best that can be done here is to attempt to convey some facts and impressions of American politics as background for the coming chapters. Aside from some discussion of the federal system, no attempt is made here to describe governmental institutions in the fifty states. Each state has a chief executive, a legislature, a judicial system, and many departments and agencies to carry out state programs and administer state laws. Anyone interested in public administration in a particular state should, of course, be familiar with the institutions of that state and how they operate. In gaining familiarity the questions posed explicitly and implicitly in the following sections might provide a useful guide. For example, Presidential-congressional relationships are briefly discussed. A person interested in any particular state might very well want to understand the relationship that exists between a governor and the state legislature just as he might want to know what resources a governor has available to influence state administrative organizations.

---

1. There are enormous numbers of textbooks in American politics. Any student who has not had a course in American politics might want to supplement this chapter by skimming one or more of them.

But, again, the explicit focus here is on the federal system and the national government.

The Federal System

No one can begin to understand public administration in the United States without some understanding of the federal system of government.[2] That the United States is a country of many governments is well-known. How these governments (national, state, and local) relate to one another is not so obvious, but is of great importance. The relationships that exist between governments have an effect both on what governments do and how well they do it.

In the very early years of our government there may have existed what has been called *dual federalism*. This meant in practice that the national government tended to its business; the states tended to theirs; and the two didn't meet. If dual federalism ever existed in pure form (it probably didn't) it had given way by the early nineteenth century to *cooperative federalism*, the form (or practice) that continues and continues to expand to this day. Cooperative federalism simply means that the national government and the state governments (and the local governments too) work with each other in achieving public purposes—the construction and operation of a welfare system, a highway system, an educational system, and so on. It is possible to find a variety of terms in the literature of federalism that try to describe present relationships and future trends. Marble-cake federalism, creative federalism, and new federalism are among the most common terms describing these interactions.

There are a number of subsidiary points to be made. First, the role played by the national government has constantly increased in importance. Its role grew explosively in the 1930s and again during the 1960s. (Concurrently, of course, the role of the public sector in national life has increased, and the importance of the instruments of national government—the President, the

---

2. Among the many books on federalism are three relatively brief ones: William H. Riker, *Federalism: Origin, Operation, Significance* (New York: Little Brown, & Co., 1964); Daniel Elazar, *American Federalism: A View from the States* (New York: Thomas Y. Crowell, 1972); and Richard H. Leach, *American Federalism* (New York: W. W. Norton, 1970). The many reports and studies of the Advisory Commission on Intergovernmental Relations provide much information about the current operation of the United States federal system.

Congress, the Courts, and the bureaucracy—has substantially increased. More on this later.) The growing role of the national government has been clearly described by James Sundquist.

> In the nineteen sixties the American federal system entered a new phase. Through a series of dramatic enactments, the Congress asserted the national interest and authority in a wide range of governmental functions that until then had been the province exclusively or predominantly of state and local government. The new legislation not only established federal-state-local relations in entirely new fields of activity and on a vast new scale but it established new patterns of relationship as well.[3]

Why did the role of the national government expand? Any brief answer cannot help but be inaccurate, but major points can be mentioned. Today there are a number of problems—social welfare and environmental pollution to mention only two—that appear to many people to require action on a scale requiring national resources and national power. This observation leads to three separate points. First, today people seem more willing than ever to call on the national government for legislation, help, money. There is a national consciousness that was not nearly so strong at the turn of the century. A second point is that an apparently ever-increasing number of conditions are being created and/or discovered and then defined as problems that require government action or a government response. Third, the role of the national government has expanded because, with the personal and corporate income taxes, it is able to generate resources on a scale unmatched by individual state and local governments. There are other reasons for the expansion of the national role. When problems are interstate, like the pollution of a river or air traffic safety, federal activity is highly probable. When state and local governments appear unresponsive to citizen demands (civil rights is an example), the citizen may turn to Washington. When there is a perceived need for a national standard to be met (welfare) and a service to be delivered in a more uniform fashion, national action is likely.

The resources of the national government are the base for the hundreds of grant-in-aid programs that today link the national government with the state and local governments. Grants-

---

3. James Sundquist, *Making Federalism Work* (Washington: The Brookings Institution, 1969), p. 1.

in-aid from the national government today help state and local governments to educate children, move traffic, maintain order, improve housing, treat sewage, and clean air. Grants-in-aid are a way of bringing national resources to bear on problems that manifest themselves at state and local levels across the country. In a sense they represent a compromise between leaving a problem completely in state hands and giving it completely to the national government.

Grants-in-aid have two features that must be remembered. One is that they are usually accompanied by conditions of one kind or another. To be eligible for most grants a state must undertake certain activities and meet specified standards. There is, to be sure, room for a good deal of slippage and negotiation, but the fact is that grants are accompanied by conditions, or strings, or maybe red tape. A second characteristic is that grants are normally allocated on the basis of some formula—on the basis of population, the basis of need, or perhaps on a matching basis. Sometimes the state must put up a dollar of its own to get a national dollar. Sometimes it needs to put up only a dime to get 90 cents, as in the case of the interstate highway system. Obviously both the conditions and the formulas are matters over which there may be conflict with national and state spokesmen having different views and with spokesmen for rich and poor states having different views.

The growth in the national role has been accompanied by a good deal of conflict, compromise, and confusion. In political rhetoric it is common to find proposals (and pleas) for reversing the trend of events, strengthening the states, and redressing the balance of power. So far these have come to little, but there is no question that the centralization-decentralization question will be with us as long as we maintain a federal form of government. Questions about the roles and powers of the components of a federal system are an inherent part of the functioning of such a system. As this is written, in 1973, President Nixon is trying to disengage the federal government from many programs and turn them back to the states. He has also, through the strengthening of Regional Councils (one in each federal region and composed of the regional directors of federal agencies), tried to decentralize federal decision making and make it easier and quicker for state and local authorities to deal with federal agencies.

Although it is common to speak of the national government and state governments as though they represented two sides in a game, the reality is not so simple. The President, the Congress, and the courts, to say nothing of the scores of different government organizations may all have differing views and favor different practices. The national government is not a monolith. Nor is the interest of the states a single one. Within any particular state, there may be differences between governors, legislatures, and state agencies. Among states there are poor states and rich, large and small, northern and southern, urban and rural. Some states can be thought of as Democratic and some as Republican. It is such variety that makes intergovernmental relations such a complex phenomena.

What often happens is that federal agencies work out their own accommodations with counterpart organizations in the states. The Federal Highway Administration in the Department of Transportation in Washington, D.C., works with the state departments of highways. Components of the Department of Health, Education, and Welfare work with State Welfare Departments, with State Education Departments, and so on. The Law Enforcement Assistance Administration in the Department of Justice works with police departments and with regional law-enforcement councils. These examples of organizational relationships could be multiplied endlessly. In each of these relationships the distribution of power and influence between national and state agencies may vary, as may the conditions for getting a grant, the stringency with which conditions are enforced, and the formula that is used to allocate funds. Again, the complexity of intergovernmental relationships is emphasized.

The President of the United States

The President of the United States is easily the most visible figure in the national government.[4] Elected every four years, he is the Chief Executive and in a sense the head public administrator. He is also of course many other things—chief of his

---

4. A sampling of books on the President might include the following: Aaron Wildavsky, *The Presidency* (Boston: Little, Brown & Co., 1969); Clinton Rossiter, *The American Presidency* (New York: Harcourt Brace and World, 1960); Richard Neustadt, *Presidential Power* (New York: John Wiley, 1964); Thomas Cronin and Sanford Greenberg, *The Presidential Advisory System* (New York: Harper & Row, 1969); Dorothy Buckton James, *The Contemporary Presidency* (New York: Pegasus, 1969); Richard Fenno, *The President's Cabinet* (Cambridge: Harvard University Press, 1959); and Patrick Anderson, *The President's Men* (Garden City: Doubleday Anchor Books, 1969).

party, commander-in-chief of the armed forces, chief of state, and so on. As many authors have pointed out, the President is both King and Prime Minister. In the President's name, policies and programs are developed and carried out; money is spent. The President's annual State of the Union message sets out what he is going to do and what he would like to achieve. His budget shows how much money he intends to spend on countless activities. Special messages to the Congress spell out more or less specifically the details of particular proposals.

To carry out these duties the President needs help, and he finds it in many places. To a degree, he finds it in the agencies and officials of the executive branch, many of whom he appointed. (The President appoints the heads of departments and agencies and many lesser officials as well). The heads of the major departments together with certain other officials appointed by the President jointly form his cabinet, which is in some sense a presidential sounding board and advisory group. But each member has his own responsibilities and his own department to run, and his department has its own interests. The result is that the President relies for help not only on the departments and agencies of the executive branch, but on the Executive Office of the President and especially on the White House Office. The Executive Office consists of both presidential appointees and career civil servants organized into a number of different units—the White House Office, the Office of Management and Budget, the National Security Council, the Domestic Council, and so on. As we will look at these organizations in more detail later, it suffices here simply to observe that the President has a substantial personal and institutional staff to help him carry out his duties.

The President and his Executive Office should be differentiated from the executive branch of the government. Many writers speak of the executive branch and the President as though they were virtually synonymous, but it is prudent to differentiate the two. The President has a government-wide view (ideally), while the organizations of the executive branch are more specialized and more likely to have a parochial view. One of the continuing problems of the President is to get the organizations in the executive branch to do what he wants them to do. They often may resist his wishes or may simply ignore him.

Much of this book discusses from various perspectives the Presidential-executive agency relationship. At this point two observations can be made. First, in order to cope with a large bureaucracy the Presidency has become increasingly institutionalized, or organized. In a sense, the Presidency has itself been bureaucratized. (Perhaps there is some truth in the notion that only a bureaucracy can cope effectively with another one.) But to say that the Presidency has been to a degree bureaucratized is to say also that the operations of the Presidency have been specialized and routinized. And it may also be to say that increasingly the President (the man) is only a part (though to be sure, a major part) of the Presidency (the institution).

The Congress

The President must not only deal with the bureaucracy, he must also deal with the Congress.[5] The State of the Union message, the Budget, Special Messages and their accompanying draft bills—all these are just proposals until Congress has acted on them.

As every reader must know, the Congress is composed of the House of Representatives (435 members) and the Senate (100 members). The basic unit of organization in each house is the committee; there are 17 in the Senate and 21 in the House, and the committees have subcommittees. Committees in both the Senate and the House specialize in particular areas of public policy and are responsible for legislation in their areas—military affairs, finance, agriculture, and so on. Each house has an appropriations committee that is responsible for reviewing appropriations (money) bills, and the other committees deal with substantive legislation, not with appropriations. (The work of the substantive committees may, however, leave appropriations committees with no choice but to appropriate.)

The committees do much of the work of the Congress. They

---

5. For the student who wants to know more about Congress, there are available general books on the Congress and the legislative process, books on the House and Senate separately, books on various committees, and books on various practices. There are also books on Congress and the President, Congress and the Court, Congress and interest groups. A good useful introduction is Nelson Polsby, *Congress and the President* (Englewood Cliffs: Prentice-Hall, 1971). A recent collection of articles on the same subject is Ronald Moe, *Congress and the President* (Pacific Palisades: Goodyear, 1972).

review, draft, and redraft legislation. They conduct inquiries and hold hearings, and in the end kill bills or report them out for action by the whole House or Senate. Committees and frequently individual committee chairmen exercise a great deal of power, and the prudent government executive (whether bureau chief or President of the United States) has a healthy respect for what a committee can do to his program.

To say that the committees and their chairmen have power opens up a host of other topics. How do committees exercise their power? What are the consequences of committee power? How do chairmen reach their positions? How can chairmen be circumvented? Who else has power? How is power distributed in the Congress?

The first point to be made is that no bill reaches the floor of either the House or the Senate without going through a committee. The second point to be made is that many more bills are introduced than ever get to a floor vote. Most die or fail or simply drop out of sight in committee. The committees in effect serve as cemeteries for many legislative proposals. Committees may bottle up bills which they disapprove, or a chairman may simply not schedule hearings. Consideration may be so delayed that in the end time runs out before consideration is complete. If hearings are held they may be stacked with hostile witnesses who can be depended on to give testimony adverse to the pending legislation. Hostile committee members may, by the questions they direct to administration witnesses, build a record with which to defeat a bill. Of course, all these observations can be reversed; and when a committee is presented a bill that it supports, prompt and favorable treatment can be expected. The major point is that a committee composed of only a few men may in effect act for Congress. Minority rule, not majority rule, is often the fact.

Procedure in the several committees varies somewhat, as do the degree of influence and the techniques of the several committee chairmen. Some committee chairmen exercise virtually autocratic control over their committees, and some favor a more democratic style. But there is no question that the committee chairman is in charge. A congressman gets to be chairman of a committee simply by staying around a long time. The most senior member of a committee (that is, the man who has been a member of the committee longest) who is also a member of the party currently in control of the whole chamber (House or Senate) is the chairman. Of course, members may switch committees on occasion. A relatively senior member of the Senate or House may want to move up from a less prestigious committee (Post Office and Civil Service, for example) to a more prestigious committee (Armed Services or Finance are examples) and he may do so, but at some cost. If he switches committee assignments, he starts at the bottom again within the committee hierarchy.

The power of committees and their chairmen is not unqualified of course. Within committees it is possible for a chairman to be outvoted, though an astute chairman is not likely to let this happen and an autocratic chairman won't let it happen. If a committee appears to be burying a bill that many other members want to act on, both houses have procedures for getting it out, though these are not commonly used. And it is sometimes possible through a combination of skillful legislative drafting and judicious referral to get a bill sent to a committee that will treat it kindly and keep it out of the clutches of a hostile committee. Referral is the prerogative in the House of the Speaker and in the Senate of the Vice President.

In addition to committee chairmen there are others in the House and Senate who have power. Generally, more senior people have more influence than less senior people. The importance of seniority is declining and certainly is not as great as it once was, but it is still to be reckoned with. Party leaders and their assistants have positions of some influence. In the House, the Speaker is in effect the head of the majority party and exercises substantial influence both within his party and the House as a whole. In the Senate the Vice President plays a largely pro-forma role, while major roles are played by the majority and minority leaders. Indeed, in the Senate the majority leader is largely responsible for arranging the calendar and deciding when what issues will come up for debate, though he does this usually only after consulting with other interested particpants. In the House, unlike the Senate, the calendar is set by the Rules Committee. This committee and its chairman have blocked legislation by simply not granting a bill a rule, that is, by not permitting it to come to the floor for consideration.

In trying to comprehend the Congress it is not enough to notice only Congressmen and Senators. Also important are the individuals occupying staff roles. Individual Congressmen and

Senators have office staffs that help them with everything from answering mail to speechwriting to constituency relations. Committees and subcommittees also have staffs that commonly work most closely with the chairmen (majority staff) and with the ranking minority member (minority staff.) Committee staff can play a very important role in helping to decide what issues a committee will look into and what bills it will hold hearings on. Staff may also schedule witnesses to testify, and help in preparing questions to be asked by the Congressmen, and through the year maintain liaison with administrative agencies. In addition both the General Accounting Office and the Library of Congress in different ways perform research and study functions that may assist committees and individual Congressmen. The GAO audits expenditures of executive agencies and increasingly also evaluates the effectiveness of programs. The Library of Congress, as its name may suggest, provides bibliographic assistance. But this paragraph on staff must conclude with the observation that Congress as a body, to say nothing of Congressmen as individuals, enjoy nothing like the staff assistance available to the President.

These several paragraphs on the Congress may be drawn together under a single question: How does a bill become a law? In brief, a bill is drafted, introduced, and presented to the Speaker or Vice President. (Except for tax bills and, by custom, appropriations bills, legislation may originate in either house.) It is referred to the appropriate committee for consideration. Hearings may or may not be held, and the bill may or may not be reported out. If reported out, it is debated on the floor before a vote is taken. If passed, it is sent to the other house where much the same procedures take place. If similar but not identical measures are passed by both houses a conference committee composed of members from both houses meets to resolve differences. Identical measures are then presented to both houses and, if passed, the legislation is presented to the President for his signature or veto. Congress may overturn a veto.

Clearly in this process there are many points at which a bill may be killed or modified. It may be altered or doomed at any point from initial drafting to final conference. Important also is the notion that at many points in the legislative process outsiders may exercise influence. Preeminent among those who may exercise influence is the President of the United States both directly and indirectly through his staff. By the astute use of the powers and prestige of his office and the resources at his disposal, a President may influence the course of legislation and get from the Congress programs he desires and prevent favorable action on programs distasteful to him. Department secretaries, bureau heads, party leaders, and interest-group spokesmen may all attempt to influence the work of committees, the decisions of Congressmen, and the final votes of the House and Senate.

Although legislating is the most visible function of the Congress, it is by no means the only one. Congressmen are often consulted by the President and government executives before actions are taken or proposals made and in this way may have an impact on the development and implementation of public policy. Through their inquiries and investigations Congressional committees are able to review administrative performance; Congressional control of administration is a topic we shall return to. Congress serves as a forum for public debate and in some sense may fill a public information and education role. Congressmen perform numerous services for their constituents, their districts, and their states and may on occasion intercede on behalf of constituents with administrative agencies.

How well are these several roles performed? What are the most important? What is the role today of Congress in policy-making? How effective is Congress over-all? Interesting questions certainly, but largely unanswerable except on a personal and intuitive basis, which means that different authors have suggested different answers. My own view is that the significance of Congress in American public policy making has never been greater, if only because the government role in American life is today so large. The mid-twentieth-century explosion of government activity has vastly expanded the importance of Congress. But at the same time the Congress seems to be increasingly overshadowed by the President and the executive branch. The bureaucracy seems more powerful than ever, at the expense of Congress. Whether these conditions will persist is, of course, a question; but now Congress has not the expertise, information, time, or staff to make many decisions or adequately review administrative performance. The volume and complexity of the government's business today has weakened the Congress vis-à-vis the executive branch. Despite this, Congressmen are still able, as influential individuals, to perform important services for their constituents. They fulfill an ombudsman role that is vital in a bureaucratic age. The Congress with its powers has access to the administration and may humanize a bureaucracy that might otherwise be impersonal.

It is clear that at any particular time the power balance between Congress and the executive is affected by salient issues, events, and personalities. On occasions, the Congress reasserts its prerogatives, and the bureaucracy and the Presidency pull in their collective heads. Yet the trend, I think, is for bureaucratic or administrative or executive government, not Congressional government. Still, there is no question that the Congressional role in American government is vastly important, and American government executives forget this fact at their peril.

The Courts

Anyone interested in public administration, or, which may not be the same thing, taking a course in it, needs some familiarity with the judicial system, quite as much as he needs to be aware of the Presidency and the Congress.[6] Acquaintance with the judicial system is important because the actions of administrative agencies may be challenged in the courts and because courts, especially the U.S. Supreme Court, may establish rules or guidelines that govern the behavior of administrators and administrative agencies.

What is the structure of the system of courts in the United States? How are the judges that staff the courts selected? Over what matters do federal courts have jurisdiction? How do controversies come to the courts? How are decisions made and enforced? What is the role of the courts in the making of public policy? Such are the questions that it is important to consider, however briefly.

Just as every state has a chief executive officer and a state legislature, every state has a court system, generally consisting of magistrates or justices of the peace, a general trial court (superior court, district court, circuit court, or other

---

6. There are a number of books on constitutional law, but few are directly concerned with the role of the judiciary and its relations with other political institutions. The student may find useful Martin Shapiro, *The Supreme Court and Administrative Agencies* (New York: The Free Press, 1968); Sheldon Goldman and Thomas P. Jahniger, *The Federal Courts as a Political System* (New York: Harper & Row, 1971); and Robert Scigliano, *The Supreme Court and the Presidency* (New York: The Free Press, 1971).

title), perhaps appellate courts, and a Supreme Court. But in this section we will not be concerned with these state systems and will instead focus our attention on the federal court systems. At the top of this system is, of course, the United States Supreme Court, consisting of a chief justice and eight associate justices, all appointed for life by the President by and with the advice and consent of the Senate. Beneath the Supreme Court are several Circuit Courts of Appeals (with varying numbers of judges) and beneath these, the Federal District Courts. Like Supreme Court judges, the judges of these additional federal courts are appointed by the President and serve a life term. In addition to these courts, there are a number of specialized courts that have been organized by Act of Congress and are thought of as legislative rather than constitutional courts. These are the Court of Claims, the United States Court of Customs and Patent Appeals, the United States Customs Court, the United States Court of Military Appeals, and the United States Tax Court. These courts will not be described further because of their rather narrow jurisdictions, though clearly for some administrative agencies their decisions may be of substantial importance. Citizens regularly go to the Tax Court, for example, to challenge decisions of the Internal Revenue Service.

The Supreme Court is clearly the most visible federal court and the one whose decisions have widest impact; yet for all its visibility and importance, it is not easy to describe its role. It serves as the protector and defender of the country's constitution, and its role in the defense of individual rights has been great. In interpreting the constitution and protecting individual liberties, it may review and strike down legislation passed by Congress and the acts of Presidents. It can review the acts and decisions of administrative agencies and determine whether they are consistent with constitutional and legislative requirements. Clearly it is a powerful body, and there is some truth in the proposition that the constitution is what the Supreme Court says it is. One has only to look at such important decisions as the school segregation cases of the 1950s or to consider the several decisions of the 1960s that protected the rights of persons accused of crimes, or the New York Times case of 1971 which protected freedom of the press, to see that in deciding the cases that are brought to them, Supreme Court justices make the constitution grow; they make law; they make policy.

What kinds of cases come to the Supreme Court? There are two simple answers. First, those cases that the judges want to review, they do. Second, important cases. But these answers must be expanded. In some types of cases, the Supreme Court has original jurisdiction and in some others it has appellate jurisdiction, but by far most of the cases it considers it chooses. In effect the person making the appeal asks the court to review his case, and if four justices think the case in question merits the attention of the Supreme Court it is taken. The court agrees to review only a few more than 10 percent of the cases they are asked to look at. Which ones do they choose? They are likely to select cases that involve a substantial constitutional question or cases where the law is unclear, or cases involving conflicts in different circuits. They can pick and choose and avoid cases that they regard as unimportant (from a national perspective), as well decided already, or as inappropriate or poorly timed.

The circuit courts of appeal are the courts in which most appeals from the decisions of federal district courts stop. In addition to taking appeals from the district courts, it is important to note that the circuit courts also may take appeals directly from federal regulatory agencies. In other words, if a citizen (or company) thinks it has not been fairly treated by a decision of the Federal Trade Commission, the Federal Communications Commission, or some other regulatory agency, the decision may be appealed directly to a circuit court without going through the process of a district court trial. This particular appellate jurisdiction emphasizes the connection between the courts and administrative agencies, but it also demonstrates that administrative agencies themselves exercise judicial or quasi-judicial power. That is, administrative agencies in holding hearings and making decisions may act in the capacity of a district or trial court, and the record developed in the agency can be taken to an appellate court.

The federal district courts are the basic trial courts of the federal system with original jurisdiction in a variety of matters involving federal questions. They also may get involved in trying suits between citizens of different states if the amount of money involved is over $10,000. What kinds of cases come up in federal court? A brief list of examples might include the following: the trial of a man accused of transporting a stolen car across the state line; federal employees challenging their dismissal from government jobs; prospective employees arguing that the test used by the Civil Service Commission was biased; an antitrust suit involving one or more major corporations; a trial in which a newspaper is accused of printing secret material that had come into its possession; the trial of a narcotics pusher. Several observations can be made about this list. First, in all the cases, the Department of Justice is involved either in a prosecuting role or in defending the government, as in the two cases where employees or prospective employees were challenging government action. Second, in most of the cases other federal agencies are involved. The Civil Service Commission would be involved in two; the Drug Enforcement Administration would be involved in one; perhaps the Department of Defense would be involved in another. Third, many of these cases appear routine and, if appealed at all, would go no further than the circuit court of appeals. But in each, it is certainly conceivable (and in some very possible) that important constitutional questions would be raised so that an appeal could be lodged with the Supreme Court and they might accept it for review. In the end, perhaps the testing techniques of the Civil Service Commission would be ruled unconstitutional, the newspaper allowed to print the material, and the narcotics pusher let go because the evidence was obtained illegally.

In thinking about the court a few final points must be made. The crucial one is that the courts can only decide cases that are brought to them. They can not go out and search for controversies. A second point is that not all questions or controversies are *justiciable,* that is, that are not susceptible to being settled in the court. The definition of justiciable is to be sure, elastic, and what one court rules is outside its purview another court may accept, but the principle of justiciability should be remembered. A third point is that courts must rely on the executive branch to implement decisions. Particularly if a decision requires affirmative executive action (as school desegregation does), a decision alone may not mean a great deal.

Finally, for all the power of the courts, they are parts of the American political system and are affected by it. The Congress defines the jurisdiction of the court, and the President appoints the judges. The courts are insulated but by no means totally isolated. Perhaps realizing this, courts commonly combine self-restraint with their power and in recent years at least have given the President and the Congress and indeed administrative agencies substantial leeway to conduct their operations as they see fit.

Pressure Groups

The public-policy process involves not only the institutions and individuals already discussed but also an array of unofficial organizations and individuals.[7] Foremost among these are organized groups representing particular points of view and having particular goals. Any student can think of numerous examples —the National Association of Manufacturers, the American Medical Association, the American Bar Association, the National Education Association, the National Rifle Association, the AFL-CIO, the National Farmers Union, and hundreds more. Known as interest groups or pressure groups, these organizations play a part in American politics and policy making. Such organizations, often more accurately their leaders, attempt to influence public opinion, nominations and elections, legislation, executive branch organization, administrative regulations and enforcement, and top-level staffing in the executive branch.

The terms "interest group" and "pressure group" cover, of course, not only a great number of organizations but also a great variety. One can ask what features characterize an interest group; but one can also ask about differences and similarities. We can answer these questions if we keep in mind that many of the characteristics of interest groups can be thought of as variables, that is, the feature or characteristic or dimension varies from organization to organization. Consider for example an important characteristic of any interest group: size. Clearly it varies. Some groups are large and some are small. As size may be related (and certainly leaders would like to convey the impression that it is related) to votes controlled and resources available, size is an important characteristic of interest groups. Size of course is by no means the only important feature of an

---

7. A classic study of interest groups is David Truman, *The Governmental Process* (New York: Alfred A. Knopf, 1951). Also of interest are Grant McConnell, *Private Power and American Democracy* (New York: Alfred A. Knopf, 1966); Abraham Holtzman, *Interest Groups and Lobbying* (New York: Macmillan, 1966); Lewis Anthony Dexter, *How Organizations are Represented in Washington* (Indianapolis: Bobbs-Merrill, 1969); and Robert H. Salisbury, *Interest Group Politics in America* (New York: Harper & Row, 1970).

interest group. Consider the membership. Who composes the organization? Who joins it? Doctors? Lawyers? Blue collar workers? Whites? Blacks? City people? Farmers? The answer will tell you not only what measures the organization is likely to favor and disapprove but also may tell you something about the relative influence of the organization and its points of access to officials and institutions. An organization made up of middle-class and upper-class members is likely to have better access and be more influential in the policy process than an organization made up of lower-class or working-class individuals. An organization made up largely of whites is likely to have more influence than an organization made up largely of blacks. An organization made up of farmers is likely to have (and certainly to want) reasonably good relations with the United States Department of Agriculture and the agriculture committees in the Congress. Where is the National Education Association likely to want access? The National Rifle Association?

Interest groups have other characteristics that should be mentioned. Interest groups are more or less cohesive, or united. It is possible to think of organized agriculture, but a moment's thought will suggest that agriculture is a very varied enterprise and not likely to be particularly cohesive. There are farmers on 80 acres, on 800, and on 8000. There are marginal farms and business farms, family farms and corporate farms. There are all sorts of crops grown all over the United States. The legislation that helps the dairy farmer may not help the farmer whose corn provides the oil to make the margarine. The result is that there are several farm organizations, and the goals of one may not be the goals of another. Take another example. Only about 50 percent of the physicians in the country belong to the American Medical Association, which means that the views of the AMA may not be at all the views of all doctors in the country. Think of black people in the United States. There are a number of organizations representing them: the NAACP, the Urban League, CORE, and several others. These examples could be extended, but these suffice to suggest the cohesion problem and another puzzle as well. If the President, a Congressman, or a government executive says he wants to give the farmer, the doctor, or the working man what he wants, what can he mean? Do the term "the farmer" and equivalent general terms mean anything, given their variety?

There is another aspect of the cohesion problem that is

worth mentioning. When the head of an organization says that all the members of his organization will vote a particular way, will they? The answer is, No, they will not all vote a particular way. In some organizations, many will, and in others less; but it is doubtful all members will vote the indicated way. Explanations for this range from the simple fact that some members didn't get the word to the probability that some belong to other organizations that make other demands on them, to the fact that a person they respect may have given them conflicting instructions and advice, to the fact that a man's self-perceived economic interest may appear to conflict with the advice his organization gives. Labor-union leaders are likely to be a good deal more liberal on racial matters than labor-union members). The obvious question for any official or for any informed citizen when confronted with a demanding interest group leader is: Is anybody going to be following that leader?

These comments lead to another observation or two. Interest groups are commonly hierarchical organizations; there are lots of members and few leaders or lots of Indians and few chiefs. The geometric form to have in mind is the triangle or perhaps the pyramid. This is not the place to survey in detail the characteristics of hierarchical organizations, but a few important (though perhaps obvious) points need making. The people on top of an organization cannot by any means always control their membership, especially when it comes to secret voting. A second point is also important for legislators, administrators, and informed citizens. The people on top may have little idea what the membership think or want. It is customary for interest-group spokesmen to say they speak for their membership, but in fact they may be speaking for themselves, for the leadership. The other side of the coin, especially in large or dispersed organizations, is that the membership may be at best dimly aware of (and perhaps not even interested in) what the leadership is saying or doing. There may be little communication between top and bottom, and in fact for many purposes the organization may be the top. The bottom may serve simply to contribute dues and inflate the membership figure.

To come at the organization question in a somewhat different way, it is possible to view an interest group as composed of an active minority (composed of the top leadership and interested and active supporters) and a large relatively passive majority who pay their dues and do other things. If an interest group is viewed as itself a political system, then it can be divided into those few who take an active part in the group's politics and position taking and those who do not. In addition, large organizations also have paid full-time staffs supporting the leadership group—lawyers, legislative analysts, lobbyists, and writers—all perhaps overseen by an executive director.

What do interest groups do? What do they want? How do they go about getting what they want? We can begin answering these questions with another. What does the government do, or what do the institutions and agencies of the government do? Most generally, the government authorizes and distributes benefits and burdens. In turn, interest groups try to obtain benefits and avoid burdens; somewhat more clearly, leaders of groups try to obtain government action (or sometimes inaction) that will benefit the members of their group and try to ward off action that will be detrimental to their members. Examples are legion. Airlines and the natural gas industry want to charge higher rates. The automobile industry wants less stringent safety regulations and wants deadlines for improvements pushed back. The steel industry wants favorable tax treatment. The shoe industry wants to be protected from Italian imports, and the textile industry wants to be protected from Japanese imports. The National Welfare Rights Organization wants higher welfare benefits, and labor groups want a higher minimum wage. The National Rifle Association resists the very idea of firearms registration, and the Sierra Club wants wilderness land preserved. Any newspaper could provide more examples of particular groups trying to get or avoid specific government actions.

How do organizations go about achieving their ends? First, an organization may try to create a favorable public-opinion climate. An organization (interest group) may engage in institutional advertising and, if appropriate, run membership campaigns that serve also to inform the general public; and it may try to get helpful articles placed in newspapers and magazines. The railroad industry wants not only to build its own image but also, if possible, to tarnish the image of the trucking industry. (Those huge trucks are such a menace on the highway.) Consumers worried about the high price of drugs may find an article in their favorite magazine describing the substantial and expensive research programs carried on by pharmaceutical companies. In a strike, both labor and management may take to the newspapers to tell their sides of the story.

Interest group leaders try to influence legislation in Congress. Lobbyists and elected leaders provide information to congressmen, testify in committee hearings, lend (or withhold) support (money, workers, votes) in primary and general elections. Books and articles by the score have been written on the role of interest groups in the legislative process, and surely it would be hard to find any major legislation that did not attract the attention, interest, and activity of some organized groups. Often of course, groups with entirely different goals are each trying to get their way, as when labor and management conflict over labor legislation.

Equally important (and to be discussed in detail later) interest groups try to affect the administrative process. After a law is passed it has to be implemented, interpreted, and enforced. Minority groups, to take one example, are very interested in the enforcement of civil-rights statutes; if they are not enforced they are meaningless. The tax legislation of the United States is accompanied by the voluminous regulations of the Internal Revenue Service. A business group may be just as interested in these as in the tax legislation passed by Congress. The National Education Association is interested in what comes out of the Office of Education in the Department of Health, Education, and Welfare. Numerous conservation groups follow closely the activities of the Environmental Protection Agency, the Department of the Interior, the Corps of Engineers, and the Department of Agriculture. Only recently the tree-harvesting practices of the Forest Service in the Department of Agriculture have come under attack.

Consistent with their interest in administration, interest groups may try to have a hand in the executive appointment process. The AFL–CIO thinks it should have some say in the appointment of top staff in the Department of Labor or at least no one should be appointed that is unacceptable to the AFL-CIO leadership. The AMA has successfully blocked at least one appointment to the Department of Health, Education, and Welfare, and conservation groups are likely to scrutinize the record of anyone appointed to a position in the Department of the Interior. In addition to trying to influence appointments, groups may also try to alter organizational structure to their benefit. Attempts may be made to upgrade an organization's status, to create an independent organization to look after a particular problem or serve a particular group, to place a unit in the Executive Office of the President, or to turn an independent agency into a cabinet department. All of these observations will be amplified in later chapters.

One final point. In trying to get what they want groups may attempt to build alliances or coalitions and thus increase their effective strength. A variety of civil-rights, labor, and welfare organizations may band together in an effort to improve welfare legislation or in an effort to increase the minimum wage. The steel workers union may join with steel management in an effort to protect the industry from the effects of imported steel. The fight against pollution has brought together disparate groups and individuals. Of course a coalition pushing a particular program may include not only unofficial interest groups but also government agencies. The Environmental Protection Agency may join with private anti-pollution groups and congressional committee members in attempts to get more stringent legislation protecting the environment and regulating industry. On the other hand the Department of Commerce can be expected to be on the side of business in its resistance to pollution legislation that appears to do too much damage to profits.

It should be clear that coalitions are fluid affairs, and often after a particular bill is passed (or defeated) the coalitions developed around it may fade away. But new coalitions of groups both new and old may develop around new bills. So common are coalitions that coalition building can be regarded as an inherent part of the policy-development process. And indeed for a major piece of legislation to have much chance of passage it probably must be supported (or appear to be) by a variety of organizations.

Political Parties

Political parties are another part of the unofficial institutional structure of American government.[8] Like pressure groups, parties play an important role in American politics, but a different role. The direct involvement of the parties in public-policy development—at least to the extent of pressure-group involve-

---

8. Two useful books on parties are Fred Greenstein, *The American Party System and the American People* (Englewood Cliffs: Prentice-Hall, 1963) and Frank J. Sorauf, *Political Parties in the American System* (Boston: Little, Brown & Co., 1964). A classic text is V. O. Key, *Politics, Parties, and Pressure Groups* (New York: Thomas Y. Crowell, 1956).

ment—is uncommon; neither, at least at the national government level, are the party organizations heavily involved in the administration of programs. The main mission of the two major political parties in this country is the organization of elections and the control of election outcomes. Each party wants its candidates for office chosen.

But having said this, qualifications must be added. To win elections the parties—and more specifically the party candidates —must appear in platforms and statements to be more or less responsive to the major concerns of the electorate. The connection between campaigns, elections, and public policy is a complex and hazy one, but this does not mean there is no connection. Which party wins an election—especially which party wins control of the White House—may make a difference for the style of administration and the substance of public policy. Details of a party platform may shortly be forgotten (if they were ever noticed), but whether a Democrat or Republican is elected may make a difference for four years.

One reason that it makes a difference is that the composition of the two major parties differs. Surely there is overlap, and each party may try to appeal to many of the same groups and individuals. Both parties will have city members, small-town members, and farmers. Both will have members who are well-to-do and others who are middle class. Young voters will be in both parties. But in the end a coalition that is successful in electing a Republican is likely to be composed somewhat differently than a coalition that can elect a Democrat. The Democratic Party will have many more minority-group members than the Republican Party. The Republican Party will have more members who have been successful in business and industry. And because of such differences a Republican President desiring to hold together the coalition that elected him may act differently than a Democrat President trying to hold together his coalition.

Another reason that party makes a difference is that it serves as a bridge or a barrier between Congress and the President. An election that ends with a Congress and President of the same party may yield cooperation. (Of course, despite the same party label there may still be institutional defensiveness and rivalry as well as value differences.) When an election ends with the Congress of one party and the President of another, then Congress and the President may find it impossible to cooperate on very many issues and deadlocks may frequently result.

Either of these conditions may have interesting consequences for administrators and government organizations. If the President and the Congress are of the same party it may be much harder for an agency in conflict with the President to find support in Congress. By the same token, the President with Congress on his side is in a much better position to influence, control, and even discipline erring agencies and administrators. He is also of course in a position to enlarge programs, increase budgets, and take other rewarding actions with some hope that the Congress will sustain his action. When the Congress and the President are of different parties some agencies may be caught in a crossfire, while others relax in the arms of Congress. Those allied with the President may be investigated and their budgets cut. Those allied with the Congress on the other hand may be able to operate to all intents and purposes independently of the President.

There is yet a third reason that party makes a difference in government. Obviously the President who is elected is either a Republican or a Democrat, and because he holds the highest office in the land he is by definition and tradition leader of his party as well as Chief Executive. Any attempt to analyze or understand Presidential behavior must keep in mind both these roles—and of course many others. As Chief Executive the President must administer the government, but as Party Chief he must keep together and lead his party. To some extent the power and resources of the Presidency will be used by the President to strengthen his party, reward and motivate the party faithful (especially of course the contributing members), and build support for the next election. The President today does not have the supply of government jobs available for distribution that he once did, but he has some, and party membership is one criterion for selection. In a sense, the party serves as a recruiting pool. To be sure it is not the only pool—membership in it is not enough—and on occasion an astute President may dip into the other pool to get a man he wants; but activity in party politics is certainly one way to get a government job. The Chief Administrator must staff his top management positions and many others besides. The party leader turns to this party for names.

As we are not concerned in this book with electoral politics, the structure of the parties in this country need not concern us greatly, but two points should be briefly mentioned. The first point is that the party structure in this country is highly de-centralized. The state and city organizations are what count, and party leaders in states and cities that have a lot of votes have a lot of influence. In the 1960's a Democrat candidate who had some interest in Chicago votes had to reckon with Mayor Daley and his Chicago organization. A Republican candidate could not afford to ride roughshod over Governor Reagan in California. Once in office a President must keep his source of support intact. The government administrator unsympathetic to such political subtleties may be rudely awakened by a White House staffer or even by the President himself. Given the fact that so many of the activities and services of the federal govern-ment in fact go on and get delivered in the states and localities of the country, some awareness of state and local politics and its relations to the White House may stand federal program administrators in good stead. In effect, the administrators work for the President—and he may have some interest in responding to the needs and interests of state and local leaders. Thus it may be in the interest of federal administrators to do likewise.

A second point can be made briefly. Parties in this country are undisciplined and indeed incoherent. Under each party label are a host of very different political actors. In the Congress there are Republicans and Democrats on both sides of almost every issue from foreign policy to welfare. And outside of Congress one can find Republicans that look like some Democrats and vice versa. Administrators can be prepared to see Republicans in Congress substantially altering the budget prepared by a Republican Administration and Republican governors attack-ing social and economic programs originating in a Republican administration. Of course the same observation might be made of Democratic Congressmen, governors, and Presidents. A partial explanation at least is that each man in office got there (or feels he did) by his own efforts and will do what he thinks he must to stay in office. As a governor and a Congressman and a Presi-dent all have different constituencies, and each may be trying to respond to his constituency, it is no wonder that each may act differently and in the process disagree with others of the same party. The result on occasion may be conflict and confusion, with programs stymied and administrators wondering what to do next, but such is public administration in the context of Ameri-can politics.

Citizen Participation and Public Opinion

Low levels of citizen participation are a fact of American politics and government.[9] The voting turnout in American elections is not noteworthy for its height (it can be abysmally low in local and school elections), and participation in other types of political activity is noticeably low. Not more than 15 percent of the American public (and probably less) take an active part in politics. And if one focuses on the politics of public policy as differentiated from electoral politics, the percentage would be even lower. To be sure, one can view everyone who pays taxes, collects social-security benefits, goes to a national park, or otherwise has contact with a government agency as a participant in government or politics. Viewed this way, participation would be quite high. But if participation is defined not as simply conforming to law or consuming services, but rather as actively attempting to influence policies or decisions or choices, then it is surely low.

Why is participation low? There are many reasons, though all may not apply to every individual. One reason is that participation takes time away from other things. Some citizens may not want to give that time. Participation also requires attention and effort, and some may not want to give these. Another way of phrasing these observations is simply to note that participation imposes costs or requires contributions that many citizens may prefer not to make, especially if they see little benefit to be gained from the expenditure. If a citizen thinks he will have little impact, if he is already satisfied, if he thinks the efforts of others will get him what he wants—why should he participate? Of course there are other reasons for not participating. Some citizens do not vote because they cannot. There may be legal barriers (which range from residency and citizenship requirements to the disenfranchisement of prisoners and mental

---

9. Useful books for further reading in participation and public opinion include: Lester Milbraith, *Political Participation* (Chicago: Rand McNally, 1965); Anthony Downs, *An Economic Theory of Democracy* (New York: Harper & Row 1957); V. O. Key, Jr., *Public Opinion and American Democracy* (New York: Alfred A. Knopf, 1964); Robert E. Lane and David O. Sears, *Public Opinion* (Englewood Cliffs: Prentice-Hall, 1964); Angus Campbell *et al.*, *The American Voter* (New York: John Wiley, 1964).

hospital patients). There may also be economic and social barriers to participation. If a man takes an active part in politics he may lose his job. And participation may be low because it is inconvenient or because would-be participants lack information. One cannot vote if he is unaware of the election or the location of the polling place. He cannot testify at a hearing if he does not know it is being held.

The opposite question about participation also deserves attention: Why do the people who do participate do so? Citizens participate because they think they may benefit, because they can, they are interested, and they have the time. But it is also true that participation may be habit, and to some extent participation may be the result of socialization. People who participate in politics are likely to come from families that participate in politics, which means (and this may have administrative consequences) that people who have never participated are not likely to and motivating them to participate (for whatever reason) may be difficult.

Although voting and other forms of electoral and campaign participation may be the best-known kind of citizen participation, today other modes of participation seem increasingly fashionable. Advisory committees, review boards, citizen action groups, citizen (or public) members of planning bodies, task forces, commissions of various kinds—all of these are examples of citizen participation. These modes of participation are important here because they are often aimed at directly influencing bureaucratic organizations.

Large bureaucratic organizations today play a prominent role in policy-making, and electoral modes of citizen participation may seem to many no longer as appropriate or effective as they may once have been. Voting may seem beside the point when bureaucrats are not subject to election. Yet even as one mentions citizen participation in bureaucratic organizations, it is important to raise questions about its results. Bureaucrats may resist citizen participation if they view it as interference or may attempt to meet demands for participation with symbolic gestures. In addition, it should be kept in mind that many citizens may not have the skills or information necessary to participate influentially in bureaucratic organizations, even if they have the opportunity. And finally, it should be remembered that if citizen participation by some citizens appears to gain results, it may also bring reaction from others who are threatened by a change in the status quo.

Despite these questions it is also true that bureaucratic organizations (especially in democratic societies) may have much to gain from at least some modes of citizen participation. Most importantly, citizen participation may bring acceptance and legitimacy, but citizen participation may also be a way of gaining intelligence about the world outside the organization. Thus, citizen participation can be an aid in developing and adjusting policy. Given these possible benefits, bureaucratic organizations are likely to support some types of citizen participation in order to achieve some goals, but it may not satisfy all citizens who want to participate. Indeed, what an organization defines as participation may be defined by some citizens as manipulation.

Public opinion and its effect on American government can be construed as another aspect of citizen participation. Certainly today no official can afford to ignore public opinion as he makes his choices and decisions. But having said this, a number of qualifications must be suggested. First, on a great many subjects many Americans do not have opinions, certainly not strongly held opinions. This frees the official to use his judgment and that of a few others. Second, opinions on a great variety of policy matters are not collected systematically, so that though they may exist, officials do not know what they are. And third, the opinions of the public on many issues may be contradictory, as when a person thinks that taxes should be cut and better service also provided. To these comments must be added the observation that a great many Americans are quite simply uninformed about government. They may have opinions, but they are uninformed opinions, and it is a nice question how much weight they ought to be given.

Any survey is likely to find people who do not know the names of their Congressmen or who do not recognize quotations from the Bill of Rights. The record of their Congressmen or their positions on major issues will be unknown to most citizens. Detailed knowledge of government agencies and the programs they carry out is possessed by only a small minority. Government agencies deal with some citizens (lobbyists, for example) who are attentive and informed, but most citizens are not. This situation has a number of implications. One is that agencies who want or are charged with providing services to the general public may have to engage in extensive public information programs, if the public is to take advantage of the services. So too may organizations such as the Internal Revenue Service that require public cooperation to carry out their missions. On the other hand, for some agencies, public ignorance may be bliss; an organization may feel free to provide special services to some citizens or groups secure in the knowledge that what is done will not be widely noticed. Or an agency may limit demand for its services (and thus pressure on its resources) by not publicizing what it provides. It can assume that many therefore will be uninformed and undemanding.

Policy Systems

In closing this chapter it may be useful to introduce the term *policy system.* When one looks at government in the United States, whether the United States government or the government of a state or large city, it is apparent that one important feature is specialization. Organizational units are specialized, and individuals are specialized. There are police departments, welfare departments, schools and libraries, parks departments, and traffic departments. The United States Government has eleven cabinet departments, which are themselves composed of numerous more specialized units, and in addition there are more than two score independent agencies of various sizes. One can speak of a welfare bureaucracy, a national-security bureaucracy, and so on. There is, in short, quite a lot of specialization with particular organizations carrying out particular programs.

The theme of specialization can be extended to the White House (where special assistants focus on one thing or another), to the Office of Management and Budget, and to the Congress. If one takes the National Government to be a policy set, then there are a number of policy *subsets*—with members drawn from Congress, the bureaucracy and the Executive Office. Of course members of some subsets (welfare and transportation, for example) may come also from state and local government and from interest groups. Another word for subset is *subsystem.*

This concept of subset or subsystem is raised in order to suggest that much policy-making goes on within particular policy areas. In any particular policy area the balance of power may rest with bureaucrats, Congressmen, or indeed, private groups.

If one considers very long the variety of public problems that confront the government, one is likely to conclude that many of them are related to one another, albeit in complex ways. The poor person (poverty is a problem) may be unskilled or indeed illiterate (education is a problem) and also in poor health (health is another problem). He may be unemployed as well. Air pollution in a city may be a result of automobile exhaust, apartment house incinerators, electric-power generating stations, jet aircraft, and leaf burning in the fall. High infant mortality may likewise have a number of causes.

But let us now go back to the notion of policy making in a subsystem. The implication is obvious. Different organizations are independently at work on similar or related problems, and the result is the lack of coordination that citizens, politicians, journalists, and scholars so frequently see. Different organizations regulate airlines and railroads and build highways. Airlines, railroads, and highways all affect urban transportation, but anything like an integrated approach is made difficult if not impossible by the structure of policy-making. The specialization that may encourage a high level of expertise may also encourage a piecemeal approach to policy-making. The competitiveness and self-interest of bureaucratic organizations and their members (employees) enhance the problem. This is not the place to suggest remedies, if indeed they are possible. But it is important to remember that policy goes on within more or less impenetrable or insulated systems. Within the system much that goes on in the world may be ignored or scarcely considered, and one condition may be magnified and given much attention. Policies may develop (be developed) that do not fit at all well with one another, an increasingly common phenomenon as the level of government activity rises. Whether the policy-developing and executing system can be redesigned, whether it ought to be, how it might be, are all questions that today deserve attention.

3 The Policy Process

The *policy process* is a common phrase in political science, but it can be misleading. It may seem to imply that policy is made one way, through one process, but this is not so. How policy is made depends on the issues, organizations, and people involved, the amount of time available, the urgency of the question, whether there is the aura of crisis, and no doubt other considerations. Policy-making is situational. Yet it is possible to think intelligently about it, bring some order to it, and attempt to understand in a general way how policy is made. This chapter begins by discussing in a fairly general and abstract way a number of things to keep in mind about public policy and then goes on to divide policy-making into a number of steps. Clearly, to break policy-making into steps risks oversimplifying it; in real life policy-making does not follow any neat and simple diagram. But the discussion of each step should make this clear repeatedly, and the process must be dealt with in some organized way.

Perspectives on Public Policy

In the first chapter a good deal of discussion was devoted to the costs and benefits of public policy, and these notions should be recalled here. Data (and more importantly, opinion) about costs and benefits affects the development of public policies at every step. But there are in addition a number of other things to have in mind. The most important is that policy is

45

often made on the basis of limited information. Agencies do, before they know what to do. Daniel Moynihan once said of the community action part of the War on Poverty that the government did not know what it was doing.[1] This same observation could be made of a number of other programs and policies. It frequently could be no other way, given the limits on information, time, and resources and the pressure to act. And thus money is spent but often all goals are not reached, though at least some goals may be.

A second important point is just this—policies often have multiple goals, and some of them may be achieved. Think about this point for a minute. More money for federal aid to secondary education may have the following goals: expansion of the U.S. Office of Education, demonstration of the President's commitment to educational improvement, relief for the fiscal problems of state and local governments, alleviation of unemployment among teachers, gaining votes for candidates in a coming election, the solution of the high school dropout problem, the improvement of secondary school curricula. Some of these goals may well be met. But the dropout problem may remain, and students may still get out of high school untrained for a job and indeed unable to read. To put the point in a somewhat different way, the goals of some of the participants may be met, but not the goals of others. Symbolic, political, and administrative goals may be met, but not substantive goals. In any event one begins to see how risky it is to say of a program that it didn't accomplish anything. It may have accomplished quite a lot, though not perhaps what you thought it was intended to.

You can develop a list of possible goals for welfare or environmental or consumer-protection legislation. In each of these areas there are multiple goals, different actors may have different (and many) goals, and goals may conflict with one another. In the end a new welfare bill (for example) may meet some of the goals of the White House, the Department of Health, Education, and Welfare, the Senate Finance Committee, and the House Ways and Means Committee—and still leave a lot of poverty. The condition of many on welfare may not be greatly improved.

In addition to the notion of multiple goals, the student

---

1. Daniel P. Moynihan, *Maximum Feasible Misunderstanding* (New York: The Free Press, 1969), p. 170.

should note and remember such terms as unanticipated consequences, unintended consequences, and indirect effects. These
are terribly important, and the illustrations are endless. Consider
just a few possibilities. A new health insurance program may
result in increased medical care costs. An increase in the minimum wage may increase unemployment, at least in some
industries. An increase in industrial productivity may have the
same effect. A program apparently intended to bring some measure of economic security to the small farmer may mostly bring
lots of money to big farmers. A high guaranteed annual income
(say $5000) could noticeably increase consumption and have
obvious and detrimental effects on the environment, and so it
goes. The point is that a new policy may do a good deal more
than was intended—and indeed not *what* was intended. In the
urge to pass a program before the Congress adjourns or before
the next election such possibilities may receive scant attention
while the rhetoric and debate focus on what is intended.

And this gets us to another important question. What is
intended? And by whom? It is not easy to know or find out.
Public rhetoric is not the same thing as private reality. Appearance and reality, symbol and substance are pairs of words that
the student interested in policy and administration should never
forget.[2] The apparent goal of a program may be the reduction of
poverty, the real goals may be multiple and include reducing the
likelihood of violent conflict but not include a major reallocation
of resources. The apparent goal of an environmental program
may be water you can drink and air you can breathe; the real
goals may be many and include no increase in unemployment,
continued growth in the economy, and continued political support from industrial and business leaders as well as a clean
environment. There are some conflicts here, and in the end environmental actions may be limited and to some extent symbolic.
The apparent goal of a regulatory agency may be the regulation
of industry and the protection of the public. The real goal may be
the preservation of appearances while not imposing undue hardship on the industry. To repeat, the notions of symbol and
substance, of image and reality are important. Policy-making
involves the manipulation of symbols, image building, public

---

2. See Murray Edelman, *The Symbolic Use of Politics* (Urbana:
University of Illinois, 1964). See also his *Politics as Symbolic Action*
(Chicago: Markham Publishing Co., 1971).

relations, and recognition of the fact that appearances *are* important.

In trying to understand why policy is made as it is, and in trying to forecast what policy is likely to be made, the student may operate with several (or one of several) models of political and administrative reality. Which one (ones) he uses is not unimportant.[3] It is possible, for example, to view policy as made by the President and consistent with his goals, and thus by listening to the President one may feel that he knows what policy is likely to be. Conversely, by looking at policy one may feel that he can impute to the President certain goals, interests, and values. But what if the President has delegated his power, or is not interested, or has tried to exercise influence and failed? Then conclusions reached may be in error, and the model of Presidential policy-making is less than satisfactory.

Instead or in addition one can view policy as the product of agency activity and agency competition and negotiation. With this perspective, if one understands the distribution of power and interests within the bureaucracy, one may be able to forecast the direction of public policy. And conversely, in determining what policy is one may make inferences about which agencies carried the day in bureaucratic battle. With this agency perspective one would not hold out much hope for a manpower policy known to be opposed by the Department of Labor or for a proposed defense posture that noticeably downgraded the air arm of the Navy.

Again, one could view policy as developing from the interaction of individuals; and with this view one would want to know who had access to whom and what their interests were. Perhaps there are other ways of thinking of reality, but these suggestions are enough to show that how you view the world may affect both your explanations and your forecasts. Of course there is no one best way, no right way. It may help us to further understand policy-making if we divide it into stages and look at each one in turn—keeping in mind that this may make policy making seem neater than in fact it is.

---

3. For a full elaboration of this idea see Graham T. Allison, *Essence of Decision* (Boston: Little, Brown & Co., 1971).

Is There a Problem?

Problem awareness, the feeling or judgment that the status quo is unsatisfactory, is the first step in problem-solving, the first step in policy-making. The complexity of the problem-awareness process and the conflicts of this stage may be concealed, but they should not be underestimated. Many potential policies lapse at this stage because there may be little agreement that the status quo is unsatisfactory. For any major new program to come into existence—whether in welfare or in education or in transportation—a great number of persons must agree that the status quo is unsatisfactory. The agency or agencies directly concerned—the President and his staff, the Office of Management and Budget, members of Congressional committees, interest groups—all these must agree on the existence of a problem. This point deserves emphasis, because in the heterogenous American political system different men often define their problem differently. Indeed, one man's problem may be the cause of another's well-being. High prices for food may be considered a problem by housewives, agencies trying to control inflation, and some Congressmen. But high prices for agricultural products may be desired by farmers, the Department of Agriculture, and other Congressmen. The situation that seems to be a serious problem to one man may seem a minor problem to another and a benefit to a third. Lack of agreement on what the problems are explains a good deal of government inertia.

To be sure, not all changes or new programs require the same degree of support and agreement. Bureaucratic agencies may change their regulations after no more than a public hearing; and the President may issue executive orders that require only Congressional acquiescence, if that. But before there is change, the status quo must be viewed as unsatisfactory by enough of the relevant participants. (The definitions of "enough" and "relevant" depend of course on the stakes involved.)

How does dissatisfaction arise? How do bureaucratic organizations become aware of problems or performance gaps?[4] There are numerous ways. Organizations may search for problems. Military organizations especially have intelligence units, but not only military organizations want to know what changes

---

4. The phrase "performance gap," is taken from Anthony Downs, *Inside Bureaucracy* (Boston: Little, Brown & Co., 1967), p. 191.

are taking place in the world they confront, what changes they may have to adjust to.[5] The Census Bureau, the Bureau of Labor Statistics, and the Office of Education are all examples of organizations that collect information to identify problems and provide a basis for program changes. Other government organizations may use this information and may collect their own more specialized information.

Besides collecting external data, bureaucratic organizations may also collect internal data on their own performance, which may result in proposals for change. Any particular agency may be in contact with agencies (federal, state, foreign, or private) doing similar work, with professional societies, and with various clienteles—and all these contacts may bring in information that will help identify problems and lead to change proposals. Many government agencies are engaged in scientific research and development, the result of which may have a direct effect on what they propose and do.

Agency search for problems may be very limited, and the information collected may be interpreted as not indicative of any problems.[6] Search for problems may be limited for a number of reasons. There may be a shortage of resources; perhaps the management of an agency thinks there are better ways to spend money than on self-examination; when work seems to be going smoothly, it may seem silly to search for trouble. Management may sometimes feel like the patient who avoids the doctor because he is afraid of what he will be told. Optimism and a sense of self-confidence can produce a sense of security. Even when search does go on it may be over a limited area. It is possible to imagine a law-enforcement agency that collects much data on crime rates but never questions its own organizational structure or recruiting policies. It is possible to imagine a military organization that collects intelligence about the enemy but does not evaluate its own performance; and it may have no intelligence about the country that unexpectedly turns out to be an enemy. Expectations affect search. It is possible to imagine a welfare agency that is constantly hunting for fraud and mis-

---

5. A relevant and very interesting book is Harold L. Wilensky, *Organizational Intelligence* (New York: Basic Books, 1967).

6. An example is the Selective Service System. See James W. Davis, Jr., and Kenneth M. Dolbeare, *Little Groups of Neighbors* (Chicago: Markham Publishing Co., 1968).

use of funds but never wondering about the over-all impact of its program. It is possible to imagine a government agency searching for information that will demonstrate that it has done and is doing a good job.

Bureaucratic agencies may interpret what information they do obtain in a biased way. Ignorance, ideology, values, and self-interest may all affect the interpretation of information. Data on Soviet military capabilities may be interpreted by the Pentagon in such a way as to suggest the need for greater military might. A budget analyst or Congressman may look at the same information and think American capabilities quite sufficient. Data on crime rates may be interpreted by police to mean that more police are needed: others may look at the same data and conclude that the present system is a failure and scrapping it might make as much sense as enlarging it. It is hard for organizations to admit that what they are doing is wrong or irrelevant or that their performance is simply inadequate, and this fact may affect their interpretation of information. Sometimes agencies may get information that they do not understand or whose significance they do not appreciate. They may get conflicting information or information that lends itself to multiple interpretations. Facts must be given meaning, and different people and organizations may give the same facts different meanings.

Limited search and biased interpretation may both interfere with problem awareness. But in our political system and indeed in the executive branch many actors or participants initially may become aware of problems and call them to the attention of relevant agencies and political officials. In any particular policy area there are often several agencies, and the problems not found by one may be found by another.[7] The Central Intelligence Agency, the Defense Intelligence Agency, the National Security Agency, and the individual services all collect intelligence. The Bureau of the Census and the Bureau of Labor Statistics both collect socioeconomic statistics, as do other agencies. Several other examples of groups of cooperating (and competing) agencies could be given. Although these kinds

---

7. A common swear-word in administration is duplication. A word often as accurate is redundancy. A valuable article on the value of redundancy is Martin Landau, "Redundancy, Rationality, and the Problem of Duplication," *Public Administration Review* 29 (July/August 1969), pp. 346–358.

of groupings may raise visions of duplication and overlapping, it is well to remember that the policy field in the hands of only one agency may contain a lot of unexposed problems. The draft, in the hands only of the Selective Service System, is a case that comes to mind. The FBI, in the hands for so many years of one Director, is another example. But the Selective Service System and the debates about the draft in the late 1960s also demonstrate that problems can be brought to surface by Congressmen, Presidential commissions, journalists, and a wide variety of intellectuals. In a pluralistic political system the search activities of bureaucratic agencies are supplemented in many ways.

For new programs or other sorts of changes to come about it is not enough that only one participant identify a problem; a number of participants must agree that a problem exists. Such agreement may be difficult to reach. Admitting the existence of a problem—malnutrition in rural areas, increasing rates of illegitimacy, increasing environmental pollution—may have political repercussions, and the existing pattern of social benefits and burdens may be disturbed. Achieving agreement on the existence of a problem may require an educational effort. Officials, to say nothing of the public, may just be unable to interpret statistical data; or the data revealing a problem may conflict with their preferences, values, or habits. Reaction to the data on the health effects of smoking is an example. Achieving agreement that a problem exists may take time, perhaps years; but agreement can be hurried by a crisis. Senator Kefauver thought the regulation of drugs too lax, but it took deformed babies to concern enough people to support him.[8] Even several assassinations of public figures have not convinced everyone that the easy availability of firearms in this country is a problem. Is it?

Can Anything Be Done?

There is a difference between being convinced that a particular condition is a problem and being able to do anything about it. There may not be enough knowledge to carry out a solution. It is possible with available knowledge to virtually wipe out mosquitoes and malaria; it is not possible now to wipe out can-

---

8. The reference is to the thalidomide scare in the early 1960s. See Richard Harris, *The Real Voice* (New York: Macmillan, 1964).

cer or mental illness—though it is possible to carry on research activities that could lead to successful treatment and prevention programs. In the social policy areas our lack of knowledge is overwhelming, but not widely appreciated or understood. The poor performance (or outright failure) of many education, welfare, manpower, and corrections programs can often be traced to inadequate knowledge and greatly oversimplified assumptions about human behavior.[9] Will this work? How do you know? What is the evidence? are questions that should be asked of anyone with a new proposal in the social-welfare field. Frequently the evidence is skimpy or simply nonexistent. But of course it is also true that frequently the pressure "to do something" is enormous—and so we have policy-making by trial and error. (If there is no or limited or biased evaluation a trial run or pilot project can go on for a long time and even be expanded before error is discovered, if it ever is.)

In addition to inadequate knowledge, there may not be enough money or skilled manpower to carry out a program, or using resources to cope with one problem may prevent action on another. The proposed solution may be worse than the problem. Solutions to some social problems may be impossible legally or politically, assuming more or less durable cultural values and political preferences. It may be difficult, however, for agencies and officials (to say nothing of politicians) to admit that a problem is insoluble. If the problem is obvious, doing anything may be passed off as a solution.

At any one time there are likely to be more problems than resources for solutions. What kinds of problems are selected for solution? The ones that attract the interest of influential participants, those in which there appears to be the most popular interest, those that can apparently be solved cheaply, and those that promise to have a quick payoff. An election is always just around a corner. These several criteria may mean that some problems—like air pollution—may wait a long time. They are not dramatic, and effective solution may be expensive. Perhaps it is more useful to ask about a problem not whether anything can be done about it, but whether anything can be done now.

Related to the question "Can anything be done?" is another question: "Should anything be done?" Information, ideology,

---

9. See Alice Rivlin, *Systematic Thinking and Social Action* (Washington: The Brookings Institution, 1971).

and self-interest may all affect the answer. Those likely to be affected detrimentally by action may argue that nothing should be done, and they may also argue publicly that nothing can be done. General Lewis B. Hershey, for many years the Director of the Selective Service System, would admit grudgingly that the draft was unfair but add that life itself was unfair. He would admit variation among local boards but also point out variation among judges and juries. In short he would admit some problems but imply that nothing could be done about them.[10] But if some participants argue that nothing can or should be done about a particular problem, others will argue that something not only can be done but must be done. For change in the status quo to take place there has to be substantial agreement that something can and ought to be done.

What Ought to Be Done and Who Ought to Do It?

Once there is agreement to solve a problem, attention turns to what and how and who. At this stage in the program development process, alternative solutions to problems are proposed and evaluated. There may be wide agreement that institutions of higher education are in financial trouble, but is the solution to be federal grants to institutions, scholarships or loans to students, or tax benefits to parents? All these proposals are plausible and debatable alternatives. There may be widespread agreement that crimes of violence are a serious and growing problem, but what can and ought to be done? Should there be a national police force, or should state and local forces be strengthened and improved, and if so, how? Or do we know enough to do anything? Should unskilled unemployed young men be given job training in their own communities or should they leave their community for a center where they can learn new skills and new behavior patterns in a new environment? Transportation in urban areas is a problem, but is the answer mass transit or more expressways? The point is clear. Virtually any problem has several possible solutions, though any advocate may argue that there is really only one.

---

10. See, for example, General Hershey's testimony before the Committee on Armed Services, U.S. House of Representatives, *Review of the Administration and Operation of the Selective Service System,* Hearings (89th Congress, 2nd session, June 22–24, 28–30, 1966).

Naturally, alternatives will vary in their cost, effectiveness, and political acceptability, though the magnitude of these variables may be hazy. Program debates are notable for producing opinions, judgments, and conclusions, not facts. The effectiveness of proposed solutions may be especially unclear. Proposed programs resemble in some ways untested though plausible hypotheses. Advocates, however, are likely to express confidence that what they favor will work. However, certain participants in a policy debate may not want a problem solved or think there is no problem. In such a case it may appear to them wiser not to say this openly but instead to propose a course of action that they think will not affect the status quo.

Just as there are alternative solutions to problems there are alternative ways to implement solutions. Within the executive branch there are many groups of agencies in the same policy areas. Thus several agencies may be able to carry out a program. Presumably the FBI could protect the President, the Department of Interior could manage the nation's forest, and the food-stamp program could be in the Department of Health, Education, and Welfare. But in fact the Secret Service (located not in Justice but in Treasury) protects the President, the Forest Service is in the Department of Agriculture (National Parks and the Bureau of Land Management are in Interior), and the food-stamp program is in the Department of Agriculture.

Rather than giving responsibility for a new program to an existing agency it is possible (and not uncommon) to create a new agency. The National Aeronautics and Space Administration was created to manage the space program of the nation; the Office of Economic Opportunity was created to oversee a War on Poverty, though it has now fallen on hard times. The Environmental Protection Agency was created to protect the environment, and a number of organizations have been set up to fight inflation. Sometimes a new agency is created because no appropriate agency exists; more often new agencies are created to carry out new programs that existing agencies might not handle well. NASA was created to avoid military dominance of the space program, and the Atomic Energy Commission was created after World War II to give civilian control to the nuclear-energy program.

The answer to how a program should be administered or a problem solved need not involve the federal bureaucracy exclusively or at all. In the United States federal system, the states often carry out programs. The grant-in-aid in its various forms has long provided federal money to the states. For highways, health, welfare, and education, federal funds have been used to support programs administered largely by the states, though with federal conditions and federal supervision. The Federal Highway Administration has worked with state highway departments in the construction of the interstate highway system, the Office of Education has worked with state departments of education, the Social and Rehabilitation Service worked with state departments of welfare. In a sense the state bureaucracies become extensions of the federal bureaucracy. If this were not possible the federal bureaucracy might be much larger.

Another way of carrying out a program without substantially increasing the size of the federal bureaucracy is to contract for service with a private corporation or other nongovernmental organization. Today much government research and development, construction, and supplies and equipment come from contractors. The Defense Department relies heavily on the services of contractors, and NASA has played the role of supervisor to hundreds of contractors and subcontractors.

Voluntary action or voluntary compliance by citizens may be suggested as an alternative to government action. This alternative was suggested by the automobile industry before the Traffic Safety Act was passed to develop mandatory automobile safety standards. Sometimes voluntary action will be undependable or insufficient, but for some reason direct government action may appear unsatisfactory. In such cases the tax system of the government may be used to elicit or reward certain kinds of behavior. Thus, rather than receiving direct grants or direct payments, a taxpayer may be given tax credits or deductions if he uses his money in certain ways. The present income-tax system subsidizes an impressive array of private charities by making contributions to them tax deductible. If this were not the case, the health, welfare, and education programs of the government might have to be much larger. As this is written substantial attention is being given to how the income-tax system might be used to aid higher education.

Although in principle what will be done and who will do it are separable questions, in practice they get mixed up. What is going to be done is not unrelated to who will do it. Who will carry out a program is related to what is going to be done and how well. If the Department of Defense were in charge of atomic energy, it would be hard to imagine much emphasis being given to civilian applications. At the early stages of any problem/policy/program debate it is likely that a number of alternative programs will be proposed together with appropriate administrative arrangements. Existing executive branch agencies are likely to propose programs that they can carry out and benefit from. The White House or the Office of Management and Budget may suggest programs to be carried out by new or re-organized groups, and they will have their own views on how programs ought to be administered. If traditional areas of state activity (educaton, health, welfare, law enforcement, highways) are involved, state officials are likely to argue for state involvement. Increasingly, city officials want to bypass the state government in administering programs designed to aid cities. Business, industry, and fiscally conservative groups may want no direct government action at all but argue for tax measures that would reward private actions aimed at achieving desirable goals. Contractors who stand to benefit, as well as some Congressmen impressed with the efficiency of business organizations, may suggest that private contractors should be paid to handle the problem at hand, whether it be space engineering or job training.

A number of factors, not mutually exclusive, are likely to determine what proposals are made. Whether or not action is really desired is important. When Senators advocate leaving the pace of school integration to the judgment of local school officials or state authorities, it takes little imagination to know what they are after. The political, social, and economic values of policy-process participants will affect what they propose. Bureaucratic self-interest is likely to be reflected in the proposals emanating from bureaucratic organizations. They tend to propose solutions they can handle, programs that they can and should administer. Bureaucratic organizations are likely to propose solutions consistent with what they have done in the past. Brand new approaches or solutions rarely come from old-line organizations. Groups and organizations usually recommend programs and administrative arrangements they think will do them the most good or the least harm. Such factors as available resources, potential cost, and political feasibility may also affect what is proposed. Of course many organizations may engage in more or less rigorous and objective analysis of the possible consequences, costs, and benefits of alternative programs and develop their proposals accordingly; their final proposals depend on both the results of their analysis and their own goals. Just as program proposals resemble untested hypotheses, so do suggested administrative arrangements. The normal assumption is that what is proposed will work, but often this assumption rests on no strong evidence, or no evidence at all. In contrast to the testing of scientific hypotheses, programs and their administration are not often rigorously tested and discarded if they do not work.

The Final Choice

As we have seen, policy-making and program development are the occasion for conflict among various policy-process participants with different interests. Some participants may for a variety of reasons resist any change in the status quo. Perhaps they are benefitting from the status quo; perhaps they fear any change would leave them worse off than before; perhaps they don't want the government to spend more money. Other participants may desire change in the status quo, but this group may be divided into several more, with each proposing a different course of action. Given this kind of conflict the status quo is likely to remain unchanged. The status quo is likely to continue until a sufficiently large coalition has not only agreed on the need for change, but also agreed on an alternative. The first part, agreement on the need for change, is hardly simple. It is not enough that people regard the status quo as not ideal; rather they must regard it as unacceptable and they must be willing to pay a price for change. This condition is an obstacle to many proposed programs and to a good deal of change. Often the price that people are willing to pay will not purchase very much change in the status quo. Of course, if they are willing to pay repeatedly, as on the installment plan, a good deal of change may occur over time. Agreement on a particular alternative may be even harder to achieve than agreement on the need for change. It may not be reached until proponents of various alternatives are convinced that virtually anything would be better than the status quo. As long as different groups support uncompromisingly their particular positions the status quo is likely to continue.

To this discussion should be added the obvious notion that some kinds of changes are easier than others. The fewer people that must agree, the easier change will be. A change that apparently affects only a few people may be easier than one that affects many. Changes with apparently predictable consequences may be easier than changes whose possible results are unknown. A change that appears as almost no change at all is likely to be easier than something that appears revolutionary. In effect, little changes are easier than big changes, and they are more common. In American government much change, much program development, is marginal, incremental. Big changes are infrequent and unlikely.[11]

The mythology of American government has it that final program choices are made when Congress votes, or maybe when the President signs a bill. This is, as we have seen, only occasionally true. American government contains many decision-makers, and any one of them, depending on the circumstances, may make the final choice. As we know, legislation may be initiated in an executive-branch agency and be virtually rubber-stamped all along the legislative line until it comes back to the agency for implementation. Programs may be developed by the White House, agencies, special task forces, Congressional committees, or interest groups. If we discard the idea of formal choice and look instead for the meaningful choice, we may more easily see that there is no single location for choosing. Who has the last word may depend on a variety of things: the problem at hand, the proposed solutions, the groups that may be affected, the agencies concerned, the abilities and interests of their heads, the party in power—both in the White House and in Congress—and the interests and abilities of the President.

Because in our political system there are so many people who might have the last word, who in fact does have it may not be clear, and appearances may be misleading. When events turn out well there is no shortage of men who will claim responsibility and credit; when they turn out poorly it may be hard to find out whom to debit. Was the decision made in an agency by some invisible bureaucrat, or was it made by the Secretary of the department? Was it made in the Office of Management and Budget or by a White House staffer or by the President himself? Did the chairman of a Congressional committee exercise an informal but very real veto? The answers to such questions require research, not recourse to organization charts and the Con-

---

11. See the work of Charles Lindblom, especially his "The Science of Muddling Through," *Public Administration Review*, 19 (1959), pp. 70–88.

stitution. A thorough investigation into a particular program or decision may conclude that it is impossible to tell just who made what decisions.

Much important executive decision-making is unpublicized and takes place in confidential meetings. For the bureaucracy there is nothing resembling either the Congressional Record or the Congressional quarterly. The sheer volume of decision-making in the executive branch makes it even more difficult to follow. Of course, inaction is also a form of choice. Proposals may not be made by agencies, ideas may be pigeonholed in the White House, and bills in Congress may languish in committee. Further, all these inactions may go unpublicized.

For a program to be effective, consistent choices or decisions have to be made in three areas. A program has to be authorized, funded, and given to an appropriate agency for implementation. Yet these choices are not always consistent. A program may be authorized but not funded; or it may be authorized but put in the hands of an organization that will not administer it properly. Why do such things occur? A program which has been authorized may not be funded because authorization and funding are done by separate Congressional committees that may not see eye-to-eye on the need for a program. There is another explanation for inconsistencies in program budget organization. Authorizing a program with some fanfare may satisfy one group; not funding it or funding it at a low level may mollify another. Passing a law may apparently gain votes in one place; giving it to an agency that will not enforce it or giving the agency so little money that it cannot enforce it may gain votes in another place.

When all this is said, however, it should be clear that "final choices" are often not final. Inconsistencies may be ironed out next year; funding levels can be increased or cut back. Unexpected consequences may result in amendments to legislation or in the issuance of new regulations. In short, decisions made may be modified, and the modifications themselves changed in time. And in all this agencies and officials will have an interest and play a part.

PART II GETTING TO KNOW BUREAUCRACIES AND BUREAUCRATS

Part II provides information essential to understanding public administration at the national level. Chapter 4 provides a brief overview of the structure of the executive branch and the organizations that compose it, although any particular department or bureau may well have been created, abolished, or reorganized between the writing of this chapter and its publication. It is essential for anyone studying public administration (or interested in the executive branch) to have some idea of the over-all structure of the government bureaucracy. It is simpler to comprehend the policy-making process and the politics of the bureaucracy if one has some notion of the structure of departments, the differences between departments and independent agencies, and the relations between department secretaries and bureau chiefs.

Chapter 5 turns to a standard topic in public administration, personnel. Who the bureaucrats are, what they are like, and how they are recruited, paid, and promoted are among the subjects discussed. Two topics currently in the news receive attention—unionization of government employees and minority hiring. Chapter 6 and 7 take up explicitly the subject of human behavior in an organizational setting. Shelves of books and countless articles have been devoted to this subject, and these chapters are by no means a summary of available knowledge. They simply try to describe some common modes of behavior or patterns of adjustment, point to problems, and raise important questions relating to what is called organizational behavior, or administrative behavior, or bureaucratic behavior.

4 The Structure of the Executive Branch

A first glance at the table of contents of the U.S. Government Organization Manual may leave the impression that the executive branch, though large, is put together in a fairly understandable way. At the top is the President of the United States and immediately following is the Executive Office of the President with a number of different subdivisions. Then there are eleven Executive Departments, ranging from State to Transportation. (They are listed in order of age; State is the oldest department in the government, Transportation the youngest or newest.) Following the departments are a host of Independent Agencies, 51 in all, from A to V. Action is for ACTION and V of course is for the Veterans Administration. ACTION is one of the newest of the independent agencies; it was created in July 1971. "The purpose of the agency is to bring together within a single agency a number of voluntary action programs brought together from throughout the Federal Government to create a system of volunteer service which uses to the fullest advantage the energies and efforts of the Nation in the American tradition of voluntary involvement."

Any first impression of simplicity and clarity, however, will change when one begins to probe beneath the surface of the executive branch. In fact, the executive branch is a complex and confusing collection of agencies where the reality may be belied by the appearance and where questions of authority and responsibility become inextricably mixed with questions of politics, prestige, and money. In the end one may be persuaded not only that the structure of the executive branch is complex and confusing, but also that it is quite inadequate to cope with the problems the government today confronts. Because of its size and complexity units of the executive branch may be virtually autonomous or invisible and in either event uncontrollable. Yet before one can make this judgment or reject it, one must become familiar more or less with the executive branch, its components and their relationships. You may later decide that questions of structure are relatively unimportant and that to worry about structure is to divert attention from more important matters. To blame the structure of the government for failure and errors may be to miss real issues.

The President and the Executive Office

The President, on paper, is clearly the man on top and his office—the Presidency—is at the pinnacle of the Executive Branch. The President is the central figure in the executive branch and of course in his own administration. He is head of the civil service, the foreign service, and the military services. He is the superior of the heads of all the executive departments and agencies, which in effect makes him a member of numerous policy subsystems. In scores of arenas the President has a hand in resolving conflicts, making choices, giving rewards and administering discipline. In foreign affairs and national security, in taxation and economics, in health and welfare, in conservation and natural resources the President plays a role. The State of the Union message is the President's message, the Budget of the United States in a very real sense is the President's budget.

In recent years it seems clear that a major phenomenon of American politics has been the expansion of the Presidency. Today we demand more of the President than ever before and in response the Presidency has grown. The Presidency has grown also because of the powers that have been given to the President, powers often that parallel our demands, expectations, and hopes. The President is responsible for the national security and foreign affairs of the United States. To be sure this responsibility has always been his, but today atomic energy and intercontinental missiles have rendered the task incomparably more complex than in the days before World War II. The President is held responsible for the health of the economy and for the health and welfare of the nation's citizens. He is supposed to support the fight against crime and also serve as environmental protection officer. Any student can think of other things the President should do; it would be a good exercise to make a list.

The enlargement of the Presidency is surely in part a result of developments outside the Presidency to which the President has been asked to respond. But in part it is also a result of what might be called mass-media magnification. Thanks in part to the media (and of course thanks also in part to a President's willingness to use them) the President is the most continuously visible public official in the United States. He thus becomes the almost inevitable focus of criticism, discontent, and demands for action. The consequence has been Presidential enlargement.

The growth of the Presidency as been accompanied also by the institutionalization and indeed the bureaucratization of the office. Clearly no one man, even if helped by a small coterie of assistants, could possibly cope with the demands today placed on the Presidency. Thus a number of organizations have grown up around the President designed to serve his needs as well perhaps as the needs of constituencies or publics important to the President. Presidential organizations are not fixed in number and continue to develop in response both to Presidential taste and the number of expectations placed on the President. Just as the rest of the executive branch, the organizations directly assisting the President are in a state of flux. The description and discussion that follow therefore can make no claim to being more than suggestive and illustrative.

The holding organization that is the institutionalized Presidency is the Executive Office of the President. It was created in 1939 by Reorganization Order Number 1 in order to draw together (and to provide) advisors and assistants to the President. Its main component in 1939 was the Bureau of the Budget. Today that is still the largest component and surely one of the most important, though it has a new name, The Office of Management and Budget. But today there are a number of organizations in the executive office. A list of the organizations in the Executive Office may be informative, but even as you look at it remember that it is not fixed. In fact you might check this list with one in the latest Government Organization manual to see what has been added or subtracted.

Organizations within the
Executive Office of the President
The White House Office
Office of Management and Budget
Council of Economic Advisors
National Security Council
Central Intelligence Agency
Domestic Council
National Aeronautics and Space Council
Office of Economic Opportunity
Office of Energy Policy
Office of the Special Representative for Trade Negotiations
Council on Environmental Quality
Office on Telecommunications Policy
Special Action Office for Drug Abuse Prevention

The very titles of these organizations show the range of Presidential responsibility and concern and indicate the President's heavy involvement in both foreign and domestic policy. Several of the organizations suggest the close connection between public policy and economics, and several suggest the quite specialized and technical nature of many Presidential concerns. The proverbial man in the street may not know much about such matters as telecommunications policy or international trade. The President has advisors on both. And indeed he must, for what President (what one man?) could on his own handle matters as diverse as drug abuse and economic forecasting? Indeed this list suggests that an important Presidential problem is simply deciding what he needs advice on. Even on this issue he may need advice. It is little wonder that a recent book was titled *The Presidential Advisory System.*[1] In a sense the essence of the Presidential task is seeking and using (or ignoring) advice.

One more point might be made about this list of Executive Office organizations. Creating a new organization within the Executive Office or transferring an existing organization to or from the Executive Office is often a move with symbolic as well perhaps as real consequences. Creating a Council on Environmental Quality in the Executive Office or an Office of Drug Abuse is a way (if you are President) of telling the public or

---

1. Thomas E. Cronin and Sanford Greenberg, *The Presidential Advisory System* (New York: Harper & Row, 1969).

more likely a particular constituency that you are concerned about the problem at issue. Controversial or salient problems or (which may be the same thing) problems that the President is currently concerned about may be looked after by an appropriately named organization in the Executive Office. The politics of organization shows its face in the executive office as well as in the executive branch as a whole.

Several of the organizations deserve extended comments; one of these is the White House Office.[2] The men in the White House Office are personal appointees of the President and serve as his personal assistants. They maintain contact with Cabinet members, sub-Cabinet officials, bureau chiefs, Congressional leaders, party leaders, and interest group spokesmen. They gather information, communicate the President's wishes, and issue his orders. Members of the White House Office listen, read, speak, decide, and act for the President. In short they help him and extend his reach.

The staff of the White House office is not large, but it is influential. Currently the White House Office includes about two score professional staff members with such titles as Counsellor to the President, Assistant to the President, Special Consultant to the President, and Special Assistant to the President. It would be hard to say what these particular titles mean. But within the White House Office there is both specialization and hierarchy, which indicates no doubt that the Presidency along with the rest of the executive branch is a bureaucracy. There is an assistant to the President for Domestic Affairs, and there is an assistant for National Security Affairs. There is a Press Secretary, there are Congressional liaison people, and there is the equivalent of a chief of staff. One man who has held the latter position described his job in the following terms, "I have the general administrative responsibility for the operation of the White House staff—and for the President's schedule, the flow of paper to and from the President, and generally riding herd on the whole operation. . . ."[3] There may be consultants or advisers or assistants on special problems, and there are likely to be some general utility fielders. And amongst all these people there is a

---

2. A very readable book on the White House Office is Patrick Anderson, *The President's Men* (Garden City: Doubleday Anchor Book, 1969).

3. See interview with H. R. Haldeman in *U.S. News and World Report*, September 14, 1970, p. 56.

pecking order; some men are close to the President and see him frequently and others mainly see those who see the President. It might be noted also that it is not uncommon for individuals officially assigned to departments to be detailed or assigned to the White House.

It should be clear that the President has full authority to design his own office and use his staff as he will. The result is that the precise organization of the White House Office and the use to which it is put may differ over the course of a President's term and from President to President. Much depends on his background, training, and taste in politics and administration. A White House Office may be almost military in its style and structure, as in the days of President Eisenhower, or it can appear more chaotic, as in the days of Franklin Roosevelt. The staff can have a largely academic caste or a more professional and business appearance. It may be enlarged by one President and shrunk by another—and over the tenure of one President may both expand and contract.

Although many of the White House staff are relatively invisible and unknown this is not true of all; and it should be clear that the men called simply assistants and consultants may have much influence and power. The men who see the President daily and for extended periods (not all staffers do), who sift and sort the people, papers, and ideas that will reach him, and who then communicate the President's decisions and desires are obviously in positions of some power. The result is that the astute foreign ambassador may prefer the ear of the special assistant for national security affairs to the ear of the Secretary of State, and others with an interest in Presidential thinking may search for the appropriate White House contacts and channels. In the end as the power of the White House Office grows and Presidential assistants gain visibility and stature, the positions of Cabinet members and other agency heads may decline somewhat. In other words a conscious structural change that expands and professionalizes the White House Office may produce effects throughout much of the executive branch.

In his book *The President's Men*, Patrick White illustrates clearly the power of the White House staff. One man he interviewed, who had been a Presidential assistant, put the matter forcefully, "I had more power over national affairs in a few years in the White House than I could if I spent the rest of my life in the Senate." And when asked about a Cabinet post the same respondent said, "Most of them aren't worth having."[4] Overstated? No doubt. Illuminating? Certainly.

The Domestic Council is another component of the Executive Office.[5] It is new, having been in existence since July 1, 1970. The Domestic Council was created in order to give the President some means of developing and analyzing alternative policies for dealing with domestic problems. Formerly a President had to rely more or less heavily on the staffs of executive departments and agencies. The creation of the Domestic Council recognized the fact that most major problems do not fit neatly within the boundaries of single executive departments and agencies, and it recognized further that most departments already are committed to particular views of the world and to particular programs and policy solutions.

The members of the Domestic Council are the President, Vice President, and all cabinet members except the Secretary of State and the Secretary of Defense. It has an Executive Director (who may also be titled Assistant to the President) and a professional staff of about 20. It operates largely on the basis of ad-hoc committees and task forces made up of staff members and representatives of concerned agencies. The job of the Executive Director is to see that the President gets careful studies of salient issues that include necessary background material, analyze and evaluate possible alternative actions, note possible consequences, and make recommendations. The Domestic Council is still quite new and has not yet developed a firm image and reputation. It is entirely possible that a new administration would substantially reorganize it, or simply let it fade away. But the function it performs of high-level interdepartmental policy analysis is too important and probably too useful to Presidents to disappear.

The Domestic Council overlaps to some extent with the Office of Management and Budget, another major component of the Executive Office. In principle the Domestic Council is concerned with what ought to be done by the government, and the Office of Management and Budget is concerned with how it ought to be done, but obviously in practice what and how cannot be neatly separated.

---

4. Patrick Anderson, *The President's Men,* p. 2 for both quotations.
5. *The National Journal* has carried a number of articles on various units of the Executive Office in the last few years.

Created largely out of an existing organization—the Bureau of the Budget—the Office of Management and Budget (OMB) has much in common with its predecessor.[6] Its best-known and most obvious function is to review the budget requests submitted by departments and agencies and to prepare the final budget that the President submits annually to the Congress. For this purpose the OMB has a number of program divisions—national security programs, human resources programs, natural resource programs, and so on—as well as a budget-review division. In addition OMB is involved in the review of legislation, in problems of government agency organization and in management improvement. When OMB was created there was some effort made to strengthen its management and organization activities though there is some question how successful the effort has been. In any case OMB is more than simply a budget-preparer. At top levels OMB officials frequently act as general-purpose troubleshooters for the White House, and the organization as a whole is involved in such varied activities as labor relations, executive development, program evaluation, program coordination, and the development of management information systems.

The reorganization of the Bureau of the Budget and its renaming to some extent simply reflected the fact that in recent years the functions of the BOB have increasingly expanded. But the reorganization also signaled an attempt to enhance Presidential control of the budget bureaucracy, and an attempt to enhance the influence of OMB vis-à-vis the departments and agencies. On the first point, the reorganization increased the number of Presidential appointees in the OMB. The intent apparently was to make the OMB staff the President's men, even more than they had been in the BOB. On the second point, appeals from the Director of OMB on budget matters were made much more difficult. It was made very clear that the Director's decision was the President's —and to question the Director's decision was to question the

6. Relatively recent papers include James W. Davis and Randall B. Ripley, "The Bureau of the Budget and Executive Branch Agencies: Notes on their Interaction," *Journal of Politics*, vol. 29 (November 1967) pp. 749–769; Allen Schick, "The Budget Bureau That Was: Thoughts on the Rise, Decline, and Future of a Presidential Agency," *Law and Contemporary Problems;* Vol. XXV (Summer 1970) pp. 519–539; John E. Moore, "Policy Implications of the Office of Management and Budget," paper prepared for 1971 meeting of American Political Science Association.

President's judgment. Naturally even Cabinet officers do not do this very often.

Although it is not possible to consider in detail all of the remaining units in the Executive Office of the President, a few more deserve special attention. The Council of Economic Advisors (CEA) is one such.[7] Created by the Employment Act of 1946, the CEA is composed of three men appointed by the President with the advice and consent of the Senate. In addition there is a small professional staff. The main responsibilities of the Council are to advise the President on economic matters and to prepare an annual economic report analyzing economic developments and trends and making economic policy recommendations. The CEA gets involved in a variety of legislative matters and helps to develop government programs in areas ranging from the environment to manpower to regional economic development. Naturally the CEA comes into constant contact with other agencies in the Executive Office and the executive branch generally.

The relationship between the Council of Economic Advisors, the Treasury, and the Office of Management and Budget is so important and visible that the Russian word *Troika* has been adopted to distinguish three men—the chairman of CEA, the director of OMB, and the Secretary of the Treasury. This group plays an important role in the creation of economic policy. It should be noted, however, that the particular role of the CEA and its relationship with the President may depend on the personalities of the Chairman and of the other members of the Troika and their relationships with the President. As it is established by statute the President cannot easily reorganize and abolish the CEA, but his relations with it can be frequent, easy, and fruitful, or simply proper. If the Chairman is aggressive and has the confidence of the President as well as some political sense, the influence of the CEA can be substantial. If these conditions are missing, then the influence of the CEA may be less. (Obviously the reader may apply these comments in general to the heads of other departments and agencies.)

The National Security Council (NSC) was established in 1947 "to advise the President with respect to the integration of

---

7. For an account of the Council of Economic Advisers see Edward S. Flash, Jr., *Economic Advice and Presidential Leadership* (New York: Columbia University Press, 1965).

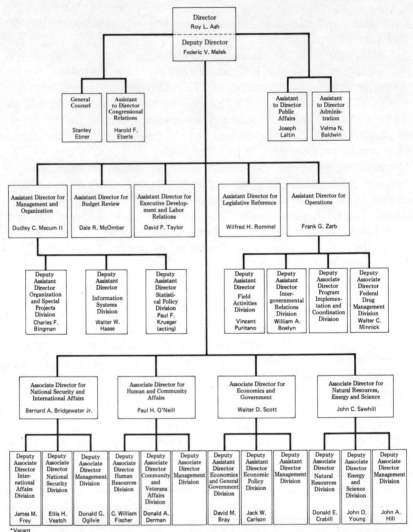

Director Roy L. Ash		
Deputy Director Federic V. Malek		

General Counsel — Stanley Ebner

Assistant to Director Congressional Relations — Harold F. Eberle

Assistant to Director Public Affairs — Joseph Laltin

Assistant to Director Administration — Velma N. Baldwin

Assistant Director for Management and Organization — Dudley C. Mecum II

Assistant Director for Budget Review — Dale R. McOmber

Assistant Director for Executive Development and Labor Relations — David P. Taylor

Assistant Director for Legislative Reference — Wilfred H. Rommel

Assistant Director for Operations — Frank G. Zarb

Deputy Assistant Director Organization and Special Projects Division — Charles F. Bingman

Deputy Assistant Director Information Systems Division — Walter W. Haase

Deputy Assistant Director Statistical Policy Division — Paul F. Krueger (acting)

Deputy Assistant Director Field Activities Division — Vincent Puritano

Deputy Assistant Director Intergovernmental Relations Division — William A. Boelyn

Deputy Associate Director Program Implementation and Coordination Division

Deputy Associate Director Federal Drug Management Division — Walter C. Minnick

Associate Director for National Security and International Affairs — Bernard A. Bridgewater Jr.

Associate Director for Human and Community Affairs — Paul H. O'Neill

Associate Director for Economics and Government — Walter D. Scott

Associate Director for Natural Resources, Energy and Science — John C. Sawhill

Deputy Associate Director International Affairs Division — James M. Frey

Deputy Associate Director National Security Division — Ellis H. Veatch

Deputy Associate Director Management Division — Donald G. Ogilvie

Deputy Associate Director Human Resources Division — C. William Fischer

Deputy Associate Director Community and Veterans Affairs Division — Donald A. Derman

Deputy Associate Director Management Division

Deputy Assistant Director Economics and General Government Division — David M. Bray

Deputy Assistant Director Economic Policy Division — Jack W. Carlson

Deputy Assistant Director Management Division

Deputy Associate Director Natural Resources Division — Donald E. Crabill

Deputy Associate Director Energy and Science Division — John D. Young

Deputy Associate Director Management Division — John A. Hill

*Vacant

Source: Office of Management and Budget

domestic, foreign, and military policies relating to the national security so as to enable the military services and the other departments and agencies of the Government to cooperate more effectively in matters involving the national security."[8] In effect the National Security Council is a high-level interdepartmental

---

8. Title 1, Section 101 of the National Security Act of 1947 as amended. Reprinted in Senator Henry M. Jackson, *The National Security Council* (New York: Praeger, 1965), p. 296.

committee with professional staff headed by the President's Assistant for National Security Affairs. The membership includes the President, the Vice President, the Secretary of State, the Secretary of Defense, the Director of the Office of Emergency Preparedness, and other officers appointed by the President. Meetings of the NSC are commonly attended by the Director of OMB, the Secretary of the Treasury, and the Chairman of the Joint Chiefs of Staff, and in the Nixon administration by the Attorney General.

When considering the functions of the National Security Council it is important to note that its precise functioning—as in the case of other Executive Office organizations—varies from Persident to President. Under President Eisenhower the National Security Council played a visible and important role in national-security policy deliberations. President Kennedy and President Johnson relied on it much less often, but it was rejuvenated during the Nixon administration. The *New York Times* reported in 1971 that the National Security Council budget was triple what it had been in 1968 and 2½ times as large as it had been in 1962.

The National Security Council was expanded and strengthened partially because of the administrative style of President Nixon, who has tried to bring more policy-initiation activity into the House and to use White House staff to control the bureaucracies, and partly because of the influence and strength of Henry Kissinger, the President's Assistant for National Security Affairs. Again the importance of individuals is emphasized in trying to understand organizational structure and functioning.

The Executive Departments

In the Executive Branch there are eleven organizations called executive departments. A major characteristic that the departments have in common is that each is headed by a Presidential appointee who is a member of the President's Cabinet. (This is not completely distinguishing, however, as other officials may also have Cabinet rank, the head of OMB for example or the Ambassador to the United Nations.) The executive departments, together with their constituent units, are responsible for most of the programs of the federal government, spend most of the money, and employ most of the people. But there are vast differences among the departments. As Table 4-1 shows,

TABLE 4-1

Executive Department: Their Budgets and Employees

Department	1971 Number of Employees	1971 Budget Outlay
Agriculture	84,252	8,560,000,000
Commerce	28,435	1,188,000,000
Defense	1,092,804	75,922,000,000
Health, Education, and Welfare	104,283	61,866,000,000
Housing and Urban Development	16,030	2,890,000,000
Interior	57,570	225,000,000
Justice	42,662	916,000,000
Labor	11,352	7,923,000,000
State	23,398	468,000,000
Transportation	68,489	7,247,000,000
Treasury	90,135	20,990,000,000

Source: The Budget of the United States, Fiscal 1973, Tables 3 and 11 (pp. 497 and 506).

the Department of Defense is at one extreme in size and the Department of Labor at the other. The budgets of the Defense Department and the State Department differ greatly. The departments also differ in age. The Department of Transportation, created in 1967, has just begun to roll or fly, so to speak. The Department of State is as old as the United States. The Departments perform different functions, serve different interests, and have different sources of support; and many of them are simply conglomerations of widely varied units. Health, Education, and Welfare is an example, and so is the Department of Commerce. Even the Department of Transportation contains such different bodies as the United States Coast Guard, the Bureau of Public Roads, and the Federal Aviation Administration. A result of course is that a Department may be almost as hard for a Secretary to administer as the executive branch is for the President to run.

To assist him in the management of his department, every Secretary has a staff composed of both political appointees and career civil servants. Usually a Secretary's deputy or undersecretary and several assistant secretaries are political appointees and have over-all responsibility for some particular function or program area. In the Department of Health, Education, and Welfare, for example, assistant secretaries are responsible for the following areas: Public Affairs, Health and Scientific Affairs, Community and Field Service, Legislation, and Planning and Evaluation. In addition there is an Assistant Secretary for Administration and Management and an Assistant Secretary, Comptroller. Each area also has deputy assistant secretaries and special assistants. At the departmental level also can be found career civil servants who staff the administrative structure— the budget office, personnel office, and so on—and who provide assistance (and sometimes no doubt resistance) to the political appointees.

Below departmental level are the constituent organizations of a department; all departments are made up of these constituent units. There is no universally applicable terminology to describe and classify these subdepartmental units, but there are some generally used terms. *Administration* is the term often used to describe a major unit within a department. An administration may be headed by an assistant secretary or by an administrator, or by a man (or woman) with another title. There is not much standardization. In the Department of Labor the Manpower Administration is headed by a man who is titled "Deputy Assistant Secretary for Manpower and Manpower Administrator." The National Oceanic and Atmospheric Administration in the Department of Commerce is headed by an administrator, as is the Health Services and Mental Health Administration in the Department of Health, Education, and Welfare. But the Social Security Administration in the same department is headed by a Commissioner, as is the Office of Education.

In addition to administrations, departments commonly have *bureaus*, which may also be constituent units of administrations. In a sense the bureaus are the blocks with which departments are built. Departments vary in the number and variety of their bureaus, and within many departments there are organizations with the position or status of a bureau but without the name. The Justice Department houses the Federal Bureau of Investigation and the Bureau of Prisons, but the Immigration and Natuarlization *Service*. The Department of the Interior claims the Bureau of Indian Affairs and the Bureau of Mines, but the Geological

Department of Health, Education, and Welfare

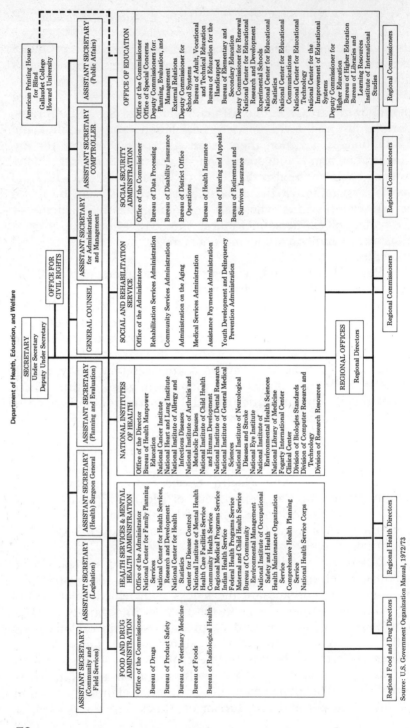

Source: U.S. Government Organization Manual, 1972/73

Survey. Such anomalies can often be traced to the prior independent existence of an organization whose name was not changed when it was brought into a department.

Bureaus, like departments, differ substantially in their size and organization. The United States Forest Service (Department of Agriculture) has a substantial field organization, thanks to the number of national forests. The National Park Service (Department of the Interior) sends its men in broad-brimmed hats wherever there are Parks or National Monuments. The FBI, the Secret Service, and the Internal Revenue Service all maintain field operation. The National Bureau of Standards, on the other hand, is located almost entirely in and around Washington, and the Patent Office is under one roof. Some bureaus are headed by political appointees who come and go with the President, if not more often; directors of other bureaus are almost permanent fixtures. At least, all bureaus are located within departments and on paper are subordinate to cabinet secretaries and often to assistant secretaries as well.

In addition to administrations and bureaus, a variety of other organizations may be attached to departments in one way or another. The Agency for International Development is part of the State Department, but in the past it was independent and even now is semi-autonomous. The National Security Agency, according to the official statement in the Government Organization Manual, was begun in 1952 "as a separately organized agency within the Department of Defense." The military departments, within the Department of Defense are simply noncabinet departments, whatever that may mean. Other apparent oddities could be pointed to with little trouble.

The Independent Agencies

About fifty agencies in the executive branch are not located within departments. These independent agencies perform some of the government's most important functions and provide some of the most important services. The Civil Service Commission, the Veterans' Administration, the General Services Administration, the Atomic Energy Commission, the National Aeronautics and Space Administration, the United States Information Agency, the Environmental Protection Agency, and the U.S. Postal Service are all examples. To be sure, a good many less well-known organizations are also included in the list of independent agencies: The Delaware River Basin Commission, The American Battle Monuments Commission, the Indian Claims Commission, and the Panama Canal Company may all serve as examples.

The many independent agencies are quite varied. Several are single-purpose organizations headed by a single individual. Seven are regulatory commissions. Some government corporations are also independent agencies, and a fourth category includes what can be called central service and control agencies.

Among the single-purpose agencies headed by a single individual are some of the better-known independent agencies: NASA, the Veterans' Administration, the Selective Service System, and the United States Information Agency. Some are as big as departments; the Veterans' Administration is bigger than the Department of Labor, and the budget of NASA has been most impressive. Like departments, most of the independent agencies with a single head are organized along hierarchical lines, but an independent agency is unlikely to present the conglomerate appearance of some departments. The critical difference between independent agencies and departments, of course, is that only departments are headed by a Cabinet member.

The independent regulatory agencies are as follows:

> Civil Aeronautics Board (CAB)
> Federal Communications Commission (FCC)
> Federal Maritime Commission (FMC)
> Federal Power Commission (FPC)
> Federal Trade Commission (FTC)
> Interstate Commerce Commission (ICC)
> Securities and Exchange Commission (SEC)

These agencies have two characteristics that set them apart from other government organizations.[9] First, they are headed not by a single commissioner or director or chief, but by a multi-member commission. Second, the commissioners serve for fixed terms, rather than at the pleasure of the President. A President

---

9. The literature on regulatory agencies is vast. Among recent items to appear are Louis M. Kohlmeier, Jr., *The Regulators: Watchdog Agencies and the Public Interest* (New York, Harper & Row, 1969) and a recent symposium on regulatory administration in *Public Administration Review,* July–August 1972, pp. 283–310. Ralph Nader's Study Group has issued reports on several agencies, including the ICC and (though not strictly speaking an independent regulatory agency) the Food and Drug Administration.

who serves two terms may have substantial impact on a regulatory agency through his appointments, but he cannot have the immediate impact that he may have on other agencies. This impact is also tempered by the requirement that he balance his appointments. He cannot appoint only members of his own party to regulatory commissions; appointments must be bipartisan. Many independent agencies are independent only in that they are not part of departments, but the regulatory agencies are independent in that they are insulated from some kinds of direct Presidential influence. Congress views the regulatory agencies as within its sphere of influence and has tried solicitously to protect the commissions from Presidential interference.

Several justifications have been suggested for the independence of the regulatory agencies, all related to what these agencies do. These agencies are charged with making and enforcing rules regulating the behavior of major industries. The Interstate Commerce Commission has to decide which railroads can run to what points, whether a railroad can cancel a particular train, and what charges railroads my levy. The Civil Aeronautics Board has similar responsibilities with regard to airlines. The Federal Communications Commission controls the issuance of radio and television licenses. The Federal Trade Commission is concerned with the propriety and accuracy of advertising, among other things. Because in carrying out such responsibilities the regulatory agencies make rules (legislate) and conduct semijudicial hearings, it may be argued, to justify their independence, that they do not belong entirely to any one branch of the government. This argument is not especially impressive, as many departments and bureaus also perform legislative and judicial functions.

Another explanation for the independence given the regulatory functions were first performed in the states by multimembered commissions. Congress used this state experience as a model when creating the Interstate Commerce Commission in 1887, and other commissions were then formed using the ICC as a model. Another reason for the independence of the agencies may be that Congress thought their functions too important to be left to the President alone.

Finally, and perhaps this is as good a reason as any, once regulation appeared inevitable, industries apparently preferred to be regulated by a specialized and relatively independent agency that they might be able to control. As it has worked out, the regulatory agencies have indeed developed close relationships with the industries over which they have jurisdiction. The clearest example of this may be the close and supportive relationship that exists between the ICC and the railroad industry, though certainly the relationship between the FCC and the broadcasting industry has not been noted for distance or coolness.

A number of the organizations in the executive branch are government corporations.[10] The U.S. Postal Service and the Tennessee Valley Authority (TVA) are perhaps the best known examples, but the Federal Deposit Insurance Corporation, the Federal Home Loan Bank Corporation, and the Panama Canal Company also illustrate this kind of organization. The government corporations provide services that are quasicommercial in character, and in their structure and powers they bear some resemblance to business corporations. They have more flexibility in their operations than government departments, bureaus, or other independent agencies; and their relations with the President and Congress are marked by an absence of many routine controls.

> A department must apply elaborate procedures in estimating its future financial needs and in obtaining appropriations from Congress. It enjoys no assurance of continuity in its programs, for once a year it must seek funds from a Congress that is sometimes friendly and sometimes inexplicably capricious. It must hire its employees subject to intricate procedures and regulations fixed by the Civil Service Commission. In spending money it must take care lest it violate the voluminous jurisprudence on the subject created in the decisions and interpretations of the Comptroller General.[11]

A government corporation has none of these departmental restrictions. Most important, the government corporations enjoy substantial financial flexibility. They are not subject to annual

---

10. For an introduction to government corporations see V. O. Key, Jr., "Government Corporations," in Fritz Morstein Marx, *Elements of Public Administration* (Englewood Cliffs: Prentice-Hall, 1959), pp. 219–245, See also Harold Seidman, "The Theory of the Autonomous Government Corporation," *Public Administration Review*, XII (1952), pp. 89–96, and also his "The Government Corporation: Organization and Control," *Public Administration Review*, XIV (1954) pp. 183–192.

11. Key, "Government Corporations," p. 220.

appropriations, and their earnings may be retained by them and poured directly back into their operations. Thus they do not every year have to ask the Office of Management and Budget, the President, and the Congress for funds.

Though government corporations are not subject to the usual financial restraints or controls, they are not uncontrolled. The provisions of the Government Corporation Control Act of 1945 ensure that government corporations are not free to do just as they please. Rather they are controlled in unique ways. Congress originally must authorize the corporate form of organization and specify what the corporation may and may not do. Congress may dissolve corporations. By legislation Congress may modify the authority or responsibilities of a corporation. Congress may or may not provide working capital to a corporation as it chooses. The operations of the corporations are reviewed annually by the President, the Bureau of the Budget, and the Congress. Government corporations must submit budget programs annually, though these are more like work plans than requests for funds. Because the corporation is not requesting funds, the Congress need not appropriate funds; but it must authorize expenditure from corporate funds.

Some departments include corporations, and these can be controlled in some measure by the department secretary. Certainly their status is different from that of ordinary bureaus, but they cannot act totally contrary to departmental policy.

Why do government corporations exist? Why is this form of organization used? The most important explanations are the need for freedom and the need for speed. As V. O. Key has suggested, the corporation is most commonly used during emergencies when speed is essential and the usual government restraints on action may hinder the response to a problem. The major objective in the creation of most government corporations has been to carry out, under emergency conditions, functions of a commercial nature clothed with a public concern."[12] Key has noted also that, when an emergency is over, the corporation created to act in it often disappears. Many depression and war-born corporations have disappeared, the Reconstruction Finance Corporation and the Defense Plant Corporation among them; but the Federal Deposit Insurance Corporation and the Federal Savings and Loan Insurance Corporation, also depression-born, have

---

12. Key, "Government Corporations," p. 224.

continued. During World War II there were a hundred corporations; today there are only about twenty.

Two executive agencies might properly be called central service and control agencies: the Civil Service Commission and the General Services Administration (GSA). These two organizations differ substantially in organization as well as in mission, but they are alike in that they provide service primarily to other government agencies rather than to the public and control other government agencies, rather than industries or members of the public. The United States Civil Service Commission was created in 1883 to administer a personnel merit system for the federal government. The Commission is composed of three members appointed by the President. Reorganization Plan 5 of 1949 provided for the designation of a chairman and vice chairman by the President. The chairman is the chief executive office of the Civil Service Commission, and since 1949 the commission has in some respects resembled an independent agency with a single administrator. The other two commissioners take part in some policy decisions and also have appellate functions, but they take little part in the day-to-day functioning of the U.S. Civil Service Commission.

O. Glenn Stahl has provided in his text on *Public Personnel Administration* a useful description of the current role and operations of the Commission.[13]

> The United States Civil Service Commission is by all odds the largest and most highly organized central personnel establishment in modern government, embracing a number of regional and subsidiary offices servicing federal installations scattered throughout the country and abroad and superintending between 800 and 900 decentralized boards of examiners manned by experts in the operating departments. Its functions cover recruitment, examining, job evaluation, training, and the administration of personnel investigations and retirement and insurance systems. Its principal role in most of these functions is that of policy making and standard setting for the decentralized personnel activities of the agencies and inspection for adequacy of agency personnel administration.

---

13. O. Glenn Stahl, *Public Personnel Administration* (New York: Harper and Row, 1962, 5th ed.), pp. 425–426.

From Stahl's description of both the service and the control functions of the Commission, it is clear that the Commission deals almost solely with other government agencies. Thanks to the increasing number of employees in the career civil service and to the increasing range of Commission activities, Herbert Kaufman has said that the Civil Service Commission is the "kingpin of federal personnel administration."[14]

> Formally, the personnel function was widely scattered. The basic framework was provided by legislation and by executive orders of the President issued under authority conferred on him by statute and by the Constitution directly. More detailed regulations were issued by the Civil Service Commission, whose staff then either executed the provisions of the regulations or exercised surveillance over the line agencies to ensure compliance. The bulk of the personnel actions in the federal government were taken by the dozens of departments and agencies that make up the executive branch, operating within the laws, rules and regulations, and under the watchful eye of the Civil Service Commission as well as with its advice, assistance, and stimulation. It was the administrators who actually appointed, assigned, promoted, transferred, trained, disciplined, and discharged government employees. After 1938, by presidential order, each major agency had a personnel office, headed by an agency personnel officer, to assist in these functions at the agency level and to serve as liaison with the Commission. In practice, however, the Commission played a key role initiating most of the legislation and Executive Orders under which it operates, its views were invariably solicited when any other source initiated proposals, it was consulted by the heads of other agencies who did not want to run afoul of its enforcement powers, and it enjoyed strong support among civil organizations and among unions and associations of federal workers. From 1958 on, its members have had six-year, over-lapping terms instead of serving at the pleasure of the President. In the partitioned world of federal personnel management,

---

14. Herbert Kaufman, "The Growth of the Federal Personnel System," in Wallace Sayre (ed.), *The Federal Government Service* (Englewood Cliffs: Prentice-Hall, 1965), p. 56.

there was probably no single dominant force, but the Civil Service Commission was unquestionably the central figure.

The government organization in charge of logistics is the General Services Administration. A list of the major units of GSA gives some ideal range of its responsibilities:

Federal Supply Service
Defense Materials Service (stockpiles)
Public Building Service
Transportation and Communication Service
Utilization and Disposal Service
National Archives and Records Service

The list, however, does not make clear the control responsibilities of the GSA; they are important. Executive branch agencies may not acquire whatever supplies they wish; they must take supplies of the quality provided by the Supply Service and in the quantities allocated by GSA. Agencies are not free to acquire their own space but must occupy space occupied and managed by the Public Buildings Service. Federal agencies must rely on automobiles and communications facilities provided by the Transportation and Communication Service, and what they do with their records is of interest to the National Archives and Records Service. The power of the GSA should not of course be overstated; within its area of responsibility there is room for negotiation and bargaining and indeed evasion. GSA no more has absolute control over agencies than does the Office of Management and Budget or the Civil Service Commission. But when the Office of Management and Budget and the President are on its side, its rules and regulations cannot be ignored with impunity.

What Difference Do the Differences Make?

So far a number of different types of organizations have been noted, and we have also seen that there are substantial differences between organizations of the same type. At this point you might ask, so what? What difference does it make? The answer is that variations among organizations in size, mission, organization, and so on effect their relative political strength, which is important if an agency is to get what it wants and avoid what it doesn't. An agency may want to avoid being merged into another, it may want a budget increase, it may want to keep responsibility for a popular program and not have it transferred to another agency, it may not want to administer an unpopular and in its view unworkable law, it may want to win a challenge from the Civil Service Commission, it may want. . . . And in such circumstances political strength, ability to influence congressional committees or the Office of Management and Budget or the White House is important. What are the bases of agency strength?[15] There are several.

One source of strength certainly is size. If all other things were equal—to be sure, they never are—the larger agency could be expected to be stronger than the smaller agency. A larger budget may be better able to sustain a rewarding public-relations program and successful congressional liaison. The larger agency may be delivering benefits to more people, and it may have projects in more states and Congressional districts—so more Congressmen have an interest in its well-being. But even as these points are made it is clear that, in addition to size, mission and location are important. An organization located just in Washington will have less clout than an organization that is widely scattered. Employees in many states and districts, projects in many locations, service delivery to a variety of beneficiaries across the country—all these serve to strengthen an agency.

There are other points to be made. The Cabinet Department, just because it is headed by a member of the Cabinet, is likely to be in a stronger position than an independent agency or a department constituent. There are of course exceptions; still, in conflicts over budget or program, Labor and HEW often won over OEO. (OEO, like OMB, was in the Executive Office, though it did not have anything like the influence of OMB.) To win conflicts over logistics the GSA must have allies to defeat Cabinet departments. Of course the leadership in an organization cannot be ignored. Some administrators are simply more politically astute than others and a skilled leader in an independent agency may win over a neophyte who happens for whatever reason to be a Cabinet secretary.

The employees of an organization and its clientele may also add or detract from its political strength. An organization composed of articulate well-educated professional people may be

---

15. See in addition to the text discussion Francis E. Rourke, "Variations in Agency Power," in the second edition of his *Bureaucratic Power in National Politics* (Boston: Little, Brown & Co., 1972), pp. 240–262.

more influential than one composed heavily of clerical or blue-collar workers. On the other hand, if the latter are well organized they may carry weight, especially in pay and personnel matters. An organization that serves an influential clientele can have influence quite disproportionate to its size. And an organization that is delivering benefits may be in a somewhat stronger position than one that is regulating or extracting. But of course who is being affected is important. An organization giving benefits to a low-status group—a welfare organization—may not carry the weight of an organization whose programs benefit the elderly or the suburban middle class.

Some summary comments are in order. Clearly there is no single basis of power; an agency that lacks one resource base may have another that more than compensates. It is hard to imagine an agency without any resources, but their distribution is far from even and some agencies may be well-off while others aren't. To understand policy making and administration one needs some understanding of the distribution of power within the bureaucracy—both among organizations and among individuals. One needs also, of course, some notion of their goals and interests. This is an important reason for having a firm grasp on the structure and nomenclature of the executive branch. It is hard to understand the game with no knowledge of the players. But in the end it is important to emphasize that the distribution of power, of status, of influence, is not static. As administrators and administrations come and go, as new problems arise and others fade from the front pages, as new groups organize and others lose strength, as public taste and opinion appear to shift, the structure of the executive branch will change, and so will the distribution of power within it.

5 Executive Branch Personnel

There is a subject of study (and an administrative activity) called personnel administration. This chapter is not, or is not intended to be, a condensation of that subject. It does contain information about some important topics that concern the people who work in the executive branch of the government. It begins with some description of the federal work force and comments briefly on grades and pay. It then moves on to consider the recruitment of political appointees and career civil servants, and concludes with some consideration of political activity in the civil service and trends in unionization.

The Federal Work Force

The federal government is the largest single employer in the nation; there are about 2,500,000 civilian government employees and most of these work in the Executive Branch.[1] (Currently the costs of the civilian payroll amount to somewhat less than 11 percent of the federal budget.) Employees of the executive branch are distributed not only among many organizations but also throughout the United States and around the world. A glance at the telephone book of any city will reveal many federal organizations. The State of California contains al-

---

1. Information on federal employment can be found in the current volume of *Special Analysis of the U.S. Government Budget,* issued annually by the Superintendent of Documents, U.S. Government Printing Office.

most as many federal employees as Washington, D.C.; and Illinois, New York, Texas, and Pennsylvania all have well over 100,000 federal employees within their borders. One implication is that the federal government is not necessarily government by some bureaucrat in far off Washington, D.C. Federal employees located throughout the United States and working where they live may be just as aware of local conditions as comparable state and local government employees, and perhaps more so. Another obvious implication of the size and spread of the work force is the job and payroll impact (potential and actual) of the federal government. Congressmen and Senators vie for federal installations and projects because they mean jobs and money for constituents. An additional point worth emphasizing in this context is that if it were not for federal grants-in-aid to state and local governments and contracts to a variety of vendors the federal work force might be much larger than it is. As matters stand it is accurate to think of much of the work force, especially in such departments as HEW and HUD, as the federal supervisory and review force, with the work being done by other organizations.

Although it is possible to view the federal government as one large employer (the largest in the country), it is also possible to view it as several employers. In a sense each of the departments and agencies can be viewed as an employer, though the employees of most of them are covered by uniform entrance requirements and conditions of work set by the United States Civil Service Commission. Some federal employees, however, work in organizations that are not part of the regular civil service, but instead have their own personnel systems. That is, they have their own rules and standards for hiring, retaining, promoting, and dismissing. The FBI, for example, has its own personnel system, as do the Central Intelligence Agency and the National Security Agency. The Atomic Energy Commission has its own personnel system, as do the Tennessee Valley Authority and the United States Postal Service. The Foreign Service in the Department of State is separate from the regular civil service. The uniformed services are of course not part of the civil service; besides the regular armed forces, these include the Coast Guard, the Coast and Geodetic Survey, and the Public Health Service. The Department of Medicine and Surgery in the Veterans Administration is also separate from the regular civil service.

Although there might appear to be a number of organizations not under civil service, these do not include in total many employees. Most federal employees are in the competitive civil service; those that are not are in what is known as the excepted service. These include, in addition to those in organizations with their own merit systems, those persons who hold positions excepted from competitive examination. People in key policy-making positions are in the excepted service, as are people holding positions for which it is not practicable to give an examination. Government lawyers are never hired on the basis of a competitive examination since it is against the law to expend public funds to examine attorneys.

Just as the armed forces have their ranks, from private to general, so do the Civil Service and the organizations independent of the Civil Service. In the Civil Service the grades go from GS (General Schedule) 1 to GS 18. Clerical and subprofessional people occupy the lower grades, Grades 12 through 15 can be thought of as middle management and professional grades. Grades 16 through 18 are known as the supergrades. College graduates start at the 5 or 7 level, depending on their qualifications, and students with graduate study may start at 7, 9, or 11, depending on what they have studied, how long they studied it, and other considerations. Pay, as might be surmised, varies between grades and also within grades, depending on length of service. Today a college graduate can begin at around $10,000 a year. A middle-management official may make $20,000 or more, and a top-level civil servant may make as much as $36,-000 a year. (It should be pointed out that beginning with the Salary Act of 1962 an attempt has been made to ensure that employees in different systems who do equivalent work are paid at equivalent rates.) For many years after World War II, the low salaries paid by the government were a frequent handicap in recruiting and retaining able people, particularly in the upper grades. Such appears not to be true any longer. From 1962 through 1971 there were 10 salary increases for federal employees, and the future no doubt holds more. Of course there may still be individual employees who find they can make more money in the private sector than in the government, but there are doubtless others in opposite circumstances. Indeed so far are low government salaries from being a widespread problem that there is beginning to be some complaint that government salaries have risen too fast and are perhaps too high.[2] This may at

---

2. See for example Taylor Branch, "The Rising Profits of Public Service," *Washington Monthly*, March 1971, pp. 25–32.

least be an indication that comparability with pay levels outside government has about been reached.

Federal employees hold a variety of jobs. They are scattered through a variety of occupations and professional specialties. Today scientists, engineers, economists, lawyers, doctors, and educators all work for the federal government, and more than half of all employees are in professional, technical, and related occupations. A recent analysis of the federal work force, for example, yielded the following results:[3]

TABLE 5-1

Occupations of Federal Professional Employees	
Professional, Technical and Kindred	50.9%
Engineering, Medicine, Science and Math	13.0
All other Professional	5.1
ADP, Scientific and Technical Support	6.7
Personnel, Budget, and General Administration	5.3
All other Administrative and Technical	13.1
Government Occupations	7.7

And not long ago the Bureau of the Budget (now the Office of Management and Budget) reported:

> Changes have taken place in the position structure as a result of changes in the character of the Government's workload and in the employee skills required to deal with it. For example, between 1954 and 1965, greater specialization and emphasis on research and development led to an increase of 53 percent in the number of engineers in the Federal Service, and an 83 percent increase in the number of physical scientists. During this period, the Government's need for professional medical personnel rose 31 percent and for biological scientists, 46 percent. At the same time, the expanded efforts to reduce employment and to increase productivity—in many cases shifting from manual to semi-automatic or automatic processing methods—decreased the need for unskilled employees.[4]

---

3. Taken from a U.S. Civil Service Commission pamphlet, "The Federal Career Service," issued in 1969.

4. This quotation is from page 30, *Special Analysis, Budget of the United States*, Fiscal Year 1967.

A somewhat fuller picture of the variety of occupations in the Executive Branch is provided by Table 5-2. Postal occupations account for by far the largest number of white-collar jobs, but there are a substantial number of employees in other occupational groups. (There are also a number of employees in a variety of blue-collar occupations, but data showing the distribution of the blue-collar work force are not included here.)

TABLE 5-2

White-Collar Workers in the Federal Government,
by Major Occupation Group, 1971

Postal (1970 figure; 1971 figure not available)	594,800
General administration, clerical and office services	434,900
Engineering and architecture	150,400
Accounting and budget	106,100
Medical, hospital, dental and public health	98,800
Supply	69,200
Business and industry	64,900
Legal and kindred	46,600
Physical sciences	44,400
Biological sciences	43,200
Personnel management and industrial relations	36,300
Investigation	43,600
Social science, psychology, and welfare	35,500
Transportation	41,500
Education	28,900
Commodity quality control, inspection and grading	20,100
Information and arts	19,400
Equipment, facilities, and service	16,900
Mathematics and statistics	13,800
Library and archives	8,400
Veterinary medical science	2,300
Copyright, patent, and trade-mark	1,700
Miscellaneous occupations	44,200
Total	1,966,100

Source: Statistical Abstract of the U.S., 1973, 93rd edition, Table 645, p. 404.

Additional data further illustrate the occupational distribution of federal employees and emphasize the diversity of jobs and skills. An analysis of federal executives published by the Civil Service Commission in 1972 contained a table showing the distribution of federal executives by occupational category.[5]

Table 5-3

Occupations of Federal Executives

Occupational Group	Percent of Federal Executives
Social Science	4
Personnel	2
Administration	23
Biological Sciences	3
Fiscal	4
Health and medicine	3
Engineering	11
Legal	13
Information and arts	1
Business and industry	2
Physical sciences	13
Mathematics and statistics	3
Education	1
Transportation	1
Public Law positions in science and engineering	12
All other positions	4

Source: United States Civil Service Commission, Bureau of Executive Manpower, *Executive Manpower in the Federal Service* (Washington: U.S. G.P.O., 1972) p. 5, table 8.

These data show that not all top level federal employees are administrators, which was also the finding of John J. Corson and R. Shale Paul, who inquired specifically (by means of questionnaires and interviews) into the activities of the top 5,000 career

---

5. See the report issued January 1972 by the Bureau of Executive Manpower, U.S. Civil Service Commission, *Executive Manpower in the Federal Service.*

civil servants.[6] They were able to classify senior civil servants into three main groups. Thirty-five percent of the top civil servants were classified as program managers; that is, they served as bureau chiefs or division directors or office heads and were responsible for carrying out programs. Another 35 percent were engaged in such activities as budgeting, personnel administration, management analysis, or other types of administrative support work. The remaining 30 percent were working simply as professionals—lawyers, economists, scientists, engineers, and so on.

What might be thought of as the professionalization of the federal service has a number of implications. The data emphasize the increasingly difficult position of the unskilled or semi-skilled worker. There are fewer and fewer places to which he can turn for a job, fewer and fewer jobs available. Additionally, the professionalization of the civil service is likely to alter the distribution of grades (more in the upper grades and fewer in the lower grades), and unless the size of the civil service is reduced the personnel costs of the government may go up. There are likely to be other implications as well. It is possible that professionals will be more mobile, moving from organization to organization and from problem to problem, than government employees have been in the past, and they may be less willing to be routinized. Loyal to their profession and socialized into it, they may not be tightly bound to the organization they happen to be working for. They may demand (certainly prefer) a good deal of individual (professional) autonomy and discretion over their time. They are likely to resist close direction or supervision. And many professionals may value highly what appear to them to be "rational" approaches to problem solving and may resist the intrusion of "politics" into their activities. All of which is simply to suggest that the professionalization of the public service may have substantial consequences for its operation and results.[7]

In addition to looking at the distribution of the federal work force among occupational groups or among organizations or

---

6. John J. Corson and R. Shale Paul, *Men Near the Top* (Baltimore: The Johns Hopkins Press, 1966).

7. For an extended discussion along these lines see Frederick C. Mosher, "The Public Service in a Temporary Society," *Public Administration Review,* January/February 1971, pp. 47–62.

among the states, it is possible to describe it in several other ways. Data are available on such obvious characteristics as age, education, length of service, career mobility, and a number of other characteristics, though it need not all be presented here. It is available in a number of Civil Service Commission publications and elsewhere. But some general observations are in order. The federal work force has not been particularly mobile. Many executives make their careers completely within one bureau of an agency; this is especially true in those organizations that have a strong career orientation—like the Forest Service or the Coast Guard—but it is common throughout the federal service. The implications of this for organizational rigidity and innovation are worth considering. Federal executives are well educated. Eighty-five percent of federal employees above the grade of GS 15 have at least a bachelor's degree, and over half have a master's degree or better, though most have had no education since entering federal service. Two thirds of federal executives have more than 20 years of service and, the largest groups (44%) are in the age category of 45 to 54 years. Such data suggest that government executives are really not very different from executives or professionals engaged in comparable work in private industry.

Two other characteristics of the work force deserve emphasis. Not surprisingly, very few high-level federal jobs are occupied by women. There are 28,000 federal employees in grade 15 and higher, and fewer than 600 are women. To put the point another way, 98 percent of the persons in grade 15 and above are men; 2 percent are women. And what women there are cluster in particular occupations. Over a third of these women are medical officers. But if women are scarce in senior grades, such is hardly the case at the lower levels. Indeed, over 45 percent of the employees in grades 1 through 7 are women, and over three quarters of the employees in grades 2, 3, and 4 are women. This obvious imbalance has many explanations, of course. Women predominate in the relatively low-paid clerical field, and also fewer women are likely to make a long-term career in the federal service. In addition fewer women go to law school or medical school than men, to say nothing of there being fewer women than men in such fields as business administration, science, and engineering. Some of this results from personal choice, some from role socialization, and no doubt some from discrimination in college and graduate school. But when all these explanations are in, there still exists the strong possibility that at least in some circumstances the small number of women in the upper grades of the civil service can be explained by discrimination in the employing agency. "It's a man's world" still applies.[8]

Not only are there few women in the upper ranks of the civil service, there are also comparatively few members of minority groups—blacks, Spanish-speaking people, American Indians, and so on. In 1967 there were over 5000 supergrade positions in the federal service; less than 100 were filled by minority-group members. More recently an analysis of the position of blacks in the Cabinet departments shows that they uniformly fare less well than whites. Table 5-4 shows that in no Cabinet department are more than 9 percent of the black employees making more than $15,000 a year, and in many it is

TABLE 5-4

Blacks in Cabinet Departments

Department	All Employees	Black Employees	Number of Blacks Earning $15,000
State	21,373	12.9%	3.1%
Treasury	93,478	14.7	2.0
Defense (civilian)	1,052,288	11.4	2.0
Justice	37,459	9.2	1.4
Post Office	706,563	19.3	4.3
Interior	66,331	5.2	.9
Agriculture	86,526	5.8	1.8
Commerce	28,042	16.7	3.7
Labor	10,136	26.4	9.0
HEW	104,131	21.1	4.0
HUD	14,224	18.6	6.3
Transportation	62,278	6.2	1.7

Source: Civil Service Commission Data, Table from *Business Week*, August 28, 1971, p. 36.

8. In addition to data available from Civil Service Commission reports, see Helene S. Markoff, "The Federal Women's Program," *Public Administration Review*, March/April 1972, pp. 144–151; see also a news report in *Science*, "Inside HEW: Women Protest Sex Discrimination," October 15, 1971, pp. 270–274.

much lower than this. The table also shows of course substantial differences among organizations. (Perhaps one way to explain this is to look at the composition of the Congressional committees that have jurisdiction over the departments. The House Agriculture Committee is headed by a man from Mississippi.)

Another table shows clearly the concentration of minority employment in the lower grades. Indeed it shows that the proportion of minority employment declines consistently and steadily from grade 1 to grade 7.

TABLE 5-5

Minority Group Employment
Percent Within Each Grade, November 30, 1969

Grade	Total Employment	Minority Employment	Percent Within Each Grade
1	1,919	1,512	60.0
2	23,222	8,277	35.6
3	114,952	33,817	29.4
4	171,955	40,230	23.4
5	153,010	31,252	20.4
6	74,182	12,089	16.3
7	112,833	14,732	13.1
Total	652,073	141,549	21.7

Source: U.S. Civil Service Commerce pamphlet, "Upward Mobility for Lower Level Employees," issued 1970.

There are many explanations for this situation, but no doubt among the most important are the weaker educational preparation of many minority-group members (and discrimination in education) and discrimination in recruiting and promotion. The U.S. Civil Rights Commission has been quite concerned by figures such as these and has urged that corrective action be taken. The U.S. Civil Service Commission also has been concerned, but in the end the solution to the problem rests heavily with the departments and agencies of the government and with American society.[9]

9. For a lengthy treatment of the problem see Samuel Krislov, *The Negro in Federal Employment: The Quest for Equal Opportunity* (Minneapolis: University of Minnesota Press, 1967). See also *Federal Civil*

Political Executives
And Their Recruitment

By far the majority of those working in the executive branch are civil servants, but many of the most important positions in the executive branch at the Cabinet and sub-Cabinet level are filled directly by the President. Article II, Section 2 of the United States Constitution, which deals with the President's appointment power, says:

> He shall nominate and by and with the advice and consent of the Senate, shall appoint ambassadors, other public ministers and consuls, judges of the Supreme Court, and all other officers of the United States, whose appointments are not herein otherwise provided for, and which shall be established by law; but the Congress may by law vest the appointment of such inferior officers, as they think proper, in the President alone, in the courts or law, or in the heads of departments.

> The President shall have power to fill up all vacancies that may happen during the recess of the Senate, by granting commissions which shall expire at the end of their next session.

Consistent with this authority the President appoints Cabinet secretaries and sub-Cabinet officials, heads of independent agencies and regulatory commissions, some bureau chiefs, and scores of other officials. In a paper written in 1967 Laurin Henry noted that there were between 150 and 250 principal presidential appointees, the precise number depending on the definition of principal.

> Depending on the strictness of the definition, one counts to between 150 to 250 of these principal officials before entering the zone of several hundred lesser presidential appointees such as ambassadors, federal attorneys, mem-

---

Rights Enforcement Effort: A Report of the United States Commission on Civil Rights (Washington: U.S. G.P.O., 1971) and the *Federal Civil Rights Enforcement Effort: One Year Later* (Washington: U.S. G.P.O., 1971). Both of these reports have sections focused on the effort (and lack of effort) of government agencies and the U.S. Civil Service Commission.

bers of minor boards and commissions, and others who are traditionally considered more important for patronage than for policy reasons.[10]

When all the others are added there are perhaps 2500 presidential appointees. With some exceptions (the immediate White House staff is an obvious one) the President's power to appoint is qualified by the Senate's power to consent or demur, but this qualification is often not a crucial one, particularly for major posts. The President has the initiative, and the Senate demurs infrequently. Partially, of course, this is because the President is unlikely to nominate someone he thinks the Senate is likely to disapprove.

Although the President has the power to appoint top-level officials, he in effect must share this power. Interest groups, the President's own party, state Congressional delegations, the President's own advisors, and members of the Cabinet, to say nothing of the press, may all have views that they do not shy from expressing. The President cannot heed everyone, but he is unlikely to ignore everyone. And in the end he may not appoint or may withdraw an appointment, because someone or some group objected strenuously. To forestall this it is not uncommon for a President to check initially with interested groups to seek their views and the names of likely appointees.

It should be understood that when the President does not appoint a man of his own choice, a man who shares his views, he may make more difficult for himself the task of influencing the direction of policy and program. But it should also be understood that when a President makes appointments he may be trying to gain Congressional votes and group and public support. These he may need as much as he needs efficiency, economy, and competence.

A complaint made on occasion (no matter which party is in the White House) is that politics dictates appointments, and the most common Presidential reply of course is that it does not. Obviously no President is likely to admit that partisan political considerations affect his choices for his office, and just as obviously they may. That is politics. Instructive sentences

---

10. Laurin L. Henry, "The Presidency, Executive Staffing, and the Federal Bureaucracy," paper prepared for 1967 meeting of the American Political Science Association, p. 2.

appear in a recent press report describing the search for executives in the Nixon administration.

> According to Mr. Malek (Frederic Malek, White House staff member in charge of Executive Search) what he and the Executive Search team look for are individuals with exceptional intellectual ability, talent for managing people, and enough "flexibility to operate in a political arena." By flexibility he means understanding of the public and Congressional pressures that affect governmental decision making.
>
> Even though Mr. Malek asserted that partisan politics has nothing to do with Executive Search, few Democrats seem to make it through the selection process.[11]

Two major studies that shed some light on the political appointment process are Richard Fenno's *The President's Cabinet* and Dean Mann's *The Assistant Secretaries*.[12] (Before any new administration is very old there are likely to be descriptions in the press of how that President is searching for men.) Fenno's wide-ranging book includes a chapter on Cabinet appointments that is quite informative. Discussing in some detail the variables that affect appointment, Fenno illustrates clearly how complex, varied, and hard to describe the political appointment process is. In his discussion he gives attention to the availability and balance. He asks "Who is available for Cabinet Office?" and answers by suggesting that availability is made up of five factors: party, personal loyalty, geography, socioeconomic factors, and specialized talents.

Although membership in the President's party is usually thought of as a *sine qua non*, it is not always a requirement, and it is certainly not sufficient. American parties are too varied for party identification to mean a great deal in terms of policy preference. Robert McNamara and Douglas Dillon, both Republicans, appeared comfortable in the Cabinet of President John F. Kennedy, and John Connally, a Democrat at the time, was Secretary of the Treasury in the Nixon administration. Still, it

---

11. See the article by James Naughton, "Nixon's Talent Hunter Also Wields Executive Hatchet," *New York Times,* July 12, 1971.

12. Richard F. Fenno, *The President's Cabinet* (New York: Random House, Vintage Books, 1959). Dean E. Mann, *The Assistant Secretaries* (Washington: The Brookings Institution, 1965).

must be admitted that it is conventional for a President to give Cabinet posts—particularly those dealing with domestic matters —to members of his own party.

Personal loyalty is another qualification, especially important after appointment. Many Presidents have appointed virtual strangers to Cabinet posts, but they expect loyalty and policy support after appointment. For some posts geographic residence may be important. The Secretary of the Interior often comes from the West (if a nominee comes from the East, eyebrows may go up and mutters will be heard from Western interests and Senators) and the Secretary of Agriculture from an agricultural area. Iowa with its corn has produced more Secretaries of Agriculture than any other state. The Secretaries of Commerce and Labor ordinarily come from industrial states. Of course it is not enough that a prospective Cabinet member come from the appropriate area; he must also be supported by the appropriate groups, whether business, labor, or agriculture.

What can be said about the importance of specialized talent? Although this may be more important at the sub-Cabinet level, it cannot be neglected at the Cabinet level. The most obvious case is the Attorney General's position; the occupant must be a lawyer. The Secretary of State often, though by no means always, has wide experience in international affairs and diplomacy. Increasingly, management sophistication seems not only relevant but necessary in the Department of Defense. Financial experience is often sought when a Secretary of Treasury is recruited. Surely in some cases appropriate skills and experience are more definable than in others, but most posts are likely to be associated with some particular mix of skills and experience. Still, any President is fairly free to do what he chooses in these matters. He may, for example, appoint as a secretary a man with political experience and then select a deputy who can provide management strength. President Nixon appointed a Congressman to head the Department of Defense, Melvin Laird, and thus provided the Department its political skill. The post of deputy went to an industrialist, David Packard, and thus management skill was also assured at top levels.

With all these factors to consider, a President must consider one more: How will a prospective appointee fit into his Cabinet? Will there be too many Easterners, too many businessmen? There is of course no particular figure which the President may not exceed, and no figure he must reach. But he does have to be sensitive to the over-all appearance of the Cabinet. Does it present a balanced appearance, or for one reason or another does it appear lopsided or unrepresentative? A President cannot be concerned only with the individual characteristics of a potential Cabinet member; he must also consider how each one will fit into the whole.

Dean Mann has explored in detail the appointment of sub-Cabinet officials in his book, *The Assistant Secretaries*. His research suggests that presidential appointments are likely to be Presidential in form only.

> Although the recruitment process in each administration reflects the personality and political orientation of its Chief Executive, practice and expediency dictate that presidential control over appointments has to be shared with others who also have a stake in the administrative branch of the government. In some instances even for appointments only two echelons below the President, his responsibility has been delegated to such a degree that he has often been able only to ratify (and with rarity, to veto) choices made by others.[13]

Who are these others? The most important "others" are agency and department heads, who may and often do select their own subordinates. Party officials may also play a part in selecting or approving sub-Cabinet officials, and so too may pressure-group leaders. Congressmen have their favorites. Although the part played by Congressmen and by party and pressure-group representatives is usually not so great as the part played by the President and by department and agency heads, their interest does mean that sub-Cabinet appointments, just like Cabinet posts, may be the subject of some negotiation. Trades may be made, and some bargains struck.

This is not to say that every job is hotly contested, but merely that Presidents and Cabinet Secretaries cannot do precisely as they please. Rather, they operate within looser or tighter limits. A well-organized and influential clientele may tighten the limits; a relatively invisible post may be filled largely at the pleasure of the recruiter. A President may give some jobs to personal friends and long-time supporters. A Secretary may do likewise. But the demands of politics and policy militate against all or indeed many posts being filled in this friendly way.

---

13. Mann, *Assistant Secretaries*, p. 76.

It is hard to go beyond these few general points. As Mann and Doig emphasize, the recruitment process is diverse and complex—and given the numbers of posts involved, the numbers of policy and program areas, and the variety of Presidents, it could be no other way. An additional observation from the *Assistant Secretaries* is in order here.

> The selection of men for the second echelon of the President's executive team reflects many of the basic characteristics and values of the American political system. Having responded over the years to the cross pressures of conflicting interests—executive and legislative, business and professional, public and private—the process appears haphazard, for no formal procedure has been devised for locating, classifying, and enticing qualified men into these positions. An even more important point is that no system has been evolved for preparing potential candidates adequately for their duties in office. As a result, the government is largely dependent on untrained people to fill its policy making positions.[14]

This situation may have adverse consequences for the quality of governmental decision-making. It may also mean that career people, who are trained and experienced, may be called on for advice and decisions more often than they otherwise would be. The inexperience and brief tenure of political appointees mean that much important work is in the hands of career civil servants.

Recruitment to the Civil Service

Since 1883 increasing numbers of civil servants have been recruited by means of competitive examinations. Today the government announces more than 20,000 examinations and hires well over 200,000 people a year. Most of the examinations are given by the various agencies of the government, under the supervision of the Civil Service Commission. One of the most important of these is the Federal Service Entrance Examination (the FSEE), an examination designed for college graduates who are interested in federal government employment. It is designed to be taken by liberal arts students, and those who pass it may

---

14. *Ibid.*, p. 264.

be appointed to any of more than 200 types of jobs in 50 federal agencies. It is administered several times a year at numerous locations throughout the country. An applicant may also take a Management Interne examination. If an applicant passes both these examinations, he can be considered for a higher grade and is frequently offered the opportunity to participate in a management training program.

A continuing problem that confronts the Civil Service Commission is whether the tests it uses (including the FSEE) actually allow the selection of the most qualified people. This problem has three parts: (1) What is the nature of the job in question? (2) What skills, aptitudes, knowledge, and attitudes are required to do it? and (3) Does the test being used actually measure these requirements? These questions may be fairly simple to answer if clerical jobs are in question. Obviously a typist may need to type 60 words a minute, and performance test measuring this ability are simple to design. Other clerical and some blue-collar positions may be equally amenable to examination. But what about a management analyst, a budget examiner, an investigator, a physicist, or an air traffic controller? What aptitudes and attitudes and knowledge are required for these jobs, and how can they be measured or even detected?

The examination problem has other dimensions that complicate it further. It is possible that all those who do well on a test may also do well on a particular job, and thus one may be tempted to relax. But what about those who do not do well on the examination? Would they nonetheless have performed well on the job? Unless they are given a chance it is impossible to say. Yet this is not what commonly happens; only those who do well on a test (the FSEE for example) are recruited. Further, there is little evidence that high performance on the FSEE is related to high performance on the job. That there may be problems with the FSEE should not be surprising. It would rather be surprising if one examination were able satisfactorily to select persons for over 200 different positions.

Perhaps the most serious charge that has been brought against the Federal Service Entrance Examination is that it discriminates on the basis of race. In February 1971 a group of black federal employees filed suit in Federal District Court charging that the FSEE was culturally and racially discriminatory. The suit contended that the examination "has served systematically to exclude qualified blacks and members of other minority groups from obtaining managerial and professional level positions in the Federal service, and has by other means denied plaintiffs and their class equal employment opportunities."[15] A major contention of the plaintiffs was that ability to score well on such tests as the FSEE " is obviously related to the cultural background of the individual taking the examination." In addition to this case, which is pending as this is written, the Civil Service Commission has also found the FSEE being criticised by both the Equal Employment Opportunity Commission and the Civil Rights Commission.[16]

A very hard question, probably one that has not been answered satisfactorily, is how to recruit on the basis of merit and not discriminate. What compromises, if any, must be made? It is at least an arguable position that if members of minority groups are excluded from federal service as a consequence of using traditional testing procedures then the testing procedures must fall. An alternative practice might be a lengthy probationary period, on-the-job training, and meaningful performance evaluation. But the practice of performance evaluation might also lead to charges of discrimination.

The examination phase of recruitment is only one aspect of the process. Another aspect is the initial application, and here too there may be problems—or at least questions. One difficulty is knowing about agency needs and job vacancies. Although an applicant may have to take only one test he may have to inquire about jobs at numerous places, and in an initial interview he may find that all a recruiter can do is express interest. The paper-work itself may deter at least some people from applying for federal service, as they see their images of bureaucracy confirmed.

In 1964 Franklin Kilpatrick, Milton Cummings, and Kent Jennings discussed the unattractiveness of federal employment to many able people in their book, *The Image of the Federal Service.*

---

15. Taken from an article in the *New York Times,* February 5, 1971, by Paul Delaney, "Suit Alleges Bias Job Testing."

16. *New York Times,* September 26, 1971. See also the reports of the Commission on Civil Rights, *The Federal Civil Rights Enforcement Effort,* and the followup report, *One Year Later.* For a critical study of the FSEE see "The Validity and Discriminatory Impact of the Federal Service Entrance Examination" (Washington: The Urban Institute, 1971).

The appeal of federal employment is lowest among those kinds of employed adults for whom the government's qualitative needs are the greatest in the future. In general, those persons with better education, higher occupational attainments, and more technical skills feel that federal employment would seriously lower their occupational satisfaction. On the other hand, those with less education, lower occupational attainments, and less technical skills feel that government would not seriously hurt their occupational satisfaction, and would, in some cases, raise it.[17]

College students and graduate students also tended to feel that federal employment would be less advantageous for them than other positions they expected to take.

The authors point out that job security, steady income, and retirement benefits are what people think federal employment has to offer, but these benefits are congruent with the values of people with lower, not higher, levels of attainment. Federal employment appealed least to those who are the scarcest and hardest to find. In this discussion, *The Image of the Federal Service* is pointing to an important recruitment problem.

Another phase of recruitment is suitability. Who is suitable for federal employment? To put the question another way, what might render a person unsuitable for federal employment? The final answer varies with the agency, the position, and likely the person making the final determination. Thus only general observations are possible. The Civil Service Commission and employing agencies are interested in determining that persons "privileged to be employed by the Government are of good conduct and character and are reliable, trustworthy and loyal."[18] To this end most persons entering federal service are subject to a background investigation of varying thoroughness depending on the sensitiveness of their prospective position. For a sensitive position requiring a full field investigation (carried out usually by Civil Service Commission investigators), character, habits, morals, associations, reputation, and loyalty will all be gone

---

17. Franklin P. Kilpatrick, Milton C. Cummings, Jr., and M. Kent Jennings, *The Image of the Federal Service* (Washington: The Brookings Institution, 1964), p. 117.

18. See a pamphlet issued by the U.S. Civil Service Commission titled, "The Investigative and Suitability Evaluation Programs of the U.S. Civil Service Commission," March 1969, p. 1.

into and a variety of persons interviewed. Obviously a number of questions can be raised. For example, will evidence of homosexuality be considered disqualifying? How about a youthful flirtation with marijuana? Cheating in college? The list might be extended, but there is no need to do so. The point is that standards are neither clear nor uniform and may be open to dispute—both academically and in the courts. Moreover, they may be (indeed surely are) in flux as social mores change. The reader might ask himself what behavior patterns or life styles ought to be disqualifying (any?) and then ask whether he thinks everyone would agree.

Two topics that can be raised in conjunction with recruitment are retention and promotion. Every year, just as people are recruited, other people leave the federal service for a variety of reasons. Personnel turnover, or "turbulence" as it is sometimes called, cannot be avoided totally, of course. Always there will be employees who find positions outside the federal service that they think for one reason or another will suit them better— better pay, better location, better working conditions, more status, and so on. Always there will be some people who for a number of reasons are dissatisfied with their current position. Some turnover no doubt is beneficial in an organization; it may prevent stagnation, facilitate change and innovation, and perhaps improve effectiveness—though of course much may depend on which staff members "turn over." An organization with low or virtually no turnover is likely to be a fairly dusty, musty place. But turnover may also have its costs; new members of an organization must spend some time in formal or informal on-the-job training before they are in a position to contribute at a higher level of effectiveness. A reputation for high turnover may lead to questions about the organization as a place to work and difficulty in recruitment. Among federal organizations turnover rates vary a good deal; even within units in a single executive department the variation may be substantial. But this means that at any one time a number of federal managers—and perhaps the Civil Service Commission and the Office of Management and Budget—will be trying to lower their turnover rates. Others at the same time should be trying to raise theirs. Steps in either direction may involve altering working conditions, manipulating the incentive system, and perhaps adjusting retirement conditions. In any particular organization the turnover rate, the causes and consequences, and whether it needs altering may all be questions for empirical research.

Promotion can be viewed as a special case of recruitment; promotion involves recruiting someone for a higher-level post. Little empirical research has been reported concerning the recruitment practices of federal agencies, though occasional commentary has focused on the Foreign Service and scattered other organizations. The result is that only general observations are possible. The first of course is that more research into promotion practices is desirable. Aside from this what else can be pointed out? The first point to be made is that given the relatively limited mobility within the federal service and the commonness of careers within a single organization it is to be expected that in many organizations senior positions are filled from below. In other words recruitment is from a fairly limited pool. This may be beneficial to morale and ensure that the person promoted is familiar with the organization and the organization with the person promoted, and these are not small advantages. But at the same time promotion from within may mean that talented outsiders are passed over while organizational traditions and rigidities are maintained. Indeed whether or not an outsider is brought in to fill a post may say something about organizational attitudes toward change.

How are people selected to fill higher posts? On what basis are people promoted? The answers may affect the substance of public policy and the image of government agencies as places to work. Written exams are not common, though unwritten or unassembled examinations may be used. Clearly important are a person's past record and how that is evaluated by those responsible. As some people are likely to be passed over and evaluation is likely to be subjective (and certainly likely to appear so), evaluation is likely to be the cause of dispute and debate. There is also room for racial, sexual, and other kinds of discrimination, especially because, among other things, promotion is likely to be a function of acquaintance and familiarity. Clearly in a merit system promotion should be on the basis of merit, but what does merit mean? Does it mean that to be promoted a man must be rated excellent by his superior? That only reflects on past performance. In any event, how meaningful are the ratings and how competent is the supervisor? Does it mean that he should have a college degree? If so, then what is the connection between a degree and performance? And what if promotion on the basis of merit automatically excludes some groups or classes? The point clearly is that promotion practices, as much as recruitment practices, cannot be relegated solely to the pages of personnel administration texts. Promotion practices in a federal agency may affect the substance of policy over time, they may themselves become the subject of political dispute, or they may set an example of fair employment practices. Clearly, promotion practices deserve more attention than they have received in public administration research.

The Political Activity of Public Employees

Although career employees in the executive branch may engage in some of the partisan political activities open to other citizens, there are certain restrictions on their activities.[19] Career employees may vote and express their opinions privately on political matters, but they may not engage in overt partisan activity or act as the public representative of a party or political party faction.

> No person employed in the executive branch of the federal government, or in any agency or department thereof, shall use his official authority or influence for the purpose of interfering with an election or affecting the result thereof. No person occupying a position in the competitive service shall take any active part in political management or political campaigns, except as may be provided by or pursuant to statute. All such persons shall retain the right to vote as they may choose and to express their opinions on all political subjects and candidates.[20]

A number of other activities are specifically prohibited. The Hatch Act of 1939, which forbade political activity for civil servants, gave the force of law to a long array of Civil Service

---

19. A recent provocatively titled article appeared in the *Wall Street Journal*, March 17, 1972, "If You Want to Work For the Government, Hide that Dart Board."

20. Section 4.1 of Civil Service Rule IV, quoted in "Political Activity of Federal Officers and Employees," U.S. Civil Service Commission Pamphlet 20, May 1966, p. 3.

Commission decisions and rules permitting or prohibiting a variety of specific activities. For example, career employees may not solicit contributions for campaigns or be compelled to contribute to campaigns. They may not be delegates to party conventions or serve on party committees or run for public office.

Why do such rules, and there are many more, exist? They exist partially as a reaction to patronage politics and the spoils system and represent an attempt to neutralize the civil service. Moreover, it could be argued that they represent a Congressional attempt to weaken the power of the President and to protect Congressmen. Another reason or justification for the limitations on career employees is that they, particularly upper-level career civil servants, have to work closely with political employees who are members of one party or another. Communication and cooperation between political appointees and career civil servants may be easier when the career men are not publicly identified with and committed to a particular party. Republicans may have enough difficulty working with career officials who have just worked with and for Democratic office holders for eight years. If the career officials had publicly supported the Democrats and campaigned for them, the difficulties would be greater; cooperation might be completely impossible.

Given their existence, how effective are the rules regulating and limiting political activities? There are no clear answers. If we assume that to be effective regulations must be understood, then it would appear that many of the regulations are not very effective. As Table 5-6 shows, data collected for the Commission on Political Activity of Government Personnel indicate that there is much confusion about what is permitted and what is not. Indeed, as the Commission pointed out in its report, "64.1 percent of the Federal employees understand five or less of the restrictions of the law. Only 35.8 percent understand six or more of the restrictions and no employee understands more than eight out of the ten." In other words, not one employee surveyed responded correctly to all ten items. Because of this confusion the Commission recommended a simplification and liberalization of the present Civil Service Commission rules governing political activity.

Faced with compelling evidence that the existing law unduly confuses and restricts more than 4.5 million

TABLE 5-6

Percentage Responses of Federal Employees As to What Political Activities They Think They "Can" and "Cannot" Do Under Present Hatch Act Rules

Activity	Can	Cannot	Not Sure
a. Make a speech at a rally held by a political party	15.8	69.4	14.6
b. Put a political sticker on his own car	63.0	24.4	12.5
c. Hold office in a political party organization	8.5	80.6	10.7
d. Run for state or national office	8.9	81.0	9.6
e. Write a letter to his senator or congressman	96.0	1.5	2.2
f. Drive people to the polls on election day	45.0	40.5	14.2
g. Run for a school board position where people are not candidates for either major party	66.5	15.8	17.3
h. Become actively involved in local issues such as civil rights and taxes	49.5	32.6	17.3
i. Participate in voter registration drives	48.1	35.6	16.0
j. Distribute campaign materials for a party or candidate	18.6	71.2	10.1

Source: Report of the Commission on Political Activity of Government Personnel, Findings and Recommendations, Volume One, Table 1. The data were collected and analyzed for the Commission by the Survey Research Center of the University of Michigan. Items a, c, d, f, i, and j are prohibited by law and the rest are permitted.

Federal, State, and local public employees, this Commission proposes a new approach. It recommends that Congress eliminate the confusing array of do's and don'ts by clearly defining permitted activities and prohibitions in the statute. The prohibitions would be only those that Congress finds necessary to protect employees against actions that would threaten the integrity, efficiency, and the impartiality of the public service.[21]

There might well be some risk in such a policy, but it should be remembered that at least some civil servants engage in prohibited activities now, if only because they do not know they are prohibited, and government does not seem much the worse for it.[22] Then too, most citizens of the United States, even though under no restrictions, do little more than vote—and numbers do not even do that. Unless it is assumed that civil servants as a group are substantially different from most citizens, it is safe to assume that even if the law is liberalized most civil servants will continue to do little more than vote.[23]

Although they are not unimportant, questions about the effectiveness and reform of Hatch Act rules may seem to some a bit out of date, as in very recent years some civil servants in some of the agencies (notably HEW) have engaged in political activities that had little to do with activity of the traditional political-party sort. Welfare and civil rights advocates (or activists) have taken public stands in favor of particular actions and in opposition to policies of the administration in power and have justified their actions on the ground of both professionalism and personal conscience. A journalistic description of recent developments provides a picture of this new kind of political activity.

> Disaffection over the Vietnam war is probably deeper and more widespread in HEW than in any other federal agency. Many HEW employees were attracted to the department by its new social action programs and are "politicized" in a way that makes them a new breed of bureau-

---

21. *Report of the Commission on Political Activity of Government Personnel,* vol. 1 (Washington: U.S. G.P.O., 1968), p. 21.

22. It might be noted that in 1972 the National Association of Letter Carriers and a number of individual federal employees asked the Supreme Court to rule the Hatch Act unconstitutional. In June 1973 the Court upheld the Hatch Act and made it plain that Congress could justifiably prohibit federal employees from participating in a variety of political activities.

23. For data comparing the level of political activity of civil servants with that of the public in general see Gary Halter, "The Effects of the Hatch Act on the Political Participation of Federal Employees," *Midwest Journal of Political Science,* Vol. 16, No. 4 (1972), pp. 723–729.

crat. They are not drawn to the kind of overt partisan activity that is prohibited in the Hatch Act. Their efforts are directed against the war and in behalf of social programs. Many of them actively reject the concept of the politically neutral government employee and suggest that under the old criteria the perfect civil servant is an Eichmann. Like their contemporaries in the universities, many young professionals are sharply questioning authority. And upper-echelon administrators are grappling in varying ways with demands from dissidents for a share in making policy decisions.[24]

One need not, of course, point only to HEW. At various times activists, or dissidents, or young Turks have appeared in the Office of Economic Opportunity, in the Justice Department, and in the State Department.

This apparently new variety of political activity reflects the current popularity of participative democracy and participative management and its appearance within the government bureaucracies. It raises a number of questions that are not dealt with by the Hatch Act. What are the political activity rights of career civil servants? What are the limits of dissent within governmental agencies? Do they vary with the position held by the dissenter? Is a civil servant bound to support the administration he is working under, and if he cannot should he leave quietly or with voice?[25] What kinds of sanctions (and inducements) may superiors hold out in order to achieve one voice at best and at least consent by silence? The answers to these questions are not apparent, but some relevant observations are possible. Civil servants may increasingly be members of professions that have codes of ethics, and they may as individuals be bound by their own consciences. They may want to do what they believe to be in the public interest. But it is also clear that in the end the man they work for, the President, is the one the people chose and he is the one responsible, together with the people he appoints. The democratic model would seem to demand that the bureaucracy be responsive to those politically responsible to the electorate. Yet if this is so it at least raises

24. See "HEW: The Department That Lost Its Head" in *Science,* Vol. 168, June 19, 1970, p. 1432.

25. Well worth reading is Albert Hirschman, *Exit, Voice, and Loyalty* (Cambridge: Harvard University Press, 1970).

a question about the appropriateness of the democratic model for structuring internal bureaucratic decision-making. For bureaucrats to be able to decide what is right and in the public interest, for all the appearance it may have of democratic management, may be the essence of government by bureaucrats. But enough of such questions. It is clear that the political behavior of civil servants raises complex issues.

It should be mentioned that political appointees are not subject to the restrictions that limit the political activity of career civil servants. Indeed they are often expected to contribute to the party war chest and to attend dinners and rallies. They may speak in support of their party, and they may defend themselves and the administration and its policies before Congress. Precisely how active political appointees are depends on their own predilections, the position they hold, and the view of the President they serve. What is certain is that no political appointee could attack in public the policies of the party in power and continue to hold his position for long. If political activity, in other words, appeared to conflict with loyalty to the administration, it would be curtailed or the appointee would be dismissed.

The Unionization of Federal Employees

In recent years the unionization of federal employees has rapidly expanded. If one looks for example at the American Federation of Government Employees one finds that in 1964 its membership was 139,000; in 1966 it was 200,000; by 1970 it was 482,000; and it is still growing. By the end of 1970 about one half of the federal work force was organized in one union or another. And although not quantifiable, militance seems also to be growing. Strikes, work stoppages, and slowdowns are the evidence.

For many years the position of the federal government, that is, management, with regard to the organization of federal employees seemed to range somewhere between neutrality and hostility. This changed in 1962 when President John F. Kennedy issued Executive Order 10988 legitimating and clarifying the role of unions in the federal government. This order made clear the employee's right to membership in a labor organization. It delineated different forms of recognition that might be accorded employee organizations, and it set out the kinds of matters that

Source: From the Table of Contents, U.S. Government Organization Manual 1972/73

were appropriate for labor management discussions—employee grievances, the work environment, and the scheduling of work are examples. On the other hand, the order continued the prohibition against strikes by federal employees, declared that closed and union shops were inappropriate, and indicated that conditions of employment fixed by the Congress were not matters to be negotiated by labor and agency management. But though such limits existed, the order by President Kennedy made clear that government labor unions were legitimate and useful and should be recognized. It may be noted that prior to issuing his executive order President Kennedy had appointed a Task Force on Employee Management Relations in the Federal Service and had sent a memorandum setting up the Task Force to all heads of departments and agencies stating his views on federal employee organizations.

> The right of all employees of the federal government to join and participate in the activities of employee organizations and to seek to improve working conditions and the resolution of grievances should be recognized by management officials at all levels in all departments and agencies. The participation of federal employees in the formulation and implementation of employee policies and procedures affecting them contributes to the effective conduct of public business.[26]

In 1967 President Johnson appointed a committee to examine the experience of five years that had elapsed since E.O. 10988 was issued. In particular there was interest in broadening the scope of collective bargaining and in setting up machinery to settle management labor disputes. Nothing came of this review, however, and it remained for President Nixon to issue Executive Order 11491 and revoke E.O. 10988. The right to join a union was reiterated, and the system of labor-management relations within the federal service was brought even closer to the private model.

> Specifically, the new Order created a Federal Labor Relations Council, consisting of the Chairman of the U.S. Civil Service Commission, the Secretary of Labor, and the Director of the Office of Management and Budget, to decide major policy issues; strengthened the exclusive bargaining agents by eliminating other forms of union recognition; gave the Assistant Secretary of Labor for Labor Management Relations a key role in deciding bargaining unit, representation, and unfair labor practice cases; prohibited union or agency shops; authorized binding arbitration of grievances; and created a Federal Service Impasses

---

26. Quoted in Chester A. Newland, "Trends in Public Employee Unionization," *Journal of Politics*, vol. 26 (1964), p. 588.

Panel to settle negotiation impasses either by itself or
with the assistance of fact finders or arbitrators.[27]

It should be clear, however, that the prohibition against striking
was retained, and the Executive Order specifically states that
employees are not required to join. In September 1971 President
Nixon issued Executive Order 11616, which amended E.O.
11491 and among other things regularized further the handling
of grievances.

Like unions generally, government unions are interested
in improving the well-being, especially the material well-being
of their members. They are concerned about working conditions,
appointments and promotions, discipline, and of course pay and
fringe benefits. These concerns come out clearly in the newspapers that unions publish for their membership, and they
appear also in the hearings that Congress holds periodically to
consider government pay bills.

Union spokesmen come to argue the poverty of their condition and the need for improvement. The attendance of the
union spokesmen at the hearings raises an important point.
In matters of pay, public employee unions cannot bargain with
management (as unions do in private business) because management can make no commitments. Pay raises come from Congress, and unions therefore go to Congress. Because unions
must bargain with Congress, and often with the President, the
Civil Service Commission, and the Office of Management and
Budget, it is obvious that they are politically active groups.

That government unions are increasingly militant is evi-
denced by the strikes that have occurred in various organizations
in recent years. Although strikes are forbidden, they have occurred in the Post Office and the Federal Aviation Administration. And in 1970 the following paragraphs appeared on the
front pages of the Wall Street Journal.

Three years ago a local official of the American Federation
of Government Employees told a visitor that someday his
union might be forced to strike the Social Security Ad-

---

27. Richard J. Murphy, "The Difference of a Decade: The Federal
Government," *Public Administration Review,* March/April 1972, p. 110.
This issue of PAR contains a symposium on collective bargaining in the
public service.

ministration headquarters in Baltimore, despite a strict law to the contrary.

At that time, the prospect of such a development seemed rather dim. But the illegal strike by postal workers that began last week and persisted yesterday may have changed all that. Now federal officials are faced with the grim possibility that the widespread mail strike—the first major walkout against the Federal Government—could trigger strikes by other Civil servants in the sprawling bureaucracy.[28]

Although strikes did not multiply then, they still may. The very possibility of strikes by federal civil servants raises important questions of public policy. One question is whether civil servants should be prohibited from striking. But this is a relatively meaningless or perhaps trivial question. They are prohibited from striking, but they have gone on strike. Perhaps the real questions concern strategies both for avoiding strikes and for dealing with strikes once they occur. This is not the place to suggest answers to these questions, but it is important that they be considered. It is worthwhile stressing the point, as the prohibition against strikes could lead to failure to think about them. It may be that planning for strikes against the government is to think about the unthinkable, but that clearly is required. Participative politics, political activism, dissent, labor militance, worker frustration, management insensitivity—all these may lead to strikes.

Conclusion

The decade of the seventies is likely to be a time of problems and challenges in the civil service. Employees seem more militant and more likely to organize and take action than ever before. Both union activity and relatively unconventional political activity have hit highs in recent years. Whether administrators will be able to cope with these developments and how they ought to will be important questions. Minority group members and women will be pressing more than ever for jobs equal to those previously accorded white males, and these de-

---

28. *Wall Street Journal*, March 24, 1970.

mands will be very difficult to accommodate without widespread compliance from federal managers and, perhaps even more important, an increasing supply of federal jobs. It is hard to enforce equal employment opportunity in the absence of much employment. But tight budgets are likely over the next few years, which may make both innovation and expansion difficult. And to these obvious problems can be added others—the image problem, the examining problem, the employment suitability problem. Even the fact that so many officials make their careers in a single agency and enjoy a high level job security may be problems in an era of rapid social and technological change.

Surely it is clear that these several problems in the field of personnel can be viewed as important public policy problems. And a useful exercise may be for you to consider likely responses. Obviously there are several possibilities. For example, it is possible to imagine that the responses of government organizations to these problems will be quite modest. If what the government does can be viewed as the product of organizations carrying out their routines, then it is possible to imagine that the routines of today will continue to be carried out tomorrow, even though they may no longer be appropriate. It is possible that the Civil Service Commission will make proposals that are ignored by agency administrators in the field, so that while policy changes, practice doesn't. At least not rapidly. Finally it is worth suggesting that you may wish to consider several of the problems described in this chapter in the light of the description of public policy provided in Chapter 3.

6 Individuals in Organizations

This chapter continues the focus on personnel of the preceding chapter, but from a very different perspective. Attention shifts now from conditions of federal employment to the attitudes and behavior of people in executive-branch organizations. These topics are important for anyone concerned with how regulations and laws are interpreted and enforced, programs implemented and "the public" served. It is common to speak of "the government" or "the administration" doing this or that, of this organization or that carrying out (or not carrying out) programs. But in the end it is individuals who meet the public, write memoranda, assess the alternatives, make the choices, enforce the laws. Some attention to individuals and how they act in organizational settings therefore seems important.

Approaches and Assumptions

Individual behavior in organizations can be viewed from many perspectives, with obviously varying implications for management. The perspective dominant in the early part of this century has been variously characterized as the *machine* model or the *scientific management* model. Associated primarily with the name of Frederick Taylor, this approach to administration allowed little room for individual variability, viewing men as essentially extensions of and in may ways similar to the machines they operated. In the machine model orders flowed down the hierarchy, and there was little room for worker participation in organization decisions.

A second and very different approach to administration has come to be known as the *human relations* approach. It emphasized the importance of individual values and feelings and called attention to the importance of emotional and nonrational considerations in organizational functioning. The human relations approach was a reaction to the machine approach that grew out of the findings of a famous body of social research, the Hawthorne experiments. As Amitai Etzioni has summarized them, the most important conclusions of these experiments were:[1]

1. The level of production is set by social norms, not by physiological capacities.

2. Non-economic rewards and sanctions significantly affect the behavior of the workers and largely limit the effect of economic incentive plans.

3. Often workers do not act or react as individuals but as members of groups.

4. Informal leadership may be more influential than formal leadership.

5. Communication between ranks is important, as are democratic leadership and participation by lower ranks in decision-making.

The human relations approach to administration has gained much popularity, and scores of books have emphasized the importance of good human relations and participative management. But, no doubt predictably, there has also been reaction and skepticism, just as there was to the machine model. Some observers have seen in human relations, at least potentially, a tool management could use to manipulate employees and achieve its own purposes. Also, although the vision of human relations seems to be harmonious organization, it may be that within organizations there are real conflicts of interest (management versus labor is an obvious one), which all the human relations in the world will not get rid of. Conflict can serve useful purposes. Then, too, questions can be raised about which issues are actually amenable to participative decision-making—especially when in government the Congress may set both or-

---

1. Amitai Etzioni, *Modern Organizations* (Englewood Cliffs: Prentice-Hall, 1964), pp. 34–38.

ganizational goals and working conditions. In short, human relations does not appear to have all the answers, though it may have as many or more than scientific management.

The view taken here, insofar as a single view is taken, might be called the *political model* or the *political approach*. In essence, an organization is viewed as a coalition of actors whose interests are by no means identical, who mutually benefit (economically, politically, socially, and/or psychologically) from membership.[2] When they cease to benefit or when the costs of membership outweight the benefits, they may quit. The job of management is to attempt by the manipulation of costs and benefits both to hold the coalition together and to accomplish the mission of the organization. It is worth noting that these activities are to an extent separable; while a personnel adminis- trator may carry out many activities associated with keeping members in an organization, other individuals in other manage- ment roles may focus their energies more exclusively on mission accomplishment. It is also important to recognize that it is possible for an organization to become preoccupied with main- taining itself, without accomplishing the mission that was its original *raison d'être*.

It is possible to come at the problem of understanding human behavior in organizations by considering various as- sumptions about behavior and the management strategies that these assumptions lead to.[3] For example, one might assume a fairly simple economic model of man and arrive fairly quickly at conclusions about the value of economic incentives. One could assume that man was primarily a social animal and arrive fairly quickly at conclusions about the importance of social relationships. One might make other assumptions about human motivation and behavior that would have implications for the behavior of management. It is worth noting, however, that managers and policy makers frequently do not make their assumptions explicit; they are in due course disappointed when they do not get from employees the behavior they expected. Pay

---

2. This view of organizations is consistent with much of the ex- change-theory literature. See, for example, Mancur Olson, Jr., *The Logic of Collective Action*, (Cambridge: Harvard University Press, 1965). See also Richard M. Cyert and James G. March, *A Behavioral Theory of the Firm* (Englewood Cliffs: Prentice-Hall, 1963).

3. See for example Edgar Schein, *Organizational Psychology* (Engle- wood Cliffs: Prentice-Hall, 1965), pp. 47–63.

raises, for example, often seem to contain an implicit theory of economic motivation that if made explicit would be instantly questioned as perhaps erroneous and in any case simplistic.

One can also assume, of course, that human behavior is complex and flows from a variety of motives. What influences one man at one time may not work again for another man. This complex perspective leads to skepticism, caution, and inquiry, which are sensible stances given the state of social knowledge. But managers must still act. For the sake of speed and simplicity they may act as though man were only economically motivated, which may work often enough to be sensible. A manager may assume man is a social animal, which may also work. Another common simplifying assumption is that individuals are self-interested.[4] Members may not be very clear about what is in their interest, and members of different organizations may define their interests differently. Still it seems reasonable, useful, and prudent to assert that members of executive-branch organizations are interested in protecting and promoting their own interests and positions. This single simple assumption has obvious implications for such topics as communication, evaluation (it is likely a man will evaluate his own work positively), inspection, and motivation. The assumption points to other problems, too, not the least of which are those associated with the delegation of authority by self-interested superiors to self-interested subordinates. It should be emphasized, of course, that self-interested behavior is not necessarily antithetical to an organization's or a superior's interest. Organizational interest and member self-interest may indeed be congruent, but as they are not the same, they in some ways diverge. If so, members may follow their own interest in such matters and quit, relax, distort, cover up.

Roles, Behavior, and Compliance

The organizations of the executive branch are groups of people brought and kept together for the accomplishment of some specific purpose or purposes. (To be sure this seemingly simple statement must be qualified. An organization may have purposes in addition to or instead of its official stated purpose;

---

4. See Anthony Downs, *Inside Bureaucracy* (Boston: Little, Brown, & Co., 1967).

after its creation for one purpose its purpose may change or additional purposes develop.) In any organization there are various positions and roles, and the people filling them act and interact with one another in a variety of ways and for various reasons.

The distinction between position and role is often not easy to understand. A position amounts to a more or less detailed prescription of the behavior required of a particular organization member. A role is what the member of the organization actually does. It may seem at first that organization position and organization role are two names for the same thing, but this is not necessarily the case. A role—that is, actual performance—is affected in part by the formal position prescription, but only in part. Behavior is also affected by the informal and unwritten expectations and desires of other organization members and perhaps in some circumstances of nonmembers as well.[5]

The relationship between the written rules and informal expectations is by no means clear and simple. For some situations there may be no written rules but only unwritten and more or less informal norms or expectations; in other circumstances both written (formal) rules and informal norms or expectations may guide behavior. In the latter case they may reinforce one another, or they may conflict. It is hazardous to predict individual behavior on the basis only of written rules. Behavior is not necessarily consistent with rules, and issuing new rules may have little or no effect on behavior.

Performance in a role is also the result of a member's own interpretation of it, his attitudes and values, and his own ability and willingness to do what is expected. Because performance is affected by so many variables, it is hazardous to assume that organization members are actually doing what their formal position descriptions say they are. Position descriptions may have more to do with wished-for than real behavior. In real life men in identical positions may be doing very different things, and a

---

5. For a discussion of various demands on the individual in an organizational role see Daniel J. Levinson, "Role, Personality, and Social Structure in the Organizational Setting," *Journal of Abnormal and Social Psychology* 58 (1959) pp. 170–180. A major study using concepts of role theory is Neal Gross *et al., Explorations in Role Analysis* (New York: John Wiley and Sons, 1958).

man who steps into another's position may fill it differently;
no man in an organization may quite live up to the formal prescription of his position.

Two concepts associated with the idea of role deserve
particular attention. We may first observe that a particular organization member may be expected to play several organizational roles. He may have to be both an analyst of programs
and an advocate for them. He may have to be both a follower
and a leader, and he may have to be manager, lobbyist, and
professional. At the extreme any member may suffer from an
overload and be unable to perform all the roles expected of him;
it is also possible that different roles will conflict with one
another. When *role conflict* occurs, an organizational member
may be unable adequately to perform the roles in conflict.
Although this observation seems obvious, it is frequently over-
looked, as when department staff members, traditionally program
advocates, are expected also to be objective analysts of program
effectiveness. Whether because of overload or role conflict, when
a man is expected to play multiple roles some may get short-
changed. It is also worth suggesting that the total mix of roles a
man is expected to fill may affect his performance in each of them.

The possibility of variation in role behavior is enhanced in
any organization where there are subgroups or work groups
composed of only some members of the total organization.
Ideally, the several subgroups will work together to achieve an
organizational mission or purpose. But for a variety of reasons
this may not happen. Because of distance, differences in
specialty and status, or more idiosyncratic reasons, communication between subgroups may be faulty or nonexistent. Within
any particular subgroup norms may develop that conflict with
those of other work groups or the organization as a whole. If
this happens, the performance of the organization may suffer.
Workers, for example, may find it in their own interest to hold
down production or encourage lax rule enforcement, but though
this may be in their own interest, it may not be in the interest
of the organization as a whole or of management, which can
be viewed as another work group.

It should be clear by now why a common problem in organization is compliance with organizational rules. Because an
organization member may be cross-pressured and confronted
with conflicting expectations, no one can assume automatic
obedience to rules. The President cannot assume compliance, and

netiher can a bureau chief. All who want compliance must work to try to get it, and run the risk of failing.

Compliance would indeed be difficult if organizations did not have sanctions, both positive and negative, with which to reward and punish. Written rules may be accompanied by a system of formal discipline, but there may also be informal sanctions. Members of an organization may be rewarded for conforming to organizational norms with everything from acceptance, respect, and friendship to choice assignments, promotions, and more money. The executive who conforms to the norms of an organization, who fits in, may be rewarded with loyalty; the executive who ignores the norms of an organization may be rewarded with mutiny and its modern-day equivalents. Negative sanctions have to be reckoned with by any member of a social system. Obviously the senior members of an organization control some sanctions; they can use the formal discipline system to get rules obeyed. But junior members also have their sanctions. By slowing down, by striking, by sabotaging, or perhaps just by following rules to the letter, junior members can make their displeasure known. Again, compliance is problematic.

It is possible to relate the problem of compliance to other activities or organizational functions. Recruitment, for example, may be designed to yield more predictable performance and greater homogeneity in an organization. Training and socialization may obviously affect compliance, though it is worth noting that socialization (informal instruction about how to act and get along) may contradict the lessons learned in formal training programs. Supervision, inspection, and control may all have an affect on the way an individual performs his role or roles.[6]

A Look at Individual Differences

"This book is about the organization man." So begins a famous book, *The Organization Man*. The author, William H. Whyte, describes the subject of his book this way:[7]

---

6. An excellent case study of compliance is Herbert Kaufman, *The Forest Ranger* (Baltimore: Johns Hopkins University Press, 1960).

7. William H. Whyte, *The Organization Man* (New York: Simon and Schuster, 1956), p. 3.

> If the term is vague, it is because I can think of no other
> way to describe the people I am talking about. They are
> not the workers, nor are they the white collar people in
> the usual, clerk sense of the word. These people only work
> for The Organization. The ones I am talking about *belong*
> to it as well. They are the ones of our middle class who
> have left home, spiritually as well as physically, to take
> the vows of organization life, and it is they who are the
> mind and soul of our great self-perpetuating institutions.

With such language Whyte describes one pattern of adjustment
to work in bureaucratic organizations. It would be a mistake,
however, to think that it is the only pattern; many social scientists have looked inside organizations and used a variety of
terms to describe the various behavior patterns they have found.

In a popular book written some years after Whyte's, Robert
Presthus divided organizational members into three types—the
upward mobiles, the ambivalents, and the indifferents.[8]

> The upward mobiles are typically distinguished by high
> morale; their level of job satisfaction is high. Indeed the
> process and criteria by which they are selected insures that
> they will have an unfailing optimism. The reasons for this
> are clear. They identify strongly with the organization and
> derive strength from their involvement. Their dividends
> also include disproportionate shares of the organization's
> rewards in power, income, and ego reinforcement.

Unlike the upward mobiles, the indifferents, according to Presthus, do not identify with the organization. "The indifferents
are those who have come to terms with their work environment
by withdrawal and by a redirection of their interests toward off-
the-job satisfactions."[9] Further, Presthus wrote, "The typical
indifferent has rejected majority values of success and power.
While the upward mobile strives for such values, obtainable
today mainly through big organizations, the indifferent seeks
that security which the organization can also provide for those
who merely go 'along.' "[10]

---

8. Robert Presthus, *The Organizational Society* (New York: Alfred
A. Knopf, 1962), p. 167.

9. Presthus, *Organizational Society*, p. 208.

10. Presthus, *Organizational Society*, p. 208.

In the middle, between the upward mobiles and the in-differents, are the ambivalents. The ambivalent wants the prizes or rewards given by the organization, but he does not, as it were, want to play the game to get them. Perhaps he cannot. Presthus writes:[11]

> On the one hand, he wants success yet resists paying the price in collectively validated behavior. On the other, he disdains success, as popularly defined, yet feels that his individuality must be validated by others. Unable to reject or to rise above majority values, he is also unable or unwilling to play the roles required to achieve them. While the upward mobile is sustained by status rewards and great expectations, and the indifferent accommodates by limiting his aspirations, the ambivalent is chronically disturbed.

Presthus ascribes to the ambivalent, despite his seeming confusion, an important organizational role, that of critic and innovator.[12]

> Despite his inability to meet bureaucratic demands, the ambivalent type plays a critical social role, namely that of providing the insight, motivation, and dialectic that inspire change. His innovating role is often obscured because the authority, leadership, and money needed to institutionalize change remain in the hands of organizational elites. Nevertheless, few ideals or institutions escape his critical scrutiny. In his view custom is no guarantee of either rationality or legitimacy. This perception is sharpened by his inability to accept charismatic traditional bases of authority: rationality alone provides a compelling standard.

The concepts "cosmopolitan" and "local" also help us understand how individuals may adjust to work in a bureaucratic organization. These words have been used by several scholars to describe organization members who identify with the organization in which they work (locals) and organization members who identify with some external group (cosmopolitans). This dichot-

---

11. Presthus, *Organizational Society*, p. 281.
12. Presthus, *Organizational Society*, p. 258.

omy, of course, is not unlike the trichotomy proposed by Presthus. "In the context of Merton's distinction, the upward mobile is typically a 'local.' Unlike the 'cosmopolitan' who has a broad disciplinary interest or national perspective, his interests and aspirations are tied to his own organization. Always loyal, he regards its rules and actions as 'the best way' to handle large numbers of people."[13] If the local and the upward mobile can be equated, so perhaps can the ambivalent and the cosmopolitan. Alvin Gouldner has described the cosmopolitan as low on loyalty to the employing organization, likely to use an external reference group, and high on commitment to the professional skills.[14] The ambivalent has been described in similar language. "He honors theory, knowledge, and skill. Socialization as an independent professional blinds him to legitimate, organizational needs for control and coordination. Believing explicitly that both motivation and expertise come from within he resists bureaucratic rules and supervision."[15]

Other studies, using other language, have focused on similar patterns of adaption. Leonard Reissman's "Role Conceptions in Bureaucracy," for example, sets out to determine what the civil servant conceives his social role to be.[16] In data he collected in a state civil service Reissman found four ideal types of role conception.

> 1. Functional bureaucrat—seeks recognition from professional group outside of bureaucracy—just happens to work for the government—faces outward and away from the bureaucracy—active in professional societies—guided by standards of success of the profession.
> 2. Specialist bureaucrat—resembles functional bureaucrat but more aware of bureaucracy—seeks recognition from department and people with whom he works—overly meticulous about the rules and regulations, he attempts always to remain safely within these limits.

---

13. Presthus, *Organizational Society*, p. 179.

14. Alvin W. Gouldner, "Cosmopolitans and Locals: Toward an Analysis of Latent Social Roles" *Administrative Science Quarterly*, 2 (1957–8), pp. 281–306 and pp. 444–480.

15. Presthus, *Organizational Society*, p. 259.

16. Leonard Reissman, "A Study of Role Conception in Bureaucracy," *Social Forces*, 27 (1949), pp. 305–310.

3. Service bureaucrat—oriented in terms of bureaucratic structure but seeks recognition from outside group.

4. Job bureaucrat—immersed entirely in structure—seeks recognition along departmental rather than professional lines—improvement of operating efficiency becomes an end in itself.

These four patterns of adaptation are similar to those noted by the investigators. Dwaine Marvick, analyzing data collected in a government research organization, found what he called institutionalists, specialists, and hybrids.[17] As defined by him these different patterns of career identification resemble the job bureaucrat, the functional bureaucrat, and the specialist bureaucrat that Reissman described. (Marvick did not distinguish a service bureaucrat.) The cosmopolitan and the local, the specialist and institutionalist, the functional bureaucrat and the job bureaucrat are different terms that describe the same dichotomy: weak identification with the employing organization and strong identification with it. It may be more accurate to view organizational identification as existing on a continuum with the ends marked strong and weak.

Another aspect of individual behavior within bureaucratic organizations can be clearly if inelegantly described as "rule-following behavior." This behavior can be viewed as a continuum running from "always obeys the rules" to "seldom obeys the rules." Presthus noted that the ambivalent resisted bureaucratic rules and supervision while the upward mobile accepted them. Reissman suggested that the specialist bureaucrat was "overly meticulous about rules and regulations." An article which appeared some years ago described how different Navy disbursing officers adjusted to rules.[18] "The Regulation type approximates the true bureaucrat in that he remains impervious to rank, informal structures, and the orders of his superiors, but goes further in employing the narrowest possible interpretation of every regulation. For fear of the General Accounting Office his rule is, 'When in doubt, don't.'" Officers described as realists, on the

---

17. Dwaine Marvick, *Career Perspectives in a Bureaucratic Setting* (Ann Arbor: University of Michigan Press, 1954).

18. Ralph H. Turner, "The Navy Disbursing Officer as a Bureaucrat," *American Sociological Review*, 12 (1947) pp. 342–348.

other hand, saw the regulations "as illogical concatenations of procedures, restrictions, and interpretations, frequently ambiguous, sometimes contradictory, and often, when strictly applied, defeating the purpose for which they were constructed."[19]

Some, but not necessarily all, organization members will resemble the model of the archtypal bureaucrat described so well by Merton in his classic "Bureaucratic Structure and Personality."[20] Surely some may conscientiously obey and enforce every single rule no matter what the situation or consequences, but not all will. Moreover, whether a person obeys the rules may not necessarily depend on the strength of his identification with his organization. An upward mobile, for example, may pay little attention to formal rules and regulations if such behavior is the norm in his organization. If one knew only that a man was strongly identified with his organization, it would be unsafe to predict his rule-following behavior. It would be safe to predict only that he would conform to the norms of his organization.

A little imagination can produce more labels to describe the ways in which organization members have adapted to the various demands of organizational life.[21] The more involved and the less involved or, much less neutrally, stakhonovite and slacker are terms that could be used to describe, respectively, the members who work 12 hours a day on nights and week-ends and those who barely work eight hours for five days and find the thought of extra work repugnant. Technique-oriented and task-oriented are terms that can be used to emphasize the fact that some organization members are concerned with procedure and others are concerned with meeting a goal no matter how. The terms innovators and conservers might describe differing attitudes toward change. Clearly, organization members may adjust in a variety of ways to their organizations, and different organi-

---

19. Turner, Navy Disbursing Officer, p. 347, both quotations.
20. Robert K. Merton, "Bureaucratic Structure and Personality," in his *Social Theory and Social Structure* (Glencoe: The Free Press, 1957), pp. 195–206.
21. See the extensive discussion of various patterns of adaptation in Bertram M. Gross, *The Managing of Organizations* (New York: The Free Press, 1964), Vol. 1, Chapter 16. Anthony Downs devotes Chapter IX of his *Inside Bureaucracy* to a discussion of specific types of officials. Among the types he mentions are climbers, conservers, advocates, zealots, and statesmen.

zations make different demands. Consequently the word bureaucrat contains little behavioral information; it cannot mean much more than organizational member. The stereotype of the bureaucrat is a person concerned about security, obedient and rule-following, and not very forceful or imaginative. However, if the phrase organization member is substituted for the word bureaucrat, it is easy to see just how inaccurate the stereotype may be.

Leader Behavior

It seems worthwhile, after considering patterns of adaptation to organizational life, to give some special consideration to leader behavior. Most studies of leadership divide leader behavior into two types—autocratic and democratic. Stanley Seashore calls these types authoritarian and participative.[22]

> In general, there are two basic approaches to the management of an organization—the "participative" approach based upon group decision, mutual discussion of common problems and shared responsibility, and the "authoritarian" approach based upon strong individual leadership.

This dichotomy can be seen in some of the most significant work on leadership, the work done in the late 1940s and 1950s by investigators at Ohio State University. Although much of their work concerned leadership in small groups, some dealt specifically with executives and heads of formal organizations. Initially, leader behavior was conceived as existing on a number of dimensions, but finally two major dimensions or components of leadership were separated. Carroll Shartle has noted that these two dimensions are sometimes referred to as the *human relations* and the *get the work out* dimensions.[23]

Closely related to the study and description of leadership is the study of the relationship between leader behavior and situation. Early in the Ohio State studies Stogdill and Shartle published an article in which they argued that leadership must be studied "as a relationship between persons, and as an aspect of

22. Stanley E. Seashore, "Administrative Leadership and Organizational Effectiveness," in Rensis Likert and Samuel P. Hayes, Jr., (eds.), *Some Applications of Behavioral Research* (Paris: UNESCO, 1957), p. 47.

23. Carroll L. Shartle, *Executive Performance and Leadership* (Englewood Cliffs, N.J.: Prentice-Hall, Inc., 1956), pp. 116–123.

organizational activities, structures, and goals."[24] Other writers also concerned with the situation have argued that the pattern of behavior an executive chooses should be governed by the kind of enterprise he is managing.[25] Probably most observers would agree that the situation affects the behavior of a leader, but Alex Bavelas has further suggested that the situation affects who will become a leader. In an article dealing with leadership and its situation, he wrote that "almost any member of a group may become its leader under circumstances that enable him to perform the required functions of leadership. . . ."[26] He also noted that because of differences in situation the abilities that may help a man rise to the top of an organization may prove a "positive detriment" once he reaches the top.

Although the preceding paragraphs mention only a few relevant studies, students of organization have given much attention to the division between democratic, people-oriented participative leaders and autocratic, authoritarian, production-oriented leaders. Of course, executive behavior may not be so readily classifiable as these types suggest. Stanley Seashore has noted that consideration and initiation are independent of each other and that a person might be high on one end and either high or low on the other.[27] Certainly an executive can favor both good human relations and high production, but there is much room for variation in emphasis. Because their leaders and their tasks vary, organizations in the executive branch may resemble either democratic political systems or authoritarian political systems. Which they resemble may have consequences for their ability to recruit, their relations with other executive branch organizations, and their relations with Congress and their clienteles.

---

24. See Ralph M. Stodgill and Carroll L. Shartle, *Patterns of Administrative Performance* (Columbus: Bureau of Business Research, College of Commerce and Administration, Ohio State University, 1956), p. 286.

25. See, for example, Robert Tannenbaum and W. H. Schmidt, "How to Choose a Leadership Pattern," *Harvard Business Review* 36 (March–April 1958), pp. 95–101; and also Robert T. Golembiewski, "Three Styles of Leadership and Their Uses," *Personnel*, 38 (July–August 1961), pp. 34–43.

26. Alex Bavelas, "Leadership: Man and Function," *Administrative Science Quarterly* 4 (1960), p. 494.

27. Seashore, "Administrative Leadership," p. 16.

Acting and Game-playing in Organizations

Organization members as actors in roles suggests a provocative way of viewing behavior in organizations: It is acting, a performance, and it is possible to draw on the language of the theatre for help in understanding behavior in organizations.[28] Though actors in the same role may play the part differently, interpret it differently, and convey different impressions they speak lines for the role they are in. The role limits their discretion and makes their performance more or less predictable. In interdepartmental committees representatives of various departments will likely espouse a departmental position; within limits their lines are likely to be predictable. They are playing the role of departmental representative. In other situations, too, in dealing with the Secretary's office, with the Office of Management or Budget, or in a Congressional hearing, individuals will play the roles dictated by their institutional position. When management meets with labor the spokesmen for the two sides play roles. And each may act differently than he might as a private individual not representing institutional interests. Within the organization members may also play roles, and give performances for the benefit of peers, superiors, subordinates, visitors, and others. This observation suggests that for the observer to be able to in-interpret behavior and speech he must know something of the intended audience. It is worth emphasizing that organization members play for many audiences and may play differently for each. It is worth noting that problems may arise if the players must play to a mixed audience, or if the play given to one audience—say, a clientele group—becomes known to another audience—say, a Congressional committee for whom another play is intended.

Acting in an organizational setting is not a matter of lines only. Different parts and roles are associated also with different kinds of behavior, expressions, and tones, and perhaps with different dress and symbols. The setting is important in the bureaucratic play. Large well-furnished offices and limousines go with some roles, and it may be that this kind of setting helps a chief to act or play like one. Others may also show deference to a

---

28. For a provocative treatment see Erving Goffman, *The Presentation of Self in Everyday Life* (Garden City: Doubleday Anchor Books, 1959).

superior thanks in part to a setting. A change in scene may be one way to alter performance.

Any major performance in the theatre is preceded by rehearsals, and this is true also in organizational life. Practice sessions, dry runs, rehearsals may precede everything from an inspection by a senior officer to a Congressional hearing. The aim is for the performance to come off without embarrassment and to convey the impression that what is seen is what is real. (Managers who want to convey the impression of being on their toes may see that unannounced inspections are carried out, and they may thus get a more accurate impression of reality.) The language of the theater suggests that some behavior is on stage and other behavior goes on backstage—behavior not intended for the audience, whether the head of the organization, a budget analyst, or a Congressman. Thanks to various systems and schemes for classification and organizational norms, much backstage behavior is kept there, but unannounced visits, ambitious journalists, investigating Congressmen, and disgruntled employees all on occasion may cause the curtains to fall and reveal the backstage happenings.

One can also view organizational life as a game and the members as players. There may be sides or teams, or each player may act independently. The organization as a game suggests rules, of course, with points, fouls, time periods, and in the end winning and losing. The job for an analyst may be to discover the rules (as in chess different positions may be governed by different rules), the actions that get points and lose them, the strategies for winning games, and what winning means. We need not extend this metaphor further, though the reader may want to toy further with the implications. The purpose is served if with this notion, as with the theatre language, understanding of behavior in organizations is enhanced.

7 Executive Organizations Examined

Although they differ in size, resources, purposes, organizational structure, and numerous other ways the organizations of the executive branch have much in common. They are all complex social organizations. They are virtually all organized along hierarchical lines, and they exhibit in varying degrees the traditional bureaucratic characteristics—specialization, impersonality, rules, recruitment and promotion on the basis of merit, and so on.[1] In addition they all are faced with the problem of distributing authority and resources among members. In each, communication is important, and each must deal with problems of search and change. It is such topics that this chapter is devoted to in order to improve your ability both to explain and to forecast the behavior of bureaucratic organizations and their members.[2]

---

1. The characteristics of bureaucratic organizations were first discussed systematically by Max Weber. Countless numbers of other observers have also written on the subject. For one summary article see Richard H. Hall, "The Concept of Bureaucracy: An Empirical Assessment," *American Journal of Sociology*, 69 (1963), pp. 32–40.

2. For the reader who wants to go further in reading about formal organizations, there are a number of useful books. Among the most useful surveys are James G. March and Herbert Simon, *Organizations* (New York: John Wiley and Sons, 1958); Peter M. Blau and W. Richard Scott, *Formal Organizations* (San Francisco: Chandler Publishing Co., 1962); Theodore Caplow, *Principles of Organization* (New York: Harcourt, Brace

Politics and Authority in Organizations

In trying to develop an understanding of bureaucratic organizations, of how they operate, and of how their members interact with one another it is useful to remember the word politics and the term political behavior. A useful assumption is that behavior in bureaucratic organizations is political behavior—in an organizational rather than in a state or city setting.[3] But what does this mean, and what are the implications of this assumption?

We may start with the meaning of politics. Most generally and perhaps not very satisfactorily we know that politics is a summary word dealing with power, authority, influence, and access to and control over decisions and resources. Now consider an organization. Its members have varying amounts of authority in making decisions, solving problems, distributing resources. How authority is distributed, who exercises authority over what, and how effectively they do so are important (and political) questions. An individual's interest in expanding his authority is one of the important motivating forces in organizational behavior, and the competition between individuals in authority and for authority is an important source of organizational conflict. We need not assume, however, that all organization members will participate actively in an organization's politics or that all will want to expand their authority. Robert Presthus has written of upward mobiles, describing them as those who actively seek the rewards of the organization and identify with it.[4] Perhaps we can simply remember that any organization is likely to have in it organizational politicians, people interested in expanding their power and running the organization, and also numbers of people who simply work in the organization—organizational citizens, perhaps.

Authority in organizations is not distributed evenly or ran-

---

and World, Inc. 1964); James G. March (ed.) *Handbook of Organizations* (Chicago: Rand McNally and Co., 1965); Daniel Katz and Robert L. Kahn, *The Social Psychology of Organizations* (New York: John Wiley and Sons, Inc., 1966); and Anthony Downs, *Inside Bureaucracy* (Boston: Little, Brown and Co., 1967). All of these books contain extensive bibliographies.

3. See Herbert Kaufman, "Organization Theory and Political Theory," *American Political Science Review*, LVII (1964), pp. 5–14.

4. Robert Presthus, *The Organizational Society* (New York: Alfred A. Knopf, 1962), p. 167.

domly, with the obvious result that some organization members have more than others. Why does authority accrue to some organization members and not to others? There are a number of reasons. Some members relish authority—or at least the salary and perquisities that normally come with it—and actively seek it. But this is hardly the only reason. The hierarchical structure of a bureaucratic organization virtually guarantees the uneven distribution of power, although those holding office on paper may in fact have little authority. Age, seniority, and professional or technical expertise are sources of authority as well. In addition, men in authority may delegate or share authority with others. An executive pressed for time may share his responsibilities with an assistant. Authority may be shared as a training technique to prepare a subordinate for more responsibility. Doubtless there are other possible explanations for the uneven distribution of authority, but it is clear that authority may accrue to different organization members for different reasons.

Further, in an attempt to enlist employee support for other reasons, authority over at least some matters may be broadly shared throughout an organization. The common phrase for this is participative management. The apparent meaning is that employees participate in running the organization.

There are two or three follow-on points to be made. First, the uneven distribution of authority in an organization and the different reasons for authority in an organization commonly provide both the setting and the fuel for organization cleavages and conflict. Scientists may find themselves in conflict with administrators; budget officials with a responsibility for saving money may find themselves in conflict with program officers responsible for program results. Senior officials may find themselves in conflict with young Turks with fresh ideas. Despite the hierarchical appearance of bureaucratic organizations, the resolution of such internal conflicts is as likely to be a matter of politics—of negotiation, bargaining, and compromise—as it is a matter of administrative fiat. A second major point or observation is that cleavages and conflicts within organizations often result in coalition-building. Members with similar views or goals come together with the intention of increasing their influence. From another point of view of course the whole organization can be viewed as a coalition or alliance composed of members each of whom has some independence and authority. Perhaps a corollary is that the superior-subordinate relationship is a mutual-acceptance relationship. While it is clear that superiors normally have authority over their subordinates, it is also the case that subordinates commonly can restrain, limit, or influence the actions of superiors. In a very real sense subordinates have authority over superiors.

So far, organization conflict has been mentioned several times, but it may be well to mention specifically several common causes of organizational conflict and the lines along which conflict commonly breaks out. Pay, hours, and working conditions are of course common causes for conflict between what are usually thought of as labor and management or unions and management. In this respect government organizations are not different from private organizations. Differences over organizational structure and decision-making procedures may occur. There may be conflict over the allocation of resources. And there may be conflict over organizational goals and future plans. The lines of conflict may occur along age, seniority, rank, or professional dimensions, to mention only the most obvious. In addition, the importance of perceived self-interest must be remembered.

Affecting an organization's politics and related to distribution of authority is an organization's status system. The private office, the larger office, the wooden desk, the private secretary, the phone extension, the rug, the sofa—all of these are the accoutrements of bureaucratic status. In a status-conscious bureaucracy a larger desk may have the same effect as a raise, and the large office that comes with a promotion may be as important as the promotion itself. A promotion not accompanied with the traditional perquisites may seem hollow. The status symbols associated with differences in rank legitimate the communications that pass back and forth in the organization. In the army, insignia of rank make it clear who may give orders and who must obey them. In civilian organizations, too, the symbols of office make it clear whose words must be listened to. Status symbols tell those who see them that the person displaying them "is someone."

A status system is useful (and indeed inevitable), but there are costs associated with a status system. It may lead to inflexibility and be an obstacle to innovation. The observations and ideas of men with relatively low status may be undervalued (perhaps ignored), and the ideas and opinions of men with relatively high status may be overvalued. Status may also be a source of conflict. Men with high status are likely to want to preserve it and thus may resist any changes that might alter their status.

People who are well off may want to continue in that state. Even if a chief executive sees a need to reorganize or shift personnel he may avoid doing so if the changes would effect the status of personnel; he may realize that such change would be opposed and even if successful might lower morale, productivity, and increase turnover. When status is involved executives are likely to move cautiously.

In thinking about politics in organizations, one more point should be kept in mind. Just as there are varying kinds of national political systems, so there are varying kinds of organizational political systems. A research laboratory staffed largely with Ph.D.'s might at one extreme exhibit little hierarchy, few rules, and much freedom and equality. A police or military organization may have much less freedom, the emphasis on hierarchy may be much more marked, and there may be many more rules to be rigidly adhered to. Just as among national states, there are varying degrees of absoluteness among organizations.

Some Economic Considerations

Just as we can conceive of bureaucratic organizations as political systems and understand that bureaucratic or administrative behavior is political behavior, so we can also view bureaucracies as economic systems and interpret administrative behavior as economic behavior.[5] Within the organizational setting the members buy and sell; they exchange things of value. These simple statements have several implications for the relations between organization members; to view behavior in organizations as economic behavior casts additional light on bureaucratic behavior.

Members of an organization sell their effort, their skill, their knowledge, their loyalty to the organization that employs them in exchange for things they want or value. Most obviously, of course, members of an organization work for wages. But this may not be all the compensation or reward they want. They may

5. See Chester I. Barnard, *The Functions of the Executive* (Cambridge: Harvard University Press, 1938), Chapter IX; see also Peter B. Clark and James Q. Wilson, "Incentive Systems: A Theory of Organization," *Administrative Science Quarterly*, 6 (1961), pp. 129–166. In addition, see George Homans, *Social Behavior: Its Elementary Forms* (New York: Harcourt, Brace & World, Inc., 1961); and Peter Blau, *Exchange and Power in Social Life* (New York: John Wiley and Sons, 1964).

also want free time, lax rule enforcement, housing, pleasant working conditions, or a number of other things. Whether job seekers take a job and keep it is determined in large part by whether it appears to offer them what they want and whether they are willing to give (and can) what the job requires.

What determines what a job-seeker asks for? His own assessment of his worth, his economic needs, his preferences and values, and the information he has on what competing job-seekers are asking. What determines what an organization will offer a job-seeker? The resources available, the skills and experience of the job-seeker, the needs of the organization, and what other employers are offering. It is a plausible assumption that both parties to the relationship want to benefit as much as they can and contribute no more than necessary. Both employer and employee may engage in some sort of intuitive cost-benefit analysis. The terms of the exchange, if terms are reached, are likely to be the result of bargaining, negotiating, shopping, and analysis. The term economizing comes to mind, as does the term mutual adjustment.

Initially one may expect job seekers to take the job that on balance they find most attractive, that is, that provides the mix of pay, benefits, and working conditions that they find appealing. Inaccurate information or ill-informed expectations may of course produce disappointment and a severed relationship. Some job-seekers, under pressure and given a limited selection, may take jobs they do not find attractive and move out when they can. And some may raise their demands once on the job—and leave if their demands are unfulfilled.

A general assumption is that an exchange relationship is likely to continue so long as both parties to it think they are benefitting. If or when either party thinks he is not getting what he expected the relationship will become unstable and may be ended if new mutually satisfactory terms cannot be reached.[6] (This point should be kept in mind when considering the organization as a coalition.) To illustrate the point consider the

---

6. What is expected may include not only pay and working conditions but also particular policies. For a provocative discussion of what may happen when a member disapproves of organizational policies see Albert Hirschman, *Exit, Voice, and Loyalty* (Cambridge: Harvard University Press, 1970).

case of an organizational member who adjusts upward his requirements, suggesting the withdrawal of his services if his requests goes unmet. Will his request be met? The answer depends in part on the value of his services, their supply, and the ease with which he can be replaced at his present or lower rate. The answer depends in part on the resources (or the slack) available to the organization.[7] And the answer depends in part on the particular demands and their consistency with government regulations and organization policy.

Of course, not only the employee may alter demands. An organization (management) may increase expectations, asking longer hours, more productivity, fewer errors. It may require an employee to move, to undergo training, or in other ways alter initial expectations. Such changes obviously alter the terms of exchange, and the employee faced with changed expectations may demand additional rewards, if indeed an offer of increased compensation does not accompany the increased expectations. But there is a complication. Additional rewards may have diminishing value. The more money a man is making, the less making another dollar may mean, and similar statements could be made about other resources. The result is that it may be hard for employers to motivate satisfied employees. If a man does not want more money, he may be unwilling to work at night or for longer hours if money will be the reward.

It is worthwhile to comment briefly on some of the reasons for changes in demand. Employees may alter their demands as they gain seniority and experience and at least think that they have become more valuable to the organization they work in. They may raise their demands on the organization they work in if another organization makes an attractive offer. Demands may alter if it is apparent that the organization has resources to pay more. Demands may go up in response to increased need for funds, if individual or family circumstances change. An employer may increase his demands for a number of reasons. An increased workload but no increase in budget is not uncommon. An organizational emergency or crisis may result in extraordinary demands on employees. An organization may simply ex-

---

7. For a discussion of slack see Richard M. Cyert and James G. March, *A Behavioral Theory of the Firm* (Englewood Cliffs: Prentice-Hall, Inc. 1963), pp. 36–38.

pect more from employees as they acquire more experience. All these possibilities suggest the potential for change, the instability, in the exchange relationship.

The economic perspective calls our attention to other features of the employee-employer relationship. If an employer has a personnel budget fixed in the short run, it may be used in a number of ways. It may be used to pay several employees a relatively low wage or a few employees a relatively high wage. And within limits these may be substitutable. Or perhaps the funds can be used at least in part on machinery instead of men. The possibility of substituting one man for another or machinery for men may be an important consideration when terms of an exchange are brought into question. Instead of paying more, an employer may choose to substitute. Recognizing that a substitution is possible an employee may not make or press demands.

The notion of substitutability may also apply to the resources, rewards, or incentives that an organization uses. The most common incentive is money. But more free time may substitute. Or more money may make up for close supervision and little personal independence. The employer will offer what he has, and the employee will try to get what he wants or values. The cost-benefit concept still applies.

This section has emphasized an economic perspective and the suggestion that bureaucrats are economic men, but it would be a major mistake to think that the sole reason men work is economic or that they are only economically motivated. Neither could be further from the truth. In his work and life a man is motivated by a complex of reasons and seeks a variety of benefits. Nevertheless it is clear that economic considerations, perhaps especially in the United States, are important. Organization man is at least in some measure economic man. Economic considerations affect employer and employee, the work they do, the decisions they make, and their relations with their peers and each other.

Communications in Organizations

Besides being in some sense a political system and an economic system, an organization is also a communication network. Members of an organization constantly communicate with one another and with individuals and groups outside. Who communicates with whom, how frequently, about what, and with what effect? The answers to these questions may say a lot not only about the functioning of the organization in general but also about its politics and economics. By studying communication patterns we can learn about the distribution of authority and influence, and by studying the information that goes back and forth we can learn about the substance of economic and political issues.

Every member of an organization can be viewed as a communicator or potential communicator of information, but of course each communicator does not communicate with everyone else in the organization. Instead each communicator communicates with a more or less clearly defined and usually limited number of others. Communication is likely to be controlled by rules that specify who should be contacted or informed about what. A low-level employee may do little more than communicate with fellow employees and his immediate superior, and any communication he has with more senior persons in the organization is likely to be indirect and carried out by his superior. That is, he goes through channels. A superior has contact with his subordinates, with his peers, and with his superior. He may also have contact with a personnel officer, a budget office, and other representatives of higher echelons in the organization. A bureau chief will have contact with his deputy and his assistants and with the heads of divisions and offices. His name is likely to appear on general orders that go to everyone in his organization. He will have contact with departmental officials and some other bureau chiefs. In general, the more senior a person is in his organization, the more widespread are his formal communications. The more complex his responsibilities, the more people from whom he must get information and the more to whom he must give information.

The reverse of the statement that everyone is a potential communicator is that everyone in an organization is a potential receiver. And just as communication is limited, so is formal or official reception limited. Formally a man can be expected to receive the information he needs to do his job, but in practice it is often extremely difficult, if not impossible, to specify what a man needs to know to do his job. A man may be flooded with information and unable to pay attention to what is necessary, or he may suffer from a dearth of information.

There is an additional communications role in any organization—the role of relay. Bureau chiefs issue orders that are transmitted through assistants and middle management down to front-line supervisors and the men. Employees ask questions and register complaints and send reports that may go through several levels. The interaction of the relay, the communicator, and the receiver can have substantial consequences for an organization. The human relay can be a source of misinterpretation, distortion, and inaccurate repeating, and indeed a relay may send a message that differs from that originally sent. Condensation, distortion, interpretation and misinterpretation, misunderstanding, and simplification may affect messages that are relayed. Imagine what can happen as reports and memoranda get condensed and condensed and condensed until finally they land on the Secretary's or President's desk.

At this point some comment on the substance of communication, or the reasons for it, is warranted. Focusing first on communications downward—from superior to subordinate—it is common to find a variety of messages. Decisions, orders, instructions, expectations, goals, information or intelligence, requests for information or reports, responses to questions—the variety of message content is great. Focusing on communication upward—from subordinate to superior—one commonly finds information and intelligence, reports, requests for assistance, questions and requests for interpretation and guidance, answers to questions. In the flow of communication back and forth between organizational units and individuals, one finds decision-making, problem-solving, learning, conflict, compromise, and conciliation. Clearly communication is important, and failure or error can have substantial consequences.

One important cause for failure, and one that may be more important in the future thanks to what is popularly called the information explosion, is information overload. In brief this means that a person (or a communication center) may be deluged with more information than he can receive, process, relay, or act on. When this happens messages sent are in effect not received. Because the consequences can be serious, organizations and executives commonly take steps to avoid overload.

Delegation, authority sharing, and specialization have been mentioned before and are relevant in this context. Priority codes —routine, priority, critical—may be placed on each communication to ensure that the most important messages get through. There remains of course the problem of how to code any particular message. Visitors are screened, messages are filtered and condensed by subordinates to save their superior's time. Such steps are undoubtedly necessary, but the risk is that because of such protection an executive will not know what he needs to know.

Of course overload is not the only cause of communication failure. Communication may fail because communicator and receiver do not speak the same language (scientist and non-scientist, lawyer and nonlawyer, or Englishman and American) or because they give different meaning to the same words. What words connote as well as what they denote is important. Values, ideologies, professional training, and social status may all act as barriers to communication. Communications from a person of low status may be ignored; from a person of high status the same statements may receive attention. Communication gaps (perhaps not quite the same thing as failures) may occur because of economy measures; communication *is* costly and the cost of communicating has to be balanced against the cost of not communicating. Absent, inadequate, or inoperative equipment may affect detrimentally all but face-to-face communication. (When failure *must* be avoided, redundancy is commonly built into a communications system; if a primary system fails, a back-up system can be used.) Given the numerous possible reasons for failure it is clear that achieving successful communication is problematic. Even if the machinery works, messages may not be adequate or accurate.

Another way to consider communication success and failure is to consider the consequences of communication. It is true of course that not all communication is intended to have an effect. Much is intended simply to inform, but much is also intended to get action. It may not. Richard Neustadt, in his book *Presidential Power*, discusses the factors that encourage compliance with presidential orders or in other language positive response to presidential communications.[8]

> The first factor favoring compliance with a Presidential order is assurance that the President has spoken.
>
> A second factor making for compliance with a President's request is clarity about his meaning.
>
> A third factor favoring compliance with a President's directive is publicity.

---

8. Richard E. Neustadt, *Presidential Power* (New York: John Wiley and Sons, 1961), pp. 19–27.

A fourth factor favoring compliance with a President's request is actual ability to carry it out.

A fifth factor making for compliance with a President's request is the sense that what he wants is his by right.

Neustadt's observations are relevant to the communications sent by a chief executive in any organization. If these conditions are not met, communications may have little effect: orders may flow but nothing will happen, which may be a definition of communication failure.

How frequently do communications take place? The easy answer is that it depends. An organization's communications rules may specify that some communications take place on a regular basis; reports will be submitted weekly or daily, semi-annually or monthly. Some communications may take place not regularly but only when specified conditions are met or when particular problems arise. In other words, communication may be both routine and *ad hoc*. The scope of authority and the specialization of an organization member will affect both how frequently he receives messages and how frequently he sends them. Location also affects frequency of communication. Communication with the person in the next office may be constant; communication with a man across the country may be less frequent. Communication technology is also important, as is cost; when long-distance telephone rates go down, the number of calls goes up. The analyst of communications may be interested in two questions dealing with frequency: How frequently are particular types of messages sent? and How frequently do particular organization members send and receive messages?

A few final points about communication need making. The first is that communication in organizations goes on both between units and between individuals. Officials and organizations (or perhaps more precisely particular officials within organizations) communicate with one another; often this is quite impersonal, especially when the communication is routine. But there is also much communication conducted between officials on an individual or personal basis, and personal relations become important. How two people get along may facilitate or hinder their communicating with one another and do the same for the organizational communications that they are carrying on. The result of course is that personal relationships may affect institutional or organizational relationships.

A second point to bear in mind is that in an organizational setting there is likely to be a good deal of informal or spontaneous communication. Such communication may appear to have nothing to do with the job at hand, except insofar as respite from a task may be necessary for continued performance of the task. But it may be that social communication supports or keeps open the communication channels that are also used for more serious matters. It may be that ability to communicate socially with someone enhances one's ability to communicate formally about the job. From another point of view spontaneous communication may occur in situations not covered by an organization's communication rules. And from another point of view informal or oral communications may precede an exchange of written documents; informal checking may occur before an order is issued.

One last observation is in order. An important aspect of communication in any organization is communication with the environment. Members of an organization communicate not only with each other but also with numerous and varied outsiders for a variety of reasons. This point should be obvious by now. It should also be obvious that communication with the environment (and with various parts of it) may be satisfactory or faulty. An organization may communicate with its environment, learn from it, respond to it. Or an organization can be more or less insulated (isolated) from its environment. If it is isolated it likely will be rigid and slow to adapt to changing circumstances and in the end may find survival difficult. Again, the importance of communication is emphasized.

Search

Search is a subject closely related to communication.[9] Search simply means hunting for information, intelligence, and clues, and this process goes on through communication. Inadequate communication or communication failure may be virtual synonyms for inadequate search and search failure. With these connections emphasized we can go on to think more carefully about search. If search means hunting for information, intelligence, or cues, we can first ask, What kinds of intelligence are

---

9. The most useful book here may be Harold Wilensky, *Organizational Intelligence* (New York: Basic Books, 1967).

searched for? Certainly intelligence bearing on organizational performance is likely to be sought, with emphasis perhaps on signs of dissatisfaction among either organization members or clients, customers, superior officials, legislators, or others. Information on what analogous agencies are doing is likely to be sought—or should be. Information on what competitors are doing and planning is likely to be sought. Each of the armed forces has interests in the operations and plans of the others. Organizations in welfare and manpower fields are affected by other organizations. Information is needed on the activities and plans of adversaries or potential adversaries, which justifies the intelligence units of police departments and the armed forces. Many organizations search for scientific and technological developments that may affect them and also for economic, political, or demographic developments or trends that may affect their mission. How much the population and economy grow in the next five or ten years may have implications for the tasks of many organizations.

Clearly an organization requires (or may require) information from a variety of sources. The collection of information, however, operates under a number of constraints which act to limit the amount of search that goes on and the effectiveness of the search that is carried out. Some of the restraints are obvious, others not. Cost is one restraint, manpower another. The manpower restraint has both quantity and quality dimensions. Not enough manpower may be available to carry on required the search (research) and meet the other current goals of the organization. In addition the personnel available may not have the skills required—statistical, linguistic, or whatever to adequately search for some sorts of information. The result of course may be gaps in search and therefore gaps in the information acquired.

Professional training may impose blinders and prevent search in particular directions.[10] Time is another restraint, as there is rarely enough time to gather all information that might in principle or theory be nice to have. Technology at any particular point in time may be another limiting factor. After the U-2 airplane was invented, the CIA could collect more intelligence than before; with reconnaissance satellites it can collect

---

10. For comment on trained incapacity see Robert Merton, *Social Theory and Social Structure* (Glencoe, Ill.: The Free Press, 1957), rev. ed., pp. 197–198.

more than it could with the U-2. At any particular time the state of technology imposes limits on what can be obtained, the type of search, or the extent of search that can be carried out. Noncooperation or secrecy imposes additional obvious restraints. It is not easy to collect information about the operations and plans of adversaries—whether in war, crime, or politics—especially since the adversaries have an obvious interest in foiling or misleading the search.

There are other obstacles to search. The sheer size of the task for many organizations means that search will be limited. In addition, satisfaction limits search. This means that organizations that think they are performing satisfactorily may not search. A corollary is that search may concentrate in areas where there is some reason to suspect trouble, as a rational economizing strategy; but of course suprise is still risked. Organizations exposed to criticism and controversy may engage in more search behavior than those that are widely accepted. Organization ideology also limits or channels search. Some ways of doing things, some routines or procedures, may be beyond question, and search for problems or alternatives will concentrate in other areas.

Just as it is important to be aware of what may limit or restrain search, it is important to recognize that other conditions support or encourage it. Some of these are simply the opposite of the restraining conditions already mentioned. Dissatisfaction, for example, encourages search. Dissatisfaction with the status quo may encourage the search for ways to improve it; when performance again reaches a satisfactory level, interest in improvement and search for alternatives may cease. Having curious, innovative, imaginative, or aggressive personnel in an organization may encourage search. A threatening environment or one perceived as threatening may encourage search. Search behavior may also be rewarded or encouraged by superiors in an organization.

In addition to the restraints and incentives that affect search it is well to recognize that search is also affected by habits, rules, procedures, and past events. Where we search for solutions to problems is not only a function of our skills and training but also related to where in the past we have found solutions. Where we search for problems is affected by where past experience has taught us to expect problems. (Such search of course may prevent us from finding new problems in areas or sectors heretofore problem-free.) Bureaucracies being what they are it is only to be expected that search procedures for routine problems will be reduced to rules and standard operating procedures: If something goes wrong in X, then Y is what you look for. Before taking this step, ascertain the views of these people. Before sending this cable, get signatures from these people.

A number of words may be mentioned which on occasion may be useful in understanding search behavior within organizations. Search may be patterned. An air-force reconnaissance patrol may always follow a specified pattern. Searches for new recruits may always follow or use the same pattern. Search may be regular, systematic, or random. Searches may be purposeful and focused—or the opposite. It may be routine or extraordinary. As just these suggestions make clear, the word search may be applied to a variety of behaviors focused on a variety of conditions and problems. If we remember that search may be for problems and also for solutions or methods of coping and that any organization may over time be confronted with any number of problems, we can understand how widespread in an organization search behavior may be.

Just because search behavior is widespread (or may be), many units in an organization (and many members) may at one time or another be engaged in it. A chief executive and his immediate staff are almost certainly going to be engaged in search. There may indeed be a research planning unit. Research and Development organizations are engaged in search, as of course are intelligence and reconnaissance units. Budget and personnel units may engage in search, as may units charged with daily operation. But routine operations are likely to take precedence over search, and organizations and staff engaged in daily routines may have little time or interest in worrying about problems in the future or over the horizon.

Change

A final topic that requires attention before this chapter is ended is change, which happens frequently in organizations even though bureaucratic organizations are often thought of as rigid and unchanging in their ways. It will simplify consideration of the topic to start with a list of questions and then provide suggestive though of course not complete or final answers. What are the dimensions or varieties of change? What are the consequences of change? Why does change occur? What motivates change? What are the obstacles to change?

It is not uncommon to see the term organizational change, but what does it mean? It refers to several varieties or types of change and to change in various degrees. Think for a minute of the changes that may take place in an organization: changes in personnel (new people or new responsibilities or new positions for the same people), changes in organizational structure (a planning unit is added, an inspection unit is added, three new deputy administrator positions are added), changes in rules or procedures, changes in goals or mission, changes in service provided (type of service, location of service, quantity and quality of service), or changes in technology (computers, closed circuit TV, aerial photography to study urban land use or agricultural crop acreage.) No doubt the reader can add other types of changes that take place, but this list is long enough to suggest the great variety of changes that may go on under the label organizational change. Of course each of these may take place in greater or lesser degree. A work force can be tripled, or a couple of people can be added. Secret Service protection could be extended to the Speaker of the House (a minor adjustment) or the presidential protection mission could be given to the FBI (a major structural change).

These various changes may be separated analytically, but of course in practice they are likely to be connected to one another. A change in mission is likely also to bring changes in personnel, changes in organizational structure, perhaps changes in technology, and so on. Indeed the initiation of a major change may require so many other changes that it may be useful to keep in mind the term "change package." When an administrator or congressman (or indeed a professor) proposes a change in size or funding level, you should ask yourself what the whole change package (including not only explicit but also implicit components) will include or look like.

This notion of relationship is a partial answer to the question of what the consequences of change are. But other answers can be suggested. A change within an organization may have both internal and external consequences. Internally organization members may have to learn new tasks or new procedures; they may be expected to behave in different ways. Some changes (automation or budget cuts) may result in some members losing their jobs or in some members gaining status or influence at the expense of others. Instant organizational changes of one kind or another may have political or economic consequences for members of an organization. Put this way the point is obvious, but it seems sometimes to be forgotten when considering the chances for acceptance and success of proposed changes. The costs of change may explain a good deal of resistance. The observer might well bring the question "Who will have to pay what?" to his consideration of change proposals.

Apparently internal changes may also have external consequences that are worth noting. More service or less service may affect client, congressional, or White House relations. Firing an employee with good friends in a congressional committee may have immediately obvious consequences. Adopting new work rules or procedures, changing the organizational structure, or adopting a new technology may also be noticed and reacted to by outsiders. Internal changes may affect an organization's base of support outside, which may have obvious consequences for its future, either beneficial or deleterious. The point of course is that apparently perfectly necessary or proper or indeed innocuous changes may not be undertaken because of the views of some interest groups or congressional committee chairmen.

The phrase "unanticipated consequences" is one to keep in mind constantly when trying to assess (guess) the consequences of proposed changes or wondering why in the world a particular change was made. In the first instance, the most careful analysis may completely fail to predict a consequence that in fact occurs. (Alternatively, to be sure, a change may not have the expected consequences. New work-training programs may NOT lower unemployment rates; more money spent on schools may not noticeably improve the reading ability of high school graduates; more police on streets may not lower crime rates.) In the second instance it may appear after the fact that a particular change should not have been made. Why was it? Simply because foresight is not as acute as hindsight. Obvious and harmful but after-the-fact consequences may have been unanticipated.

Why does change occur? What motivates change? There are many possible answers and no way to answer generally, though any particular change may be easily explained. Again, the internal-external distinction is a convenient one. Within an organization new demands and changing attitudes (demands for higher pay, better working conditions, changing feelings about unionization) may bring other changes. A work force that is more highly educated may bring changes in supervisory practices and other procedures. Externally there may be changes in the population, in the economy, in the international situation, or in the problems that a particular organization focuses on that occasion organizational changes. Competing organizations may adopt new procedures or new technologies and in effect force (encourage) their adoption by other organizations in the same policy space. Influential outsiders (budget examiners, White House personnel, congressmen and their staffs) may also have interests and opinions that are reflected in organizational changes. Professional opinion and advances in knowledge through research and development may bring changes inside an organization. The point is that for organizational change in general there are clearly a number of possible sources, and indeed there may be multiple reasons for any single change.

But of course change is not automatic. Remember here the preceding sections on communication and search. Communication failure and inadequate search both may be obstacles to change. At the extreme, an isolated (insulated) organization is likely to be an unchanging one. A chief executive who is isolated may also be unchanging. Communication, search, and change are intimately related. But lack of or inadequate communication and search are not the only obstacles to change. Satisfaction with the status quo (or at least not much dissatisfaction) may explain its retention. (Here of course, who is satisfied and dissatisfied is important). When dissatisfaction mounts, change is more likely, but lack of agreement on the direction change should take may result in retention of the status quo. The status quo may be retained by those who benefit from it or at least are comfortable in it, especially if they would lose in change. Change may be resisted because its consequences are not all known and thus some risk is run. In effect, change may be avoided as long as the status quo is tolerable; after all, change it self imposes costs.

And in the end, though change takes place, not much may change. This may happen (and frequently does) simply because of ignorance. In a number of social problem areas we do not know how to achieve what we say we want to. We try this and that, make this change and that, but nothing happens. We make changes because we simply must do something. Changes are also made symbolically, of course. Effects may not be intended even when change is made. For cosmetic reasons, to gain or keep political support, to appear flexible and innovative, an administrator may reorganize, issue new rules, hire more members of minority groups, set up citizen advisory boards, and make other changes. And in the end not much will be different. The more things change, the more things may stay the same.

Conclusion

Organizations obviously can be viewed from a variety of perspectives. Put another way, organizations have a number of dimensions. Awareness of these many dimensions can help us understand both policy making and program implementation. And although each of these dimensions is important in itself, it is important to note that they interact with and indeed merge into one another. One cannot understand much about communications in an organization without some understanding of the organization's political system. And obviously communications, search, and change relate to one another. Communication failure may result in inappropriate change or in none. And it is fruitless to search for information in the environment if it is not to be communicated to appropriate people within the organization.

It is worth noting also that some understanding of the many facets of bureaucratic organization may help us both foresee and forestall problems. Any student of organization knows that sufficient, accurate, timely information cannot be assumed. There are too many potential obstacles. Indeed there are so many that at least occasional failure is a sure thing unless extraordinary (and costly) steps are taken to prevent any failure—checking procedures, multiple channels, back-up systems, and the like. And all these may be so costly that some communication failure may be just tolerated. Of course there may be other kinds of failures too. But perhaps the most important point is that it is risky to trace failures or problems in policy development and program implementation to any single cause. To be sure communication may be involved, but there may also be such real conflicts of interest, cleavages, and shortages of resources that all the accurate communication in the world would not bring success. Indeed it is the complexity of bureaucratic organization and the consequent multiplicity of explanations for program slippage or outright failure that may be the most important single point of this chapter.

PART III THE BUREAUCRACY AND THE POLITICAL SYSTEM

The next four chapters deal even more explicity than preceding ones with political topics. The subject of Chapter 8 is "The Politics of Bureaucracy." It considers at some length the conflicts that occur in bureaucratic contexts, what causes them, what the stakes are, and how they may be resolved. This chapter emphasizes the connection between public policy and the struggles for power and resources that go on with the bureaucracy. After reading and reflecting on this chapter you should be better able to understand and interpret much of the rhetoric and many of the events that you see reported daily in the press.

Chapters 9, 10, and 11 develop in detail subjects that were first raised in Chapter 2. They focus on the relations, what characterizes them and what affects them, that exist between bureaucratic organizations and other participants in politics and policymaking. Chapter 9 deals particularly with the question of presidential control and considers both the strengths and weaknesses of the Presidency.

The presidential view of the agencies, the agency view of the President, and the possible consequences of these views are discussed in Chapter 9. Chapter 10 reviews the circumstances which bring congressional committees and executive agencies together and discusses also what affects congressional agency relations. One section in this chapter deals with the limits of judicial supervision of administrative agencies. Chapter 11 discusses agency relations with their clienteles, and the last section examines the concept of the public interest.

8 The Politics of Bureaucracy

This chapter attempts to draw together in a general and compact way some of the material that so far has been presented. In a sense it is a review chapter, but it rearranges the materials and suggests additional implications and conclusions.[1] It is also a foreword since it raises questions that will come up again in later chapters. The main subject of this chapter is conflict, a word virtually synonymous with politics. Why do conflicts occur, and what are they about? Who are the participants? How can conflicts be coped with or avoided? These are the questions. Bureaucratic conflicts frequently go unreported and unnoticed by outsiders, but they are an inevitable part of the policy process and their outcomes at least as important for policy as the outcomes of conflicts in the halls of Congress or on the campaign trail.

---

1. An extensive though increasingly dated bibliography is part of the essay "Public Bureaucracies" by Robert L. Peabody and Francis E. Rourke in James G. March (ed.), *Handbook of Organizations* (Chicago: Rand McNally, 1965), pp. 802–837. For a book with the same title as this chapter see Gordon Tullock, *The Politics of Bureaucracy* (Washington, D.C.: Public Affairs Press, 1965). Two recent readers that can be profitably scanned in conjunction with this part of the text are Francis E. Rourke, *Bureaucratic Power in National Politics* (Boston: Little, Brown and Co., 1972) and Dean Yarwood, *The National Administrative System* (New York: John Wiley and Sons, 1971).

Analyzing Bureaucratic Politics

Although by now the definition of bureaucratic politics must be clear, an emphasizing note may be worthwhile. Most simply the term refers to the attempts of individuals, groups, and organizations to achieve their goals within a bureaucratic context. It refers to the struggle for influence, for power, and for control within bureaucratic organizations. Of course it may also refer to attempts to preserve independence and autonomy and escape control. Bureaucratic organizations can be viewed as governments, as polities, as political systems; their members or groups engage in political behavior. Struggles for power go on.[2]

The analysis of politics within bureaucratic organizations is not unlike the analysis of politics in other contexts. But what is political analysis? A basic question of political analysis is "Who Governs?"[3] The question is commonly asked in studies of community politics, but it can also be asked in studies of bureaucratic politics. And just as it is common to find that officials do not always govern or at least may share power with others, it is possible to find in bureaucratic organizations that those apparently on top are not the only ones with power. Political analysis from one perspective is concerned with the distribution of power and influence. And clearly power and its distribution is an important topic in the study of bureaucratic organization.

How can one study the distribution of power? There are several ways. One can, by interviewing officials and reviewing documents and press reports, frequently discover conflicts between different individuals or groups (each pressing for a particular appointment; one favoring a reorganization and one not; each backing a favorite policy proposal). The question then is who won, who got his way. The answer to this question begins to tell us something about who has power in the bureaucracy. To be sure, there may be negotiation, bargaining, and compromises; and no one may get his way completely. Nevertheless, the study

---

2. For a scholarly discussion of this perspective see Herbert Kaufman, "Organization Theory and Political Theory," *American Political Science Review*, LVII (1964), pp. 5–14. For recent and entertaining illustrations see current issues of *The National Journal, The Washington Monthly,* and *Foreign Policy.*

3. The question is the title of a book by Robert Dahl, *Who Governs?* (New Haven: Yale University Press, 1961).

of conflicts and their resolution is one way to study the distribution of power. In the end one may discover that who wins depends on the substance of the conflict, that the same person or group always wins no matter what, or that the winner is variable but for reasons not immediately explicable. One might also discover that even though the winner varies, winning is confined to a relatively small circle and those outside the circle never win. But these are only possibilities.

One can study the distribution of influence by looking at decisions and asking "Who makes decisions about what?" Does one man or office make all decisions, or is decision-making authority spread throughout an organization? To study decision-making one must of course begin with a decision and then, by interviewing and reviewing the record, attempt to discover how the decision was made, who made it, who influenced it, why it was made. In principle the answers to such questions should throw light on the distribution of authority in a bureaucracy. But it is often very hard to reconstruct how a decision was made, who made what decision, or who influenced it. The more one delves into a particular decision the more it may appear that it emerged, happened, was made—and the particular roles of particular actors may be very hard, if not impossible, to ascertain. Still, the study of decision-making is a possible way to study the politics of bureaucracy.

Alternatively one can simply use what in community politics has been called the attribution method. That is, one simply asks members of an organization (and perhaps knowledgeable outsiders) who has power in the organization, perhaps questioning further to probe the limits of power. Or one can start with particular issue or activity areas—personnel, planning, budgeting, and so on—and ask by means of interviews or questionnaires who exercises power in these areas.

All of these techniques, here greatly oversimplified, may be open to objection, but they all emphasize that one cannot, when studying heirarchical or bureaucratic organizations, simply look at the organization chart or the department telephone book. These documents may be useful both in deciding who to talk to and in formulating initial questions, but they reveal only the formal organization. As we have noted time and time again, there is an informal organization that one must probe if there is hope of understanding the politics of bureaucracy.

Asking Who Governs? or Who Rules? or Who Has Power?

are not the only ways to approach the analysis of bureaucratic politics. The other classic question is Who Gets What? and we can expand on this by adding Why? and How?[4] This question reminds us that while politics has a lot to do with power, authority, and influence it has also a lot to do with the distribution of benefits, advantages, rewards, patronage, or simply goodies. Who gives them, who gets them, who doesn't, why? This question is familiar in other political contexts, from the community to the Congress, but it is useful also in bureaucratic contexts. Think of the possible advantages—raises, promotions, trips, less supervision, time off, choice assignments, better offices and working conditions, selection of particular projects for funding, presidential attention—the list is a long one. An analyst looking at a particular organization might want to know how the advantages were distributed and how the pattern of distribution could be explained. How are distributive or allocative decisions made? Who is rewarded? What criteria are used? Or, from the perspective of the subordinate, What do I have to do to go up? What must I not do? Whom should I know and please and whom should I not displease? This puts the problems in simple and perhaps crass terms, but this is the substance of the politics of bureaucracy. An employee who reveals embarrassing information about his organization to the Congress or a reporter or otherwise upsets a superior may be dead-ended, released, transferred to the Podunk field office, or given a series of trivial assignments.

One can approach the analysis of bureaucratic politics in still other ways. One could focus on exchange relationships, conceiving of a bureaucracy as an exchange system or perhaps as an economy or market.[5] Who is exchanging what with whom? What benefits is each participant in the exchange receiving? One could view the organization as a status system or a communication network. Who communicates with whom about what with what results? There are surely other ways to view an organization, but these examples suffice to illustrate alternative ways of studying bureaucratic politics.

---

4. Harold Lasswell, *Politics: Who Gets What, When, How* (New York: Meridian Books, 1958).

5. Peter B. Clark and James Q. Wilson, "Incentive Systems: A Theory of Organizations," *Administrative Science Quarterly*, Vol. 6 (1961), pp. 129–166.

Cleavages and Interests

It is impossible to understand the politics of bureaucracy without some awareness of the natural break lines or lines of cleavage that exist.[6] There are several, which we will now review. Two points must first be emphasized. First, conflict may develop along these lines; but although these lines may represent the major interests, groups, factions of whatever, there may be no conflict. For one reason or another an organization may be integrated and cohesive, or at least groups may share common interests and be allied. To say that age is an important variable and that there may be friction between young and old employees is not to say that it is always so. Friction may exist, but it need not. With this important caution, what are some of the common lines of cleavage? It may be helpful simply to list several and then comment on each one in turn.

Rank
Union membership
Career status
Profession or specialty
Headquarters—field
Organizational unit
Ideology
Attitudes toward change
Outside social status

The first word on the list, rank, is surely one of the most obvious lines of cleavage in a hierarchical organization. Each employee in the organization has an assigned rank; everyone knows for sure who is superior and who is subordinate, at least in form. And there may be friction between the ranks if unpleasant or undesirable instructions are given by superiors, if unpopular regulations are enforced, or if subordinates act too independently. More generally, between the ranks there may be a conflict of interest brought on by the superior's desire to maintain control and the subordinate's desire to maintain autonomy and individuality. To repeat the warning made earlier, conflict between ranks is not inevitable, but in an egalitarian society (or at least

6. The notion of cleavage comes from Chapter 3 of Edward C. Banfield and James Q. Wilson, *City Politics* (Cambridge: Harvard University Press, 1963). Bertram Gross has written about interest and conflict in Chapter 11 of *The Managing of Organizations* (New York: The Free Press of Glencoe, 1964).

in a society with egalitarian pretentions) rank differences provide a breeding ground for friction.

Dividing employees into management and labor is perhaps the most common way to summarize the rank line of cleavage, but matters may be a good deal more complex. In the federal service employees in the so called supergrades (GS 16, 17, 18) may for some purposes be viewed as one group, men in middle management (GS 13, 14, 15) viewed as another, junior administrators (GS 9 through 12) another, and so on. In the Army there are obviously officers and enlisted men, but among officers there are company-grade officers (lieutenants and captains) field-grade officers (major, lieutenant colonel) and general officers, and there are various levels of noncommissioned officers too. The point is clear—within ranks and groups of ranks there may be shared interests, and between ranks and groups of ranks there may be friction and conflict of interest. (Even within a rank there may be friction, as a number of GS 15's compete for a single GS-16 slot or compete with each other for other things. Equality does not guarantee harmony by any means.)

In addition to ranks, union membership or nonmembership may also be a major break point. In some government organizations few if any employees belong to unions, but such membership is growing. In some organizations it is widespread. It should be clear, however, that the union-nonunion dichotomy is not synonymous with labor and management. Government agencies do not operate with closed or union shops so that within any rank there may be both union and nonunion members. Between the two groups there may be friction if the two groups disagree on such matters as the legitimacy of job actions and other forms of pressure, especially if the benefits obtained by union activity accrue also to nonunion members.

Seniority is a common cleavage point. It is not uncommon to find employees with longer service thinking they are entitled to more authority, respect, and protection than newer employees, and new employees may be resentful. Seniority is a common technique for alleviating conflict over the distribution of advantages, as it is an apparently objective and easily measured characteristic. Seniority may be necessary for promotion, junior employees may be let go first, senior employees may get first choice in assignments and so on. But junior employees (who may be fresh, well-educated, and articulate) may resent what they regard as undue deference to seniority and attempt resistance in the name of competence and change. On the other hand seniority in a different organization may lead to isolation, unpleasant work, and early retirement. And this time it is the turn of senior employees to rise up and be resentful. When differences in seniority lead to differential treatment, conflict may result. The difficulty is that when differences in seniority do not lead to differential treatment, conflict may also result.

The notion of a career status may mean a variety of things. Here the term refers to the distinction that can be drawn between the long-termer (or the career employee) and the short-term employee, the (perhaps) political employee, the in-and-outer. Some organizations may be heavily or exclusively one (the White House Office is virtually all political employees) or the other (the Bureau of Standards is largely career employees), but in many organizations (HEW, for example) there is a mix. This mix may create friction, as the career employees may be able to see both further ahead and further back than new political appointees. Their perspective and thus their reaction to policy proposals and reorganizations almost surely will differ from that of new political appointees.

Different professions or specialties within an organization may clash with one another. Budget or personnel officers, may clash with the program administrators or doctors or scientists. Lawyers sensitive to court decisions and the provisions of the Bill of Rights may clash with security officers over questions of employment or retention. Specialists in different program areas may think that it is their specialty or program or division that is being short-changed and deserves greater support. Members of the uniformed services may clash with civilians (and in the past certainly have), and professional program analysts may clash with what amount to political specialists.

Employees stationed in Washington at an organization headquarters may have very different views than employees stationed in the field, whether in the United States or overseas. Those in the field may think that Washington simply does not understand what is going on out here, and Washington may think that the field just does not understand the pressure the Washington office is under from Congress or the White House— and both may be right. The potential for friction and conflict is obvious. Friction between embassies overseas and the State Department is a commonplace, and just within the United States the regional and local offices of a variety of agencies commonly grumble about directives from Washington and the unreasonableness of the action and reporting requirements.

At a more general level, there may be conflict or friction between separate organizations. At one extreme competition may exist between Cabinet level departments and major agencies, and at the other between relatively small sections or divisions or offices within a single department. Within particular policy areas (natural resources, for example) there may be a number of organizations from several departments that either compete or cooperate with one another. From another point of view rather disparate bureaus within a single department may compete with one another for their share of department resources. Or within a particular administration or bureau there may be head-quarters-field friction.

There are a number of other potential lines of conflict that can be summarized briefly as they are likely more familiar. Ideological differences or political value differences may be important, as they have been in recent years in the Department of Health, Education, and Welfare. Civil-rights or social-welfare activists recruited during one administration may gain career status and then find themselves in an administration that does not apparently share their view. Attitudes toward the need for and the acceptable pace of both organizational and social change may differ amongst the employees of a particular organization and the bureaucracy as a whole. And these differences may result in the creation of opposing cliques, factions, indeed organizations. And finally, of course, one cannot get away from the impact of social status. A common line of cleavage in any organization is race, though in any particular organization what difference it makes and how employees of different races fare is a subject for research.

Some of these several potential groupings may be congruent with another, and when this is true conflict in an organization may be exacerbated. But lines of cleavage may also cut across one another, and when this happens it can serve to modify or temper organizational conflict.

Who Wants What?

To understand the substance of bureaucratic politics, one must know who is likely to want what, what are the goals, the gains, the rewards in this game?[7] It is useful also to reverse the

---

7. See Chapter VIII, "Officials' Milieu, Motives, and Goals," of Anthony Downs, *Inside Bureaucracy*, (Boston: Little, Brown and Co., 1967).

question and consider what officials try to avoid. In thinking about these questions there are some points to keep in mind. First, the supply of rewards is likely to be limited; there will be not only winners but losers. One can then ask what losers get, how the fact of losing is treated or papered over or interpreted, and what the effect is on an organization if losers stay in it. Second, it is possible to distinguish between organizational goals and individual goals, though in practice these may overlap, and the person who achieves organizational goals may also achieve individual goals. Third, it is worth emphasizing that there is no necessary connection between skill at bureaucratic politics and job or professional skill. The successful scientist may not rise in an organization; the man who rises may be a second-rate scientist. Finally, perhaps, it should be noted that the goals mentioned should be viewed as possibilities, as likely goals. They may not all be present in any organization, but awareness of them all may help in thinking about behavior in organizations.

A common organizational goal is autonomy—independence, flexibility, discretion—and this goal has several implications. Being independent may at the limit mean being independent of the Secretary's Office, the White House and OMB, the Civil Service Commission, the General Services Administration, and the Congress. Of course no organization quite achieves this virtually total autonomy. Independence rather has to be thought of in terms of more or less and in connection with each possible source of control. Organization X may have a close relationship with appropriation committees and be independent of the OMB, organization Y may have been organized as a corporation and be independent of the Civil Service Commission. It is also useful to remember that in some matters an organization may have a great deal of discretion and in others be kept on a tight rein.

If autonomy is a likely goal, one may wonder about the strategies or tactics that lead to it; there are several possibilities. Certainly avoidance of scandal and building a reputation for probity and competence will help. Before taking office a political executive official may get the promise of a free hand with the administration taking a hands-off attitude. On the other hand, a career man long in office may become so familiar and trusted that he and by extension his agency become autonomous. It is a good hypothesis that when a man becomes an institution his agency gains independence. Building strong support in some quarters may lead to independence from others. Emphasizing the complexity of an agency's mission may aid in getting independence as may publicly interpreting attempts to control or supervise as political interference. The American people may not like autonomous bureaucracies, but they don't like politics and political interference either—whether in health, or research, or education, or whatever. Clearly there are several ways an agency may gain autonomy, but one must also leave open the possibility that agency autonomy sometimes is an unplanned result, an oversight, rather than the consequence of planning and action.

The other side of independence is of course control. How can it be achieved? These two questions yield the stuff of bureaucratic politics. Some agencies are trying to get more independence, and others are trying to get more control. Some agencies may simultaneously be trying to achieve independence from those outside and win control over those inside. It is not far from the mark to view bureaucratic politics as a continuing power struggle. In any case control should be put down with autonomy as one of the goals or prizes of bureaucratic politics.

The notion of autonomy as a prize or goal within the bureaucracy leads to two important observations. Consider the implications for anything like coordination if numbers of agencies are even modestly successful in achieving some autonomy. If each agency is "doing its own thing" (and that may be a good working definition of autonomy), coordination simply becomes impossible, except on paper. For it to exist there would have to be control, but this runs counter to the demands for autonomy and to checks and balances, separation of powers, and so on. The result is that one agency will continue to plan housing developments and another will plan freeways for the same space; the result is that a good many problems fall between stools and that the work of some agencies is cancelled by others. The government, through different bureaucracies, simultaneously reclaims land for agriculture and takes farm land out of production.

Consider also the implications of bureaucratic autonomy for everything from responsive and responsible government, to congressional control, to presidential power. Obviously there are problems and probably conflicts. They will not be resolved here, but they need to be made explicit. Many of the arguments for bureaucratic autonomy, taken by themselves, are plausible—especially arguments that point to the disadvantages of political interference, the consequences of rotating political executives and the impossibility of long-range planning, given annual budgeting and the irrationalities of the legislative process. Yet the possible consequences of these arguments for politically responsive government should be understood. To strengthen the bureaucracy, to enhance its independence (or the independence of some parts of it) is to weaken the power of Congress and the President. And by the same token, to strengthen the President may be to make or threaten to make inroads on bureaucratic autonomy. Understanding the consequences you can go ahead and pick your side, or simply stand aside. What is important is that you penetrate the surface of political and administrative rhetoric and understand the unstated consequences of strengthening one actor or another in the political arena.

Who wants what? is of course not a matter only of control and autonomy. There are other goals of prizes that must be considered. One of these is money. Budget increases are a common goal of bureaucratic organizations, though the notion of budget increase may contain within it a number of subgoals. An organization may want to protect itself from the effects of inflation; in a period of inflation a stable budget is in fact a budget cut in terms of purchasing power. A 5 or 6 percent increase may be required just to stay even with the previous year. If an organization wants to keep its share of the budget constant, dollar amounts must increase if the government budget increases. It may want to keep its share comparable to that received by similar organizations; if the Navy asks for more money it is a virtual certainty that the Air Force will. An organization may feel that its present budget permits only inadequate performance, and indeed if an organization's performance is criticized it is likely to blame inadequate resources. An organization may want to expand its mission, and to do so will need more money. The point is clear: budget increases are a common goal and may have several justifications. Needless to add, organizations are likely also to want more manpower, more space, more material.

The potential for conflict is obvious. Constitutents of departments may all want to grow, and their budgets summed will add up to much more than the department will have. In a sense they compete with one another, each trying to get as much as possible. They may also be in conflict with the department, which may want some budgets not to grow so fast and some to shrink. And if a department cuts a bureau budget, the bureau may try to get the money back. Agencies generally may find themselves in conflict with the White House and in particular the Office of Management and Budget. There a common goal may be to slow the rate of budget growth, and another goal may be to cut some agencies to the disappearing point. And of course bureaus may find themselves in conflict with Congressional appropriations committees.

In order to improve their chances of achieving and maintaining some measure of autonomy and to improve their chances of getting more money, agencies are likely also to want political support, a good image, and influential access to important decision-makers. Obviously these goals flow together and overlap; a good image—efficient, economical, well-administered, accomplishing something important—is very likely to lead to support and respect from budget analysts, Congressmen, group leaders and other participants in policy-making. An opposite image may yield unpleasant results. The obvious inference is that agencies will attempt to convey to the press, Congressmen, other officials —that is, to outsiders—a favorable image.[8] They are likely also to be deferential and responsive to those immediately involved in decisions that affect them. Once a rewarding relationship is established with congressional committees or the White House, agencies are likely to resist any move (like reorganization) that would alter or sever the relationship.

Although the discussion of organizational goals has so far focused on what organizations want to get, the notion of goal can include something to be avoided. Agencies want to get some things (as we have seen) but they also want to avoid other things. They want to avoid outside control, simply the reverse of wanting to attain autonomy. Awareness of this goal leads you to expect that agencies will commonly be critical of and resist attempts by the Office of Management and Budget, the Civil Service Commission, the General Services Administration, or the General Accounting Office to set standards or assert control. Agencies want to avoid budget cuts, they like to avoid reductions in force, and they try to avoid loss of space or other kinds of resource losses. This is perfectly predictable; even if a President says that the federal work force is to be trimmed 5 or 6 percent,

---

8. See Francis Rourke, *Secrecy and Publicity* (Baltimore: Johns Hopkins University Press, 1961) and the more recent book by David Wise, *The Politics of Lying* (New York: Random House, 1973).

it may not happen. If you watch closely you will find unpublicized exceptions, lack of compliance, and generally a good deal of slippage.

Agencies want to avoid adverse publicity and the damage it may do their image. With this goal understood it should come as no surprise to find out that errors and worse are not announced and indeed may be classified and buried. Action or inaction not congruent with the image that an agency wants to convey, action or inaction that strikes a discordant note, may not see the light of day. To be sure, the General Accounting Office, budget examiners, investigating Congressmen, and inquiring reporters are on the other side. Even the disgruntled employee, one who perhaps lost a personal fight of one kind or another, may leak information. Low morale, widespread dissatisfaction, and frustration can turn even a sensitive organization into a sieve.

One should also understand that agencies want to avoid uncertainty. They want to know what tomorrow and next year are likely to bring. One can think of uncertainty reduction as a goal, one that helps account for the development and endurance of rules, routines, and organizational ideologies. It helps account for the resistance that suggested changes may meet and the slowness that may mark the spread of innovations. When the consequences of change are not clear, that is, when there is some uncertainty about what they will bring, they are likely to be held at arms length, scrutinized, criticized, modified, and accepted slowly if at all. Uncertainty reduction also helps account for the simplified way in which officials may view the world, the simple cause-effect relations they posit, their simple models of reality. Perhaps another way of saying that officials seek to reduce uncertainty is to say that they seek simplicity and stability and try to avoid complexity and change. Of course, not all officials are like this, but the proposition is a useful aid in predicting official reaction to change proposals and understanding policy outcomes.

At the beginning of this section a distinction was made between organizational goals and individual goals, and it is time to come back to that. To this point the goals we have considered have been organizational goals, or perhaps more precisely goals individuals have for their organizations. But individuals also have goals for themselves, and in looking at bureaucratic politics you should remember them, obvious though they are. At the material level organization members want job security, reasonable levels of pay and fringe benefits, promotions in rank, pleasant working conditions, and so on. Not all employees regard these as equally important, of course, but if they are not provided or if some employees think they are unfairly treated there may be friction. In the end a job action of one kind or another may take place that impairs the functioning of the organization. In addition to material goals, employees, especially professional and managerial employees, may want a rewarding career, challenging assignments, stimulating colleagues or co-workers, a good deal of discretion and freedom in their job and over their time, and perhaps other kinds of intangible benefits. Individuals may also have particular policy preferences they want the organization to implement. There may also be actions that they do not want the organization to take.

There are in short a variety of individual goals, and individuals within an organization may expend a good deal of time and energy in trying to achieve their goals. They may ally with one another or compete; they may attempt to gain the attention of superiors and earn their favor, or they may simply work. They may with facts and argument try to persuade others to their policy views. In the end if they are not successful they may withdraw. The administrators task is to keep enough members in the organization and supportive of it that mission accomplishment is not seriously impaired. He must, if he can, use resources so that the goals of many members of the organization are met. This point suggests a link between organizational and individual goals. If an organization can increase its budget and maintain a measure of autonomy it will likely more easily meet the demands of members. A cut budget and tight outside controls may substantially reduce the flexibility of superiors in dealing with subordinates.

We might consider briefly the connection between what might be thought of as mission accomplishment and the achievement of goals such as discussed in this section. Mission accomplishment refers to such things as students educated, deaths averted, criminals arrested, housing units built, workers trained, audits conducted, irrigation systems constructed, rivers dredged, and investigations carried out. Presumably such activities can be viewed as ends—and getting more money and space and administrative flexibility can be viewed as means. But in practice there may be no measurable connection between ends and means; at most there may be a faith connection.[9] That is we believe there is a connection, and so money is appropriated in the hope that more work will be accomplished and more problems solved. But it often does not work that way. More and more money can be spent, and conditions to all appearances do not change or indeed continue to deteriorate. It would be easy to conclude that we know how to spend money but do not know how to solve problems. An agency may achieve many of its goals, and the problems it was set up to deal with may remain. But there is a further point to make, that often means become ends, and the effective goals of a bureaucracy become more money and more men and more autonomy. Difficult and complex goals—the reduction of poverty, the reduction of unemployment, the reduction of infant mortality, the reduction of crime—become transformed into simpler, more measurable goals—more money and more men. Because they may be rhetorically associated with social goods, more money and more men for one agency or another may be hard to resist, but some skepticism is frequently in order. The organizational benefits in more money and men are clear enough. The skeptical analyst may well inquire about additional benefits—and if some are claimed inquire about the evidence. What is good for the agency (more autonomy, more money, and so on) may or may not be good in a larger context. But this debate is a major part of the politics of bureaucracy.

Conflict and Conflict Resolution

It is obvious by now that there is much potential for conflict within bureaucracies. The cleavages, the various and conflicting demands and interests, the limited resources—all these make conflict all but inevitable. There is potential for conflict between individuals, within agencies, between agencies, and surely potential for conflict between operating agencies and controlling agencies like the Office of Management and Budget and the Civil

---

9. In 1971 Alice Rivlin wrote, "Little is known about how to produce more effective health, education, and other social services." See her *Systematic Thinking and Social Action* (Washington, D.C.: The Brookings Institution, 1971). For provocative views of what administrative activity accomplishes see James Q. Wilson, "The Bureaucracy Problem," *The Public Interest*, No. 6, 1967, pp. 3–9, and Peter Drucker, "The Sickness of Government," *The Public Interest,* No. 14, 1969, pp. 3–23.

Service Commission. How can conflicts be prevented? How can conflicts be resolved? What are the possible consequences of conflict? These seem important questions.[10]

Conflict prevention is a topic that provokes a number of observations. The first is that given the very real differences of interest that may exist both within and between organizations all conflicts simply cannot be prevented. Better communication and good human relations may prevent or defuse some conflicts, especially ones growing from misunderstanding or misinformation. But some conflicts of interest are very real. One set of advisors favors one approach for combatting inflation and another set favors another approach; the Navy wants to be given more money and the Office of Management and Budget wants to give it less. More communication will not easily resolve such conflicts. Indeed it is possible to imagine that more and clearer communication may simply make some conflicts sharper. Still, there are a variety of ways to prevent or forestall conflict or resolve it in very early stages.

Selective recruitment is certainly one way of reducing the potential for conflict. The development of an organizational ideology stressing loyalty and conformity to the organization and the importance of the organization's mission may reduce internal conflict. But so do the use of generalities and ambiguous language. Involving those who will be affected by a decision in the decision-making process may prevent later conflict when it is implemented, but it may not if those who have been consulted feel that they were ignored and their involvement was only *pro forma* window-dressing. Prior consultation, the use of interagency committees, and other devices for arriving at consensus may reduce conflict. Delaying decisions and not rocking the boat may also be ways of avoiding conflict, though of course those who want decisions and change may object.

While thinking of preventing conflicts, it is worth noting that conflict is not altogether a bad thing. To be sure there are costs associated with conflict, ranging from high levels of personnel turnover to waste of material resources, to security leaks, to inability to carry out a mission. But there are also often benefits attached to conflict. Conflict *may* result in innovation, in the

---

10. See the chapter by Bertram Gross cited in footnote 6. See also Lewis Coser, *The Functions of Social Conflict* (New York: The Free Press of Glencoe, 1956).

introduction of new technologies, in better communication, in the departure of personnel who ought to leave, in the more effective expenditure of resources. Sometimes a fight must precede a worthwhile change. The point is that one cannot *a priori* decide that conflict is a bad thing to be prevented at all costs.

As not all conflicts can be prevented (and in any event they are not), conflict resolution is an important activity in bureaucratic organizations and a major part of bureaucratic politics. Perhaps the first point to note is that conflicts in bureaucracies may be clarified and resolved up and down the hierarchy. The head of an agency (or his deputy) may settle, for example, disputes between the heads of major sections or divisions within the agency. (You should by now be able to name several possible kinds of conflicts that a bureau head might have to intervene in.) In disputes (or perhaps more politely, differences) between bureaus, the Department Secretary or his designate may intervene as may the Office of Management and Budget or the White House. In interagency or interdepartmental conflicts the Office of Management and Budget and the White House are likely to be involved, but this need not mean that either the director of OMB or the President himself will be involved. Lower levels of officials may first try to handle a conflict and resolve it, and only if they are unsuccessful will the conflict escalate to higher levels. The President gets only those problems that cannot be solved at lower levels. Conflicts between an agency and the Office of Management and Budget may first be discussed between a budget analyst or section chief and middle management in the agency concerned. What cannot get worked out will go up to the assistant director-assistant secretary level and some few differences may reach the Director on one side and the Secretary on the other. And in some cases the Secretary may think the need for more money or a personnel ceiling exception or new legislation is so strong and the OMB is so wrong that he will go to the President personally. The essential point to grasp is that each level in the hierarchy can in some sense be regarded as a conflict resolution point. The question for the analyst or observer is which conflicts commonly get resolved at what levels (and how) and which wind up on the President's desk.

Given the functioning of bureaucratic organizations, their emphasis on rules, procedures, and predictability, it should not be surprising to learn that routines have been established for handling the kinds of conflicts that routinely arise. In the field of personnel especially, formalized grievance procedures and an appeals system exist, going all the way up to the Commissioners of the Civil Service Commission. The field of budgeting has a host of both formal and informal standard operating procedures. The use of committees and task forces to gather information and opinion and give advice is common. And for many conflicts the Office of Management and Budget serves as final arbiter. Agencies that deal with the public (the Internal Revenue Service and the Social Security System are two examples) have a whole series of appeal and review procedures to use in cases involving conflicts between citizens and officials. And of course many types of conflicts wind up in the Congress and the Courts.

It should be clear of course that though we speak of conflict resolution the term by no means implies making both sides happy. That may be one result, and a good deal of conflict resolution involves negotiation, bargaining, and a compromise with both sides somewhat better off and more or less content. But conflict resolution may mean that the final judge comes down on one side or the other and one side wins, the other loses. After important conflicts are resolved officials may seek other positions, whole agencies may be shifted and reorganized, carriers or air wings may not get into the budget, and poverty programs can themselves wind up in poverty. The stakes involved in bureaucratic politics can be very high, and outcomes affect not only the lives and careers of individuals but also the existence of agencies and the substance of public policy. It is true that bureaucratic conflicts may not be well publicized, but that scarcely lessens their importance.

9 The Presidency and the Bureaucracy

Sections in previous chapters have provided some information about the President, the presidency, and the bureaucracy. The potential for conflict between the President and the organizations under him has been emphasized and the enlargement, the institutionalization, and the bureaucratization of the Presidency have been noted. In this chapter, in keeping with the present focus on bureaucratic politics, we consider the question of presidential control of the bureaucracy. What is the meaning of control? What affects the President's position, strengthens his influence, or diminishes it? What is associated with bureaucratic independence or allegiance to the President? What kinds of relations may exist between the President and the organizations of the Executive Branch?

A Note on Presidential Power

"The power of the President" is a common phrase and one that warrants attention in any consideration of Presidential bureaucratic relations.[1] What does it mean? Is it possible to say how much power the President possesses? Can it be measured? What effects or limits the power of the President? When bureaucrats act as the President requests, has he exercised his power?

---

1. The classic work on presidential power is the book of that title by Richard Neustadt (New York: John Wiley & Sons, 1964).

When they continue straight on course or lie at anchor as the President madly turns the wheel or pulls the throttle, is this a sign of presidential power failure? The same questions might of course be asked in a department or a bureau or in any context with a hierarchic structure. Does the chief have power? How much? What are his limits?

At first glance it seems clear that the President is powerful. He takes a hand in more problems and activities than ever in the country's history. To be sure, on occasion the President is challenged because some think that he has overreached himself, but still to all appearances the President is in command. But is he? Many texts and essays comment on the power of the President and candidates for office tell us what they will do if they are given the presidential office and can exercise its powers. Yet Presidents themselves, their staffs, and men who've held the office almost routinely tell a different story, and emphasize their disillusionment, frustration, and in fact their frequent powerlessness.[2] Faced with a huge permanent establishment, scores or thousands of organizations, and millions of employees, and even a Cabinet that may border on the accidental it is small wonder that Presidents come soon to complain about their inability to move the bureaucratic government and to call for its restructuring and other changes to make government more responsive to the people and more importantly to them.[3]

Yet to speak of presidential powerlessness may be as misleading as to speak of presidential power. Power is not something that the President has or hasn't, but rather something he has in

2. For example, see the discussion of John Kennedy's trouble with the bureaucracy in Arthur Schlesinger's *A Thousand Days* (Boston: Houghton Mifflin Co., 1965), p. 680. See also Thomas E. Cronin, "Everybody Believes in Democracy Until He Gets to the White House. . . . An Examination of White House-Department Relations," *Law and Contemporary Problems*, Vol. 35, No. 3 (Summer 1970), pp. 573–625.

3. In March 1971 President Nixon sent a message to Congress proposing a substantial reorganization of several Cabinet departments. He began his message with the sentences, "When I suggested in my State of the Union Message that most Americans today are simply fed up with government at all levels there was some surprise that such a sweeping indictment of government would come from within the government itself. Yet it is precisely there, within the government itself, that frustration with government is often most deeply experienced." For the full message and supporting documents see *Papers Relating to the President's Departmental Reorganization Program* (Washington; U.S.G.P.O., 1972), rev. ed.

some circumstances, under some conditions, over some individuals, in some agencies. The specifics must be a matter of individual investigation, but some general observations are certainly permissible. It is possible to think of the President's power vis-à-vis the bureaucracy as one dimension of a more general subject, power vis-à-vis various constituencies. These include, beside the bureaucracy, the Congress, the courts, the parties, various groups, and perhaps the public. Presidential influence (power) in each of these areas may differ, his power to persuade may fluctuate depending on the audience and the circumstances, but it is also obvious that these constituencies are by no means independent of one another. Ability to win in one area, to bring one group of constituencies to his side, may strengthen the President in dealing with others or perhaps make it less necessary to win the others. A President who lacks influence in Congress may be out of luck in a number of bureaucracies.

It is also necessary to remember that the bureaucracy is a whole with very different parts, and the President's relations with the different parts may vary. He may be able to get his way in some while being powerless in others. As it is impossible to separate bureaucracies from policies, the President's interest and activity in a policy area may affect his relations with the bureaucracy(ies) in that area. One can think most simply of foreign policy, domestic policy, economic policy, and each of these topics can be subdivided. Currently in matters of national security and foreign policy it seems clear that the President has more power than in many if not most areas of domestic policy. And it is clear that in recent administrations the President has seen more often and worked more closely with the heads of the national security departments than with the heads of such departments as agriculture and interior. (But even writing this I recall the complaints of President Roosevelt about his difficulties with the Navy and the complaints of recent Presidents about the State Department.) The domestic bureaucracies are much more on their own, less visible than the national security bureaucracies. At least (and this is perhaps more precise) recent Presidents have devoted more attention to and worked harder to try to control the national security bureaucracies. It should be noted of course that the relative independence of the domestic bureaucracies is not a matter only of lesser presidential interest. It is also true that domestic policy bureaucracies are more likely to be protected by and in alliance with major clientele groups and Congressional committees. Greater presidential interest might not change the relatively independent status of many domestic agencies. It might, however, increase friction.

If these remarks on presidential power have one single major point it is that presidential power is complex and elusive. This can be emphasized in yet another way. The power of the President refers to his ability to influence or effect behavior in ways that he desires. The President has power over someone if when he gives an order, a direction, an instruction, it is obeyed or followed—and would not have been if the order had not been given. This definition suggests some problems in assessing presidential power. Even though executives (and for that matter Congressmen) may act in ways consistent with presidential wishes, we may not assume they act that way because of what the President said. They might have acted similarly without a word spoken by the President. This fact makes caution necessary in assessing presidential power. What might on occasion pass for the power of the President may not be that at all.

But does this mean that presidential power cannot be assessed? Not at all, but surely caution is in order. By looking at statements and behavior with some care, one may tell with some degree of accuracy where presidential influence has been tried and found wanting. (The astute President of course will not widely publicize his losses and may try to make the victories of others his.) By looking at an agency over time and through administrations, we may judge whether a President affected it or not. Such assessments surely are an exercise in judgment, and different judges may vary in their ratings. Who can be positive that events turned as they did because the President spoke and acted as he did?

Why the President May Not Be in Control

It is clear in our Constitution, our law, and our folklore that the President is Chief Executive and Chief Administrator. But it is also clear in fact and practice that this is often not the case. When a President comes into office he may be a stranger to the internal workings of the executive branch, and further he may have no taste for administrative detail and the demands of bureaucratic politics. More important, the limits on his own training and knowledge, not to mention the limits on his time, may make it difficult if not impossible for him to supervise or criticise many of the agencies of government and their operations. To be sure he appoints executives and assistants and delegates responsibility to them, but they then become the ones with power and the President is only formally in charge. His own appointees may themselves be strangers to bureaucracy and largely uninformed about it. They may have no experience in the management of complex enterprises. This hampers their ability to get action or bring change. They may be isolated or in time become co-opted. Either way, bureaucratic autonomy may be maintained at the expense of presidential influence. It is worth noting that if a Secretary wants his department to be on his side, he must be on its side—and its side may not be the President's. Even if his appointees do stay with him, their numbers and their impact are likely to be limited, and the demands on them virtually unlimited. Even if plans are laid and directions issued there may be little follow up and less evaluation.[4] The agencies continue on their way.

It may be noted here that frequently the White House lacks satisfactory indicators of agency performance (and the agencies may not have any satisfactory indicators either). The White House may be hard pressed to know how well the government is working. There may of course be speculation and intuition; but frequently there is little data with which to take an agency to task. Lacking indicators of performance and standards the President in a sense is blind and in any case must often take on faith what he is told. This lack of useful indicators of performance (a new President may not appreciate this gap) is one more obstacle to presidential control.

These points deserve elaboration, and there are more points to be made. It is important to keep separate a Department Secretary's Office from the rest of his department. The President, if only because he appoints the Secretary, may stand a chance of having the Secretary and his staff stand with him, though this is by no means always so and may become less likely the farther into the term an administration goes. But even when (if) the

---

4. Joseph Wholey begins his monograph *Federal Evaluation Policy* with this sentence, "The most impressive finding about the evaluation of social programs in the federal government is that substantial work in this field has been almost nonexistent." The monograph was published by The Urban Institute, Washington, D.C., in 1970.

Secretary is with the President his career department may not be, and he may be quite unable to manage his department.[5]

Another point to have in mind is that when a President takes office he may be ill-prepared to staff political positions. The men who helped elect him may not be well fitted to run the agencies and he may wind up appointing strangers and some misfits. If he is successful in appointing men who are interested in solving problems, developing new programs, and changing old ones the energy and attitudes of such men may cause conflict with career officials and make implementation of new ideas and plans difficult if not impossible. Then, too, program developers may have skills and attitudes suited to change and innovation but not to the conduct of administrative routine. Men with ideas may not be able to get them into action.[6] In addition, the bureaucracy is increasingly professionalized and specialized. Beneficial as this may appear, it is also true that this change may act to isolate parts of the bureaucracy from each other and from the President and his executives. Professionalization and specialization may hamper communication, coordination, and control.

But these several difficulties by no means exhaust the obstacles to Presidential control. Any President is locked in, committed to much that his predecessors did. Much of the budget of the country is fixed and beyond the power of the President to alter.[7] He is committed to legislation already passed and court descisions already made. The staff of the executive branch is as we have noted mostly career and he cannot change it. There is apparently not much any particular President can do,

---

5. Secretaries of Health, Education, and Welfare and of Defense seem to have had particular trouble in influencing departmental constituent units. A quotation from David Broder's book, *The Party's Over* (New York: Harper and Row, 1972) is illustrative. "From their two sprawling buildings on Independence Avenue, the top HEW officials are supposed to coordinate the activities of 107,000 bureaucrats scattered across the nation. But the department has had nine secretaries in its first eighteen years of life and most of them have gone away muttering that it is 'an anthill' or 'anarchy in government.' Everything conceivable has been tried to bring order out of chaos, but the chaos remains." Pp. 161–162.

6. On this point see Adam Yarmolinsky, "Ideas Into Programs," *The Public Interest*, No. 2, Winter 1966, pp. 70–79.

7. Estimates of size of the fixed budget range around 80 to 85%. In addition, a new President arrives in the middle of one fiscal year and must more or less accept as given the budget for the next fiscal year that has been prepared by his predecessor.

not much he can alter. To be sure, there is overstatement here, but there is also truth. Promise what he will while running, a President takes office to discover that there is much he cannot change.

The size—in organization, programs, personnel, dollars—of the executive branch presents an enormous challenge. There is just too much for any one man, even with a staff, to be really Chief, except in law, on paper. Characteristics of bureaucracy that we have examined also bear on the substance of the Presidential role. Many of the bureaucracies have grown rigid, and there may be little that a President can do with them. Virtually all of them are committed to their programs and are carrying out their routines. A President with difficulty alters these routines or threatens the continuation and expansion of agencies and their program.

Many agencies have support, strong support, from various parts of the political system. Another name for bureaucratic politics might be alliance politics, and for some of these alliances the President simply is no match. Challenges to his apparent authority can be made successfully in some policy subsystems and some conflicts he may lose.

On Trying to Gain Control

Given the importance of presidential power and its fluctuating character it seems worthwhile to comment briefly on the tactics of control. Growth in the size and authority of the White House office and the whole Executive Office represents among other things an attempt on the part of the President (and/or his supporters) to maintain or to enhance the influence of the President over the bureaucracy. The function of a presidential staff broadly defined is to provide information and advice. How much they provide and how accurate it is is important to presidential success. But in achieving and maintaining power Presidents are not likely to rely only on information as it comes up through channels. Presidents and their staffs may also "end run," skip echelons, and go outside channels to solicit information from or give orders to men several levels down. A President may think that out-of-channel inquiring and requests on an irregular basis may enhance not only his control but also his reputation for control while exclusive reliance on the same sources will limit or diminish his control.

A President uses his staff not only to protect his own attention, energy, and time and to provide him with information and advice, but also (as he must) for follow-up. Were his own requests interpreted as orders and carried out, or were they bowed to, then ignored? Did action follow from his words? If not, why not? If so, was it the proper action with the desired effects? Asking such questions is what staff is for, and if they are not constantly following up and exhibiting a presidential interest, presidential control diminishes. This assertion must be qualified. Follow-up is commonly not the forte of White House staff. They do not do it systematically; among other reasons, there is not much publicity or political pay-off in it, and they may feel they do not have the time. They are more likely to be inventing new programs (or at least programs that are said to be new) than to be engaging in duller chores. The result is that much is started but little may be accomplished.

Part of presidential control of the bureaucracy—a large part—is affected by how the President develops, organizes, and uses his staff and what he does with his own time. But a section on the tactics of control must at least mention other topics. By shifting personnel, promoting, dismissing, and recruiting, a President may attempt to alter power balances and improve his own position in particular organizations. To the same end reorganizations may be proposed and carried out. Budgets may be raised and lowered and funds impounded. Statistics and status reports may be required. All such moves require effort and impose their own costs.

Presidential-congressional relations must be kept in mind when thinking of presidential control of the bureaucracy. If a President can get legislation he wants through Congress, if he can get (and on occasion avoid) appropriations, if he can prevent the veto of reorganizations, he improves his chances of getting what he wants from the bureaucracy. By the same token, however, failure or weakness in the Congress is likely to weaken a President's position in his own house. The President may use access to the mass media to inform the public of his position and win it to his side. Public opinion favorable to his proposals or his record enhances his position vis-à-vis the bureaucracy. A popular President, one who stands high in the polls and is likely to be around for some time, may be listened to more attentively and get more response than one whose standing is declining.

With all this said about the tactics of control it remains to emphasize the importance of a President's own knowledge and desire. A President must want to control the bureaucracy if he stands a chance of doing so, and he must know how to go about trying. In particular he must master the routines of administration, budgeting, personnel processes, and the like. If he does not do so or is not interested in trying, he may be more the victim of the bureaucracy than its head. Such mastery takes time. By the time a President has become aware of the levers and the nuances it may be almost time to leave.

Is Control Desirable?

We have considered, however briefly, both the tactics of control and the obstacles to it. But it remains to ask whether control is desirable or necessary? The question obviously has a variety of answers that depend on who responds. Where you stand depends on where you sit. There is a presidential perspective, and from it presidential leadership and control are very likely to appear desirable. The President, his staff, people loyal to him, and academics attracted to or intrigued by the Presidency may talk about the need for presidential strength, seek ways to prevent the erosion of his power, and recommend steps to enhance it. Proposals that might weaken the presidential office, intentionally or not, are likely to be resisted.

But of course the presidential perspective is not the only one. There is also a department or agency perspective and from here lip service may be given to the President's authority, but there is likely also to be resentment of presidential (especially White House staff) interference and oversight. Bureaus may resist close departmental control and agencies in general will try to protect their independence. What appears as necessary control and coordination from a White House perspective may appear as unwarranted interference from the agency view.

There is also a Congressional perspective on questions of presidential-bureaucratic relations. Here the obvious point is that between the Congress and the President there is a constitutionally based conflict of interest and steps that may be viewed as strengthening the President may be viewed as detracting from the power of the Congress. There is also a party perspective. Republicans in Congress may take a more favorable view of strengthening a Republican President than they would a Democratic President, and vice versa.

In sum, there seems no way to answer absolutely a question on the desirability of enhancing the power of the President in his relations with the bureaucracy. Where any particular official may stand will depend on what he wants to get, what he thinks his interest is, and how he thinks it will best be served.

Relations Between the President and the Bureaucracies

So far we have considered mainly the question of control, how the President may acquire it, how and why a bureaucracy may try to avoid it. But we can shift our focus and ask another question: How do the President and the bureaucracies view each other and relate to one another? The answers are complex and varied. Given the size and complexity of the American bureaucracy, to say nothing of the complexity of presidential personality, it is impossible to describe completely the variations, shades and nuances of presidential-bureaucratic relationships. Nevertheless, several observations about this relationship, first from a presidential perspective and then from a bureaucratic perspective, are suggested. Illustrations and discussion follow; the reader should provide additional questions and may want to challenge particular statements.

1. Commonly the President is uninformed about or uninterested in particular executive organizations. The details of administration may be both foreign and boring. At any particular time numerous organizations may be operating on their own, outside the President's attention. Of these it can be said he does not know what they are doing; he does not know what is going on.

2. The President may have an unfavorable image of the bureaucracy as a whole (wasteful, choked in red tape, disloyal).

3. In particular he may have an unfavorable image of particular organizations in the executive branch.

4. The President may be dissatisfied or indeed angry with the performance of a particular agency.

5. The President may feel frustrated by the bureaucracy and prevented by it or parts of it from carrying out his policies.

6. He may attempt to bypass a particular bureaucracy.

7. The President of course may think highly of and rely on some bureaucracies. He may trust some bureaucracies, even while he distrusts others.

8. The President may feel hemmed-in by but powerless to alter the bureaucracy or particular organizations.

Reference just to events of the last few years is sufficient to illustrate these several observations, and some can be illustrated in other ways. On the first point, for instance, several things can be said. Presidents have frequently been trained in the law but rarely in administration. Such a background provides little reason to suspect they will be informed about the details of the executive branch. Knowledge of the bureaucracy is not a prerequisite to running for office. The result may be, as Evans and Novack explicitly said of Richard Nixon, that a new President will know a great deal about American electoral politics (and maybe a great deal about foreign affairs or other policies) but have large gaps in his knowledge of American government.[8] In addition two other points need to be made. One is that Presidents (like the rest of us) are governed by the law of the 24-hour day; they cannot attend to everything, which means they must ignore some things. They make choices, and some things in effect are chosen out. Second, Presidents may have particular policy interests. In the areas of their policy interest they may know a good deal about the bureaucratic structure and administrative detail. But about a wide range of policy areas a President may have little interest, and the organizations in these areas may be pretty much on their own as long as they do not make obvious or threatening waves. As long as they carry out their routines they may escape presidential notice—except that their budgets may be attacked, cut, and used to provide resources for programs that do have presidential interest. And this perhaps suggests a third point, that many of the routines of government (and the organizations that carry them out) go largely unnoticed by Presidents.

The President may have an unfavorable image of the bureaucracy as a whole, for at least two reasons. A President may come into office on the heels of a man of a different party and may view the bureaucracy he inherits as tainted by 4 or 8 years of association with the opposition. This in itself would

---

8. See Rowland Evans, Jr., and Robert D. Novak, *Nixon in the White House* (New York: Vintage Books, 1972), p. 1. "His Knowledge of foreign affairs was encyclopedic and in the weeks just ahead would astonish those who had not known him before. . . . But there were deep and obvious gaps, surprising for one so long on the national scene, in his knowledge of the federal government and the Congress."

be enough to tarnish the bureaucratic image and cause a new President to consider it suspect. But in addition a President may share what seems to be a part of American political culture—an antipathy to bureaucracy, bureaucrats, and big government. He may also of course have noted during his career that at least parts of the bureaucracy carried out programs of which he did not approve or carried them out in a manner apparently wasteful or ineffectively. And this gets us to the observation that a President may have an unfavorable image of particular parts of the bureaucracy (remembering that he may not be able to do anything about the unfavorable image.) In addition to having a generally unfavorable opinion a President may for more or less specific reasons be angry or dissatisfied with the performance of a particular agency. After the Bay of Pigs disaster John Kennedy was angry (to understate the case) with the CIA and the military. They had in his view failed, and failed him.

The President may feel frustrated by the bureaucracy but be able to do little. Budgets may be increased and lowered, personnel shifted, and agencies and whole departments reorganized, and on occasion such moves may be taken as indicators of presidential frustration. But in the end little may change. A President may of course choose to bypass the bureaucracy. This can happen in a variety of ways. One is to appoint White House staff to do tasks that might otherwise be carried out in an executive branch agency. A White House National Security staff may be used instead of the State Department.[9] Alternatively a President may assign to one agency tasks or responsibilities that have formerly been carried out by another. The Central Intelligence Agency can take responsibilities from the Defense Intelligence Agency; The Office of International Security Affairs can loose power to the State Department. A commission or task force may be set up outside the government to look at problems that might otherwise be handled by an agency either in the departmental structure or in the Executive Office of the President. The President may call on private unofficial advisors instead of or in addition to his official staff. And to these ways of by passing the bureaucracy or particular bureaucracies can be added two others.

---

9. The New York Times (January 19, 1971, p. 12) reported: "The National Security Council staff budget this fiscal year runs $2.2 million, more than triple Mr. Rostow's budget in 1968 and two and a half times Mr. Bundy's in 1962." Of course, the staff was also increased appreciably.

The President may attempt to rely on state and local authority as in grant-in-aid programs or revenue sharing or may attempt to have problems solved and action taken in the private sector, voluntarily or on the basis of contracts, tax benefits, or some other means.

Of course there may be agencies that any particular President thinks highly of, but over-all a President may be more likely to feel hemmed in than helped by the bureaucracy—hemmed in, but powerless to change it in any very useful or dramatic ways.

But how do the relationships look from the bureaucracy's point of view?

1. A bureaucracy may view a President as hostile to its programs or to it. The opposite of course may also be the case.

2. A bureaucracy may view the President as uninformed, or the victim of poor advice.

3. A bureaucracy may view the President as putting politics above the public (organizational) interest and of being mainly interested in winning the next election.

4. A bureaucracy may need presidential support for its programs and its budget but find him unsympathetic.

5. A bureaucracy with the support of Congressional leaders may not need the President and can ignore him.

Hostility, neutrality, sympathy—a bureaucracy may perceive the President as having any of these attitudes. The President's attitude may be a function of his ideology, values, information, perceptions, and experience. Thus one President may be particularly interested in and sympathetic toward organizations engaged in reducing poverty; another may be interested in law-enforcement organizations. Yet another may be interested in science or in health. His attitude may be expressed in how he reacts to requests for funds, in the executives he appoints to the agency (and whether he allows vacancies to go unfilled), whether he is interested in expansion or not, and how he treats it vis-à-vis other organizations in the same policy state.

If the bureaucracy views a President as hostile, several courses are in principle open to it. It can simply endure; (only four or eight years more); it can attempt to change (new program proposals, reorganizations, budget reallocations) in ways that will attract presidential attention and support and reduce presidential hostility; or it can attempt to build up support in Congress or in public opinion that will counteract the probable effect of presidential hostility. To be sure these tactics may not be successful and agencies that encounter presidential hostility may be reorganized or abolished, have their budgets cut, or their heads replaced. As each of these moves may in some circumstances incur costs for the President, hostility may be manifested simply by doing nothing while aiding and expanding other agencies.

If an agency thinks the President is less than supportive it may reason that he is uninformed or the victim of poor advice. This may be especially the case if he rejects agency-initiated program proposals, cuts the budget, or lets personnel vacancies go unfilled. The public statements of a President about foreign countries may persuade State Department careerists or analysts in the CIA that a President is uninformed, and a President's statements about poverty and welfare may leave economists and experts in welfare reeling. Civil-rights positions may on occasion leave attorneys in the Department of Justice scratching their heads. Such reactions are hardly surprising. A President is unlikely to have all the facts, or even as many as specialists in particular organizations. He may be the victim of his own preconceptions. Even if he has the facts that the specialists do, he may, because he has a different position and a different perspective and is subject to different demands, interpret them differently. Certainly it is not true that when a President differs with specialists that he is always poorly informed; it may only be that he is differently informed or responding to multiple problems and a more complex view of the world. It remains to note the obvious. When the President and an agency are in agreement and sympathetic with one another the agency is likely to think that he is fully and properly informed. These comments have an important implication: As agencies may think that information is likely to lead to proper decisions, they may invest substantial resources in trying to inform the President (and his staff) about what it is they do and why it is important.

The differences in perspective that affect the acquisition and interpretation of information also affect the weight that is given to electoral considerations. It is almost a certainty that the President and his appointees are more likely to be sensitive to these considerations and to weigh them differently than career specialists and professional bureaucrats. This may affect everything from program decisions (content, funding, and timing) to contract announcements, to the interpretation given such things as crime rates, employment and unemployment figures, inflation rates, and other such potentially politically sensitive data. Facts are used in different ways by men in different positions; they mean different things; indeed, one man's facts may be another man's myths. In the end there is much room for presidential and bureaucratic difference of opinion and for conflict between the presidency and bureaucratic agencies. One further point to note is this: bureaucracies may try to do the President's bidding and in doing so open themselves to the charge of playing politics. They may gain his favor trying to tell him what he is known to want to hear. But attempts to gain presidential support may over time erode support from other participants in the political system. Politics as much as economics may be concerned with choice.

Two further points need making in thinking about presidential bureaucratic relations. First, some agencies may need Presidential support, because they lack natural constituencies in the United States or because they lack strong sources of Congressional support. If they need it, they may do quite a lot to get it—they may inform him of what they do and why, tell him what he wants to hear (and not mention what he doesn't), and try hard to do (or at least appear to do) what he wants done. Such agencies, those that need the President, are most subject to his influence, though it would surely be a mistake to think that he can protect them wholly from the effects of public or Congressional hostility and wrath. At the other extreme there are agencies that have such strong support in Congress that they do not need the President. No matter what he thinks or tries to do they know Congress will help them. Such agencies can ignore the President at least in substance while he is powerless to influence or alter them. Such agency-congressional coalitions are important restraints on presidential power.

10 The Bureaucracy, the Congress, and the Courts

This chapter begins with some consideration of the matters that bring the Congress into contact with organizations of the executive branch.[1] This may seem simple, even elementary, but it is crucial to an understanding of Congressional bureaucratic relations. The second section is devoted to executive agencies and the attention and activity that they direct toward Congress. In a third section the variety of relationships that may exist between Congressional committees and executive agencies are considered, as are the conditions that may give rise to them. A fourth section discusses the limits that Congress operates within, and a final section considers briefly the connections between administrative agencies and the courts.

Occasions for Contact

Legislation. The most obvious link between Congress and the executive branch is legislation. Legislation can be developed in various ways; it may be developed in an agency, at the White House, by a particular congressman, or in committee. It may even be drafted initially by some unofficial group. But no matter how it starts, legislation (the legislative process) brings Con-

---

1. A standard work on Congressional-bureaucratic relations is Joseph P. Harris, *Congressional Control of Administration* (Washington: The Brookings Institution, 1964).

gress and the agencies together. When a bill is being drafted the views of the affected agency (or agencies) will be sought and their reactions noted. Professional staff in the Congress (both committee staff and individual staff) may work with agency staff to develop a workable and satisfactory bill. (Of course they need not, and if there are important party or ideological differences it is unlikely.) Prior consultation, however, may mean the difference between legislation that is implemented after it is signed and legislation that lies dormant. The difference between a workable program and one that is an administrative nightmare may be early and continuing consultation between Hill and agency staff.

After a bill is introduced in the House or Senate it is referred to a committee. Here most bills are quietly buried. But the chairman of the committee may decide to hold hearings; and if an agency (or agencies) has an interest in the legislation, spokesmen will come to the hearing to provide their views. They can be expected, if they favor the legislation, to indicate that it is both necessary and beneficial. Inquiries may be focused on an agency's capacity to implement the legislation and agency spokesmen can be expected to respond positively if they favor the bill. Friendly congressmen may ask questions that have been pre-arranged between committee and agency staff and are designed to put the pending legislation and the agency in the best light possible. Of course if there are congressmen hostile to the agency or the legislation their questioning is likely to reveal this. All the agency can do is remain calm and deferential and hope for the best. After hearings a bill may be amended or rewritten, and agency personnel may be involved in the rewriting—though of course for political reasons they may be snubbed. When a bill is brought to the floor and debated it is possible (except under a closed rule) to alter or amend it further, and agency staff may be called on to provide information about the probable effect of the proposed amendment. (They may not know, of course, and may simply have to guess like anybody else.)

Clearly, in addition to formal testimony in committee hearings, there is likely to be a good deal of less formal contact between agency representatives and congressmen and their staffs. The volume of such contact may be affected by such considerations as the size of the agency, the amount of new legislation that it is trying to get or has an interest in, whether the Congress and the Administration are controlled by the same party, and how aggressive in the legislative process the agency spokesmen are or want to appear. The informal contact can be summed in a single word, lobbying. To get legislation they want, or to prevent legislation they do not want, agency (and White House) staff may lobby. In the departments this effort is commonly spearheaded by an Assistant Secretary for Legislation and in the White House by a Special Assistant for Congressional Liaison. It is these people that at least in principle try to sell what as a whole can be called the administration's legislative program. They provide information, bargain and negotiate, keep track of probable votes, anticipate roll calls, apply pressure where needed. Their tactics may range from a fairly straightforward demonstration of need, to seeing that a particular Senator gets a timely phone call from the President, to having past donors in a campaign suggest possible withdrawal of support if a Senator does not vote the preferred way.[2]

After a law is passed it must be implemented, which obviously is the task of the executive agencies. Congressmen may, of course, retain an interest in the details of implementation, in the substance of detailed regulations developed pursuant to general legislation, and in the possible future need for modification. In a sense, as governing shifts from legislation to administration, Congress and the executive agencies stay linked. But it is probably fair to say that agencies have a greater interest in legislation than Congress has in administration.

Budget. The need for money brings executive agencies together regularly with Congressional appropriations committees.[3] Every year agencies must come to Congress to obtain funds for the next fiscal year, and some must return during the course of a year for supplemental funds. Every agency has employees to be paid, space to be paid for, supplies to be purchased, and multiple other needs, from telephone service to travel—all so that the organization can continue and programs can be implemented. Virtually everything the government does

---

2. For more on this subject see Abraham Holtzman, *Legislative Liaison: Executive Leadership in Congress* (Chicago: Rand McNally, 1970).

3. A classic work is Aaron Wildavsky, *The Politics of the Budgetary Process* (Boston: Little, Brown & Co., 1964). See also Robert Ash Wallace, *Congressional Control of Spending* (Detroit: Wayne State University Press, 1960).

costs money. Grants are given to state and local governments in hundreds of programs; the money involved is initially part of an HEW or HUD or DOT or whatever budget request initially. Grants or subsidies are given to individuals and institutions and companies; services are provided; regulations and laws are enforced. Without funds, programs can't get off the paper they are written on.

Each January the President of the United States sends to Congress a Budget Message. In it he outlines his requests for funds for the executive agencies for the coming year. The message is but a brief summary of much lengthier and more detailed budget documents that also go to the Congress. Consideration begins in the Appropriations Committee of the House of Representatives but after largely ceremonial testimony before the whole committee by the Director of the Office of Management and Budget and the Secretary of the Treasury and perhaps other high administration officials, more specialized subcommittees that have jurisdiction over a particular agency or agencies take over.[4] These subcommittees hold hearings on the budget requests of particular agencies, and the chiefs with their staffs come to explain, defend, and justify their requests. Their expenditures in the year past and increases they propose for the coming year may be questioned, and particular congressmen may also ask about events or activities involving the agency that have come to their attention. Waste, duplication, economy, and efficiency are words that commonly arise during the course of a hearing.

After the subcommittee hearings appropriations bills are considered in executive session ("marked up"), and it is common for agencies to find their budget requests cut, if only by symbolic amounts. The subcommittee reports are commonly accepted both by the parent Appropriations Committee and by the whole House. After an appropriations bill is voted on by the House (the budget as a whole is never voted on but rather as

---

4. A lengthy study of the House Appropriations Committee is Richard F. Fenno, *The Power of the Purse: Appropriations Politics in Congress* (Boston: Little, Brown & Co., 1966). Chapters 6 and 7 deal particularly with the committee and executive agencies. A shorter and very interesting book on both appropriations committees is Michael Kirst, *Government Without Passing Laws* (Chapel Hill: University of North Carolina Press, 1969).

several separate bills), it moves to the Senate where with some variation the play is reenacted in abbreviated form.[5] Hearings are held in committee, and agency executives come to testify; they may request that cuts sustained in the House be restored. After hearings and final drafting, appropriations bills are taken to the floor for final passage. If the Senate version of an appropriations bill differs from the House version (not an uncommon occurrence), a conference between representatives of the two houses is necessary so that both houses can be presented with an identical bill for passage and signature by the President.

For all their visibility it would be wrong to think that budget-related contacts between Congress and executive officials were limited to hearings. The hearings are the occasion for formal, public contact, but much goes on behind the scenes and throughout the year. Budget officers in the agencies and the staffs of appropriations subcommittees are likely to have frequent contacts. If deviation from predicted spending patterns appears desirable or necessary during the year, the committee staff may be informed and they are likely to know in advance if requests for additional funds are going to be made. Budget staff in the agencies may work hard to keep the committee staff informed of agency activity and indeed may try to suggest questions that their chiefs would like to answer in the hearings. By the same token friendly committee staff may inform agency staff in advance about the questions likely to be asked and what to be prepared for. This account must immediately be qualified. While a cooperative relationship is certainly possible (and from an agency's point of view, given its dependent status, desirable) there can also be conflict and little communication between agency staff and congressional staff. For their own and the agency's good, agency staff may try to inform, to co-opt, to win over congressional staff and indeed congressmen themselves. But that is hardly always possible. Indeed, no matter what, some agencies may find themselves confronted with apparently implacable hostility from at least some congressmen—and one of them may be a subcommittee chairman. This can obviously happen if an agency is carrying out a program that the chair-

---

5. Appropriations activity in the Senate is the subject of Stephen Horn's *Unused Power: The Work of the Senate Committee on Appropriations* (Washington: The Brookings Institution, 1970).

man, for whatever reason, thinks is simply a waste of public funds.

It would be hard to overemphasize the importance of the appropriations process or the need it creates for executive agencies and Congressional committees to work together. Agencies may or may not have an active legislative program, they may be staffed entirely with career personnel, and they may never send a reorganization to Congress. They may be noncontroversial, and they may never be investigated. But each year they must come for money. Money is *the* link between Congress and the executive agencies.

It should be noted here that there are ways to avoid the scrutiny and displeasure of an appropriations subcommittee. They range from the corporate form of organization to the use of trust funds (as in social security) to permanent appropriations for one program or another (the program to remove surplus agricultural products) to the setting of special amounts to be appropriated in the substantive legislation. The importance of these various ways around annual budgeting is emphasized by the fact that over half the 1973 budget was made up of such uncontrollable items.[6]

Additional Reasons for Contact.   For a number of reasons agencies may decide to reorganize or the Office of Management and Budget or the President may decide that an agency or agencies should be reorganized. In two ways this process will directly involve the Congress.[7] The President may use his reorganization authority to propose changes in the structure of an organization or in its location within the executive branch. Relying on this authority the President may propose shifting an agency from one department to another or incorporating an independent agency into a department; he may propose altering jurisdictions, changing names, or expanding missions. If he uses his reorganization authority the President must submit a re-

---

6. For brief recent comment on the ways around annual budgeting see Murray L. Weidenbaum and Dan Larkins, *The Federal Budget for 1973* (Washington: American Enterprise Institute for Public Policy Research, 1972).

7. See Harold Seidman, *Politics, Position and Power: The Dynamics of Federal Organization* (New York: Oxford University Press, 1970). Chapter 2 is titled, "Executive Branch Organizations: View from the Congress."

organization plan to the Congress, and either house has sixty days in which to veto it. Commonly the Government Operations Committees of both houses hold hearings on the matter, and agency and Office of Management and Budget spokesmen come to explain and support the plan.

Alternatively, and more commonly for major reorganizations such as the creation of a new Cabinet department, Presidential proposals take the form of suggested legislation (a draft bill) that goes through the usual legislative process. The phrase "usual legislative process" includes of course not only hearings and administration testimony but also more informal (and probably more important) administration lobbying as well as lobbying by interests and groups who think themselves affected. If successful in both houses and signed by the President, the reorganization becomes law and is implemented.

Staffing also brings Congress and executive agencies together. By far the largest part of the executive branch is under some sort of career merit system, but heads of organizations and their immediate staffs are presidentially appointed and subject to confirmation by the Senate. When an appointment is made or rather when a nomination is made, confirmation hearings are held by the Senate committee having jurisdiction over the agency in which the nominee will serve. A man (or woman) nominated to be Secretary of Agriculture will be the subject of a hearing conducted by the Senate Agriculture Committee, and a new Secretary of Defense will attend a hearing held by the Senate Armed Services Committee. Commonly these hearings are simply a formality and confirmation is a foregone conclusion. But they can provide an opportunity for Senators to inquire carefully into the background, qualifications, credentials, views, and intentions of the nominee. They provide an opportunity also for members of the committee (whom the nominee will have to work with in the future) to make their views and wishes known. At a confirmation hearing committee members can criticize past policies of the department and indicate the kinds of changes they hope will take place. It should be emphasized that confirmation hearings are often a formality, and in any case they do not provide anything like an opportunity for searching inquiry or regular review. But they do provide a committee that wants it an additional chance to insert its views into the administrative process.

Congressional committees and executive branch organizations may be brought together fairly forcefully by Congressional inquiries or investigations.[8] Hearings may be held not on bills but on problems, and executive officials may be called to explain their own positions and the activities (or the lack thereof) of their organization. From a recent catalog of U.S. government publications come the following examples:

> Evaluation of Administration on Aging and conduct of White House Conference on Aging, hearings, 92nd Congress, 1st Session, by Special Senate Committee on Aging.
>
> Unemployment among older workers, hearings before subcommittee on Employment and Retirement Incomes, 92nd Congress, 1st Session.
>
> Cost and adequacy of fuel oil, hearings before the Subcommittee on Small Business, 92nd Congress, 1st Session.
>
> Proposed reduction in HUD personnel, hearings before the Subcommittee on Housing and Urban Affairs, 92nd Congress, 1st Session, to hear Secretary George Romney explain proposed reduction in personnel at Dept. of Housing and Urban Development, Oct. 26, 1971.
>
> Private Welfare and Pension Plan Study, 1971, hearings before Subcommittee on Labor, 92nd Session, 1st Session.

And this of course is only a tiny sample of the total activity. In the past House and Senate Committees have investigated topics ranging from wartime profiteering, to communists in government, to the operation of Selective Service. The range of possible topics is at least as broad as the range of current and possible future action by the United States government. The outcome of the investigation may be changed administrative regulations and behavior, increases in appropriations, proposals for new legislation to cope with newly discovered problems, or nought. Of course it is true that hearings may be conducted simply to document or publicize or dramatize conditions or problems that were already known or at least thought to exist.

While considering congressional inquiries the House and Senate Government Operations Committees deserve special men-

---

8. Many books on Congress deal with Congressional investigations. For one on that subject exclusively see Telford Taylor, *Grand Inquest: The Story of Congressional Investigations* (New York: Simon and Schuster, 1955).

tion.[9] These committees have very broad jurisdiction and can inquire into the administration of virtually any program. Members of the Senate Government Operations Committee especially have used their position to publicize their particular interests. The House Government Operations Committee has tried to distinguish administrative from policy matters (aware of course that this really isn't possible) and focus its attention on such administrative problems as waste and duplication, economy and efficiency, while leaving more substantive matters to the other committees. But as the Government Operations Committee is free to inquire into the operations of any government agency its jurisdiction overlaps that of virtually every other committee while being broader than that of any other single committee— with the obvious exception of the Appropriations Committee.

A final set of matters that brings Congressmen into contact with executive agencies can be labeled "constituent services and inquiries." Individual citizens and organizations routinely write their congressmen for help in dealing with administrative agencies. (This may make more sense that writing an agency directly; a Congressional inquiry is likely to be answered much faster than a letter from John Q. Citizen.) Did a constituent not receive a social security benefit check that he was entitled to, or is he having trouble with the Department of Agriculture? Has the Immigration and Naturalization Service apparently acted unfairly, or was a decision of the Environmental Protection Agency entirely too permissive with regard to pollution? In all these cases and hundreds more, a citizen may take his pen and write his congressman. The congressman in turn will get in touch with the agency concerned (perhaps through a staff assistant who specializes in the business) and ask for a report. He may stop there and simply tell the citizen what he found out. But he may also detect and get corrected any thoughtless, arbitrary, or improper action. A Congressional inquiry may serve to hasten decision and action: the administrative process gets nudged along, the bureaucratic log jam is broken. Because of such service the congressman can be and often is an important intermediary between agencies and citizens. The Congressman is in a position to serve as a sort of ombudsman, dealing with

---

9. See Thomas A. Henderson, *Congressional Oversight of Executive Agencies: A Study of the House Committee on Government Operation* (Gainesville: University of Florida Press, 1970).

the questions and complaints that his constituents have about governmental action and inaction of one kind or another.

The Care of Congressmen

Relations with Congress are so important that top officials (Secretaries and their immediate assistants, agency heads, and bureau chiefs) devote a substantial amount of time to communicating with and trying to inform, instruct, and persuade congressmen. Department Secretaries regularly and repeatedly testify before House and Senate committees. In addition many departments have assistant secretaries whose main or sole task is liaison with Congress. Below the departmental level specific positions for legislative liaison are less common; but bureau chiefs testify before committees, and their budget officers are frequently in contact with appropriations committee staffs.

In testimony before committees officials commonly are deferential. Cabinet secretaries are polite and respectful even when the questioning gets heated, and most have learned that it does not pay to argue or talk back. The informed official prepares carefully for a hearing, even to the point of going through a dress rehearsal. Past hearings are reviewed for clues to likely questions, and attention is paid to the home districts and the states that the committee members come from with the hope of being prepared for likely questions.

Given the importance of Congress and its committees it is small wonder that executive agencies are attentive to congressmen and allocate resources and make decisions that may benefit influential congressmen. Inquiries from congressmen are answered promptly, often with 24 hours of receipt. Research may be done for congressmen and speeches written. Bureaus and departments are more than willing to help a congressman draft legislation that pertains to them. If a congressman wants to inspect a project or facility, the concerned organization will frequently arrange the trip. Favorable decisions affecting a particular district or state (announcement of a large government contract or a new post office) may be announced through a congressman's or senator's office. And of course facilities may be put in states or districts where they may do some legislative good.

Not all executive organizations are equally well off when it comes to doing favors and building support in Congress. Perhaps best off are the armed forces; they can arrange inspection tours to European bases or the naval facilities in Hawaii. In addition they maintain facilities in numerous states and are constantly awarding contracts. They can assign many men to Congressional liaison and still accomplish their missions without strain. Smaller organizations are not able to devote such substantial resources to the cause of Congressional good will and of course many organizations carry out programs that do not lend themselves to gaining Congressional support. Still, any agency can be expected to do all it can to preserve Congressional good will or at least neutrality.

These points must (as usual) be qualified. Congressional good will is a useful shorthand term, but it does not reveal the substantial differences that can exist among congressmen, committees, and the two Houses. Action favored by one committee or some congressmen may be viewed with some displeasure or simply be anathema in other quarters of the Congress. The flexible administrator may be able to find middle ground, but he may have to decide whose support he wants and needs and whose displeasure he must live with. As important as differences within the Congress are the differences that can and do occur between the Congress and the Administration. When these occur, the agency executive is in the middle and again must choose. Congressmen may ask for information or for documents, and the President may instruct that they not be provided. The executive who carries this response to a committee hearing may be hard put to maintain strong friendships in the Congress. (The leak is a form of compromise.) And of course we must remember the goals of agencies—autonomy, growth, and others. In trying to attain these goals some compromises with Congressional cooperation may be required. The point of course is that executives, when other things are equal, try to maintain cooperative relations with Congress, but other things are commonly not equal.

Committees and Agencies: Varied Relationships

Relationships between Congressional committees and executive agencies can range from mutual admiration through benevolent neutrality and skepticism to something approaching mutual antipathy. Such a range is not surprising when we stop to consider the variety of activities the agencies carry out and the variety of views, values, and ideological positions in the Congress and the bureaucracy.

Many of the relationships are idiosyncratic, that is, they vary with the individuals, organizations, and issues involved. As personalities in the executive branch and the Congress come and go, the relations change. From all reports, HEW Secretary Finch got on poorly with House and Senate Committees, to the detriment of programs that the Administration favored. His replacement, Elliot Richardson, enjoyed at least initially much more cordial relations. But as the Nixon administration moved into its fourth year it was not clear that the Secretary of Health, Education, and Welfare could maintain simultaneously his cordial relationships with Democratic congressmen and his loyalty to a Republican administration. Clark Clifford as Secretary of Defense appears to have gotten on much better with members of Armed Services committees than did his predecessor, Robert McNamara. At a much lower level it was clear for years that J. Edgar Hoover enjoyed spectacularly good relations with the Congress; whether his successor can do as well will be a question. Not only executives leave or get replaced, of course. John Fogarty in the House and Lister Hill in the Senate for years were strong advocates of health legislation, and the National Institutes of Health in their view deserved all possible support. John Fogarty died, Lister Hill lost an election, and NIH found its situation changed.

Relations between committees and agencies do not depend entirely on the personal relations between the principles involved, though their importance should not be underestimated. A man who, for whatever reason, perhaps past Congressional experience or simply affability, gets on well with congressmen is an asset to his organization. But what else is important? Some agencies are engaged in work that congressmen are likely to benefit from directly. The classic example of course is the Corps of Engineers, an organization responsible for public-works projects in states and congressional districts across the land. It is so close to congress that many congressmen are inclined to think of it as an arm of Congress rather than part of the executive branch. Other agencies, though perhaps not benefitting Congressmen so directly, may be engaged in politically popular activities; the Social Security Administration is an example. As long as such agencies appear to be doing an effective job and serving citizens well, they are likely to get on well in Congress. (Such an agency will have trouble, however, if it suggests cutting back an apparently beneficial program.) In the field of social welfare the image of organizations is probably fairly stable, but the image of national security organizations goes up and down. In times of war or crisis the mission of the Department of Defense seems vital, and the armed forces are welcome in the halls of Congress. But in peace time the armed forces seem to many an unnecessary drain on the budget. Recently (1972), for example, even the chairman of the Senate Armed Services Committee has appeared to question increases in the Department of Defense budget.

Some agencies may appear to congressmen to be doing nothing that benefits congressmen or their constituents while at the same time they are using up tax dollars. The Agency for International Development is a prime example of an organization carrying out a program widely unpopular in the Congress. (It should be noted for the record that AID has many domestic beneficiaries. Numerous individuals, universities, and corporations have benefitted from AID employment and contracts, but this fact is not widely appreciated, and AID *is* unpopular.) The United States Information Agency is another agency carrying out a program that appears to have few domestic beneficiaries. "Welfare" and particularly Aid to Families with Dependent Children now housed at the federal level in the Social and Rehabilitation Service is an example of a domestic program that is highly unpopular, no doubt because the beneficiaries are themselves unpopular and have little political influence.

Agencies that because of their programs are unpopular quite clearly have a problem. They may cope with it by trying to achieve good personal relations between top administrators and congressmen; by trying to get the President to use his influence (a congressman may vote to support a program not because he favors it, but because it behooves him to support the President); by linking activities to popular symbols—fighting communism, getting people to work, helping mothers and children. Of course such tactics may not work, and then one may see reorganization, personnel shifts, and new titles.

To all these observations one can add that conservative congressmen are likely to view dimly organizations engaged in spending and social service, southerners may have negative attitudes about civil-rights activities and the organizations that carry them out, and liberals may be hostile to police agencies, the military, and the intelligence apparatus. Agencies must hope that the seniority system does not bring ideological opponents to the chairmanship of their committees. If it happens administrators can be thankful for two houses.

To sum these comments we need only emphasize again that the relations between congressmen and agencies are variable, but also to a degree predictable and controllable. The astute President appoints men who are likely to at least stand a chance of getting on well on the Hill. Administrators who get on well recognize the role of Congress and its real and potential power. They also recognize that congressmen must get elected and that legislative politics calls for flexibility and willingness to bargain.

The Limits on Congress

Clearly the executive branch is linked in many ways to the Congress; just as clearly there are many points at which the Congress can apply pressure on the Executive Branch with some expectation of results. It can fail to act or can act negatively on legislation, funds, and appointments. In a sense Congress has an apparently ample supply of political resources which it can use to get what it wants from the Executive agencies. But perhaps less obvious to the casual observer, Congress is also short in some critical areas.[10] And these shortages lessen the value of the resources that are possessed.

A crucial point is that congressmen frequently lack information that would help them use their power effectively and make informed choices and decisions. Compared to administrative officials, they are more likely to be information-short, which puts them at a disadvantage. In hearings they may ask no questions or irrelevant questions; they may not ask questions that result in useful information. They may not criticize because they do not know what to criticize, or they may criticize with little effect. They may not know what documents or reports or agreements to request. They may be given answers, facts and figures,

10. The limits on Congress and its future role have received a good deal of attention in recent years. A useful single place to find a variety of views is Ronald C. Moe, *Congress and the President* (Pacific Palisades: Goodyear Publishing Co., 1972).

and not be able to interpret them. These few sentences suggest the implications of the information problem.

What explains the lack of information? A number of things. Congressional resources for gathering information are limited. Individual congressmen have limited time, limited staff, limited expertise, and possibly limited interests. They are involved in campaigning, visiting back home, constituent service, committee hearings, bill writing, and numerous other things. A good deal of such activity has nothing to do with getting policy-relevant information. Even when they are learning about one problem or policy there are obviously scores of others that they are ignoring, not learning about. Congress as an institution also lacks staff and expertise. Compared just to the President, Congress is staff poor, with nothing like the Office of Management and Budget for budget review and program analysis or the Domestic Council for problem study and program development. When one looks at the executive branch as a whole, it is even plainer that the Congress is at an information-gathering disadvantage. Every agency in more or less degree has intelligence and analysis capability. This is much less true of the Congress.

It is worth emphasizing that more staff might not necessarily be helpful. Consider just the time and expertise of a congressman. He has limited time (the law of the 24-hour day) and virtually unlimited demands on it. He can quickly suffer from information overload. Even if more information were available he might not be able to absorb it and attend to it. And given his limited expertise he might not be able to comprehend it. This is not meant in any negative sense. A congressman may be a very able lawyer (very many are), but his ability to understand quickly scientific or medical information or the policy implications in sets of statistical data may be limited. Engineering data and economic studies may both be just mysteries to him.

One can come at the information problem in quite a different way by noting that between executive agencies and the Congress there may be (frequently is) some conflict of interest. Agencies want more money, Congress wants to provide less, or vice versa. Agencies want more autonomy and flexibility; Congress wants more control. Agencies want to carry out policy; Congress does not want it carried out. The result is that executive agencies may (and do) withold information from the Congress.

We have just seen that executive agencies are commonly much better equipped to collect and analyze information than

Congress is. A consequence of this is that congressmen must often rely on executive agencies for information and analysis. But this means at the extreme that Congress knows what executive agencies want it to know or are willing for it to know. Perhaps this overstates the point, but conditions move in this direction. Executive agencies provide information that it is in their interest to provide and may not provide information that would be detrimental to their interests.

On occasion agencies or officials (especially perhaps in the military and foreign policy fields) may refuse to provide information that is asked for a Congressional committee by relying on the doctrine of executive privilege.[11] Yet to do so is a sure way to exacerbate relations with the Congress, and Congress does have some power. Thus it is likely to be in the agency's interest to answer explicit requests for information, though of course they may not if the costs of doing so appear to be greater than the costs of refusal. Probably more common is the situation in which information is simply not volunteered and not knowing of its availability, congressmen don't ask for it.

The information handicaps that Congress labors under serve to substantially limit its effectiveness in controlling, checking, or supervising the executive agencies. But there are other limits that deserve at least brief mention. Between some committees or congressmen and some agencies (or their heads) there may be friendships or alliances which serve to mute criticism and limit supervision. Some agencies may be so small or routine or apparently noncontroversial that they do not attract attention and are thus free to go their autonomous way. Some agencies may have such strong constituency support that Congressional criticism would be perilous. Rather different from any of these considerations is the notion that thanks to the seniority system in Congress it is older men who are powerful in committee, and they may be among those least well equipped to understand or cope with rapid social and technological change. The committee system itself, with each committee having its

---

11. For a thorough review of executive privilege see *Executive Privilege: The Witholding of Information by the Executive,* Hearings before the Subcommittee on Separation of Powers of the Committee on Judiciary, United States Senate, 92nd Congress, 1st Session (Washington: U.S.G.P.O., 1972). In addition to testimony this volume contains several reprinted articles and a substantial bibliography.

jurisdiction, may limit the substance, effectiveness, and range of the review that can take place.

The end result is that Congressional review of administration or Congressional control of administration is not particularly effective or substantial. Or at least it often is not so. Investigations, hearings, and decisions may be symbolic assertions of authority but not have much effect on the reality of administrative behavior. It remains to add a cautionary note. Evaluation of Congressional effectiveness is clearly subjective. Others might look at Congress and the bureaucracy and judge the effectiveness of Congress very differently and more favorably.

Congress in the future is likely to be even less effective in its supervisory Congressional oversight role than it has been in the recent past. It will continue to be made up of amateurs, lack information, and be pressed for time. The administration will be both professionalized and specialized. In addition, the problems apparently demanding government action are likely to grow in number; and the scope of government activities, the size of the public sector, and the variety of government organizations and functions are likely to increase. In at least one view of the future the Congress will be increasingly at sea.

The functions of Congress, as the government becomes more professionalized, may become increasingly formal and ritualistic. The role of Congress may be to grant legitimacy to actions that it alone could neither call forth nor prevent. It may be able to investigate and inquire and no doubt will have the right to be informed. On some occasions, as now, the advice of Congress will have to be sought. But all of this will simply amount to taking care of the formalities, the amenities of political life. The Congress will be unable to alter the course of events or the will of the executive.

This of course will not happen all at once, though it is happening even now. And on occasion congressmen and others may resist, indeed try to reverse the process of erosion. One sees attempts to increase Congressional staff and create organizations for the Congress that are analogous to some of those in the Executive Office of the President. But even though the suggestion of these is highly likely, their creation—let alone effectiveness— is unlikely. Congress is not only multi-membered, it is also multi-headed. Each member there is independently elected, and it may prove to be impossible for such an organization effectively to use staff organization responsible to Congress as a whole. In any case Congressional staff organizations would surely meet (and have) the same difficulties in getting information and interpreting it that congressmen themselves have confronted.

Judicial Supervision of Administration

If it is true that Congress is limited in its ability to control the actions of administrators and administrative agencies, it is all the more true of the courts. The judicial system occupies an important place in American government, but it is important to remember that most administrative activity is not reviewed in the courts. Martin Shapiro makes this point in *The Supreme Court and Administrative Agencies*.

> . . . courts provide almost no effective check on what we typically think of as administration. When the Corps of Engineers builds a dam or when the Department of Health, Education, and Welfare prepares a research study on overcrowding in urban schools, there is almost no opportunity for judicial check on how efficiently, accurately, or fairly these agencies conduct their actual operations. The planning, research and development, spending and physical operations—hauling mail, printing money, storing grain —of administrative agencies are largely beyond the realm of judicial inspection. Indeed most of the business of large corporations—by correspondence, consultations, interoffice memos and telephone calls—all of which rarely rise to legal significance. A very large share of even those agency decisions that do directly affect the legal rights of individual citizens cannot be appealed to the courts and an even larger share are not so appealed. Thus courts do not provide much of a check on the general operations of administrative agencies, the millions of decisions, actions, and physical operations that turn words on the statute books into tuberculosis vaccines, hot meals for school children, rockets, national parks, and college dormitories.[12]

12. Martin Shapiro, *The Supreme Court and Administrative Agencies* (New York: The Free Press, 1968), p. 13.

Some administrative activity can be and often is reviewed in the courts, or course. "Roughly 20 percent of the Supreme Court's written opinions concern administrative decisions."[13] Much of the legislation that Congress passes is very general and must be implemented by rules and regulations developed by executive agencies. The courts may be asked to determine whether these elaborations are consistent with the parent statute and whether they have been properly applied, as well as whether the parent statute, the implementing rules, and the actions of the administrative agencies conform to the requirements of the Constitution.

How can the courts go about this task? When citizens are prosecuted for violations of federal law, the behavior of administrative agencies may come under scrutiny. How was evidence obtained? How was a confession, if there is one, obtained? These are crucial questions, and if federal agents have violated constitutional guarantees they are unlikely to obtain a conviction. Knowing this of course they are likely to act with circumspection, especially in cases when a prosecution is likely to flow from an investigation. If the Selective Service system takes a man to court for failing to report for induction, the court may study the work of the Selective Service system and determine that the man being prosecuted was improperly classified. If the Internal Revenue Service takes a man to court for failing to pay his taxes, the court may have an opportunity to find out how the agency collected its evidence and whether its rules are consistent with the intent of Congress. Of course citizens do not always have to be prosecuted in the courts before they can challenge an administrative agency; in some circumstances they can initiate a challenge to administrative agencies. Shapiro stresses, however, "that the overwhelmingly typical action of courts in exercising review is to refuse to substitute their own decisions for those of the agency, and that only in a handful of the thousands of agency decisions made each year is there even an effort by the adversary party to get a second decision from the courts."[14]

But it is worthwhile also to call attention to a point made by Stephen Wasby; even though few cases get to court the decisions may be noted by administrators and effect their han-

---

13. Shapiro, *Supreme Court*, p. 13.
14. Shapiro, *Supreme Court*, p. 95.

dling of future cases.[15] But this is conjecture. There is little evidence concerning either the impact of court decisions or the lack of impact on the behavior of administration. Not much is known in this area. As an illustration of the point, note that the bibliography in Wasby's book on *The Impact of the United States Supreme Court* lists only two items dealing with the impact on the President and his administration—one article and Shapiro's book. Given the substantial importance of administration, the impact on administration of the courts would seem a fruitful field for study.

15. Stephen L. Wasby, *The Impact of the United States Supreme Court: Some Perspectives* (Homewood: Dorsey Press, 1970), p. 221.

11 Organizations, Their Clients, and the Public

We move in this chapter from consideration of the relations between administrative organizations and other official participants in the political/policy process to some consideration of the relations between administrative organizations and unofficial participants. In particular, we focus on the relations between agencies and their clients. Frequently one cannot understand policy-making—either the way it is made or why it comes out the way it does—without some appreciation of the agency-client relationship. The chapter begins with some brief consideration of the role of clienteles and then moves to a discussion of agencies and their clients. This section considers the complications that confront an agency having many clients whose interests differ, and it also discusses the various functions of government agencies and the consequences these have for relations with clients. In following sections some attention is given to the tactics of support and opposition and in this context the public relations of government agencies are discussed. In a final section some brief attention is given to the concept of the public interest.

Clienteles and Their Roles

At the start we can simply say that an agency's clientele is made up of those individuals or groups directly though perhaps not obviously affected by the activities of the agency. Clients may be benefitted; they may not be. They may be served well or ill by "their" agency. They may be cohesive, well organized, rich, and influential, or only latent—a group waiting to be organized. The word clientele, at least as developed in this chapter, covers a variety of relationships. Perhaps we should ask how the concept of clientele is related to or distinguished from the notion of interest group or pressure group?[1] Clearly these terms are related, but they are not quite synonyms. The notion of clientele denotes a special relationship with a particular administrative organization. The terms, however, are not mutually exclusive. The AFL-CIO is clearly an interest group; it is also the Department of Labor's clientele group. Though organized labor may have an interest in the decisions and programs of many agencies (and lobby them), one assumes both a special interest and special access in the Department of Labor. Similar things might be said about business and the Department of Commerce, agriculture and the Department of Agriculture, banking and the Treasury.

But here we should qualify the statement that clientele groups have special access to particular administrative organizations. An organization may have many clients and their interests may conflict, making it impossible for each one to be satisfied. Agencies may respond to some groups and not to others, and may not even grant access to some. We should distinguish between actual clienteles and latent clienteles. Actual clienteles can be defined as those groups that not only have a direct interest in an agency, but also have access and are served. Latent clienteles may have a direct interest, but little access.

One major function of clienteles is agency support. In helping to shape a supportive public opinion and in testimony before committees of the Congress, spokesmen for clientele groups can show support for an agency. Agencies may get legislation they want and expanded budgets. Clienteles may provide feedback on program effects, and they can be a source of information about the environment and can help an agency adjust its program and procedures to changed conditions. Clienteles may oppose an agency and in the press and in Congressional hearings

---

1. The literature on pressure groups is large. Three useful books are David Truman, *The Governmental Process* (New York: Alfred A. Knopf, 1952); Grant McConnell, *Private Power and American Democracy* (New York: Alfred A. Knopf, 1966); and Harmon Zeigler, *Interest Groups in American Society* (Englewood Cliffs: Prentice-Hall, 1964).

can make their opposition known. One can expect agencies both to avoid this when possible and to strive for enthusiastic support. But agencies may have many different clients. Support from one may bring opposition from another. The question may then be, whose support will help more and whose opposition hurt less?

Agencies and Their Clients

One way to identify clientele groups is to recall the structure of the executive branch and find associated groups. For many departments and agencies this would appear to be a simple task. One thinks immediately of the Veterans Administration and the veterans and especially the American Legion. One thinks of the Federal Communications Commission and the broadcasting industry or the National Traffic Safety Bureau and the automobile industry. One thinks of the Department of Labor and the AFL-CIO.

But it is necessary to be careful; we saw in Chapter 2 that major social (economic? political?) groups are hardly cohesive homogeneous bodies. With a variety of economic interests and several major organized groups it is not clear immediately who the clientele of the Department of Agriculture is. Or, rather, what is clear is that the Department of Agriculture has several clienteles. The question then is who is served how—an especially important question and one loaded with political consequences when the interests of different clienteles conflict and a choice must be made. An example may emphasize the point. The United States Forest Service is a constituent agency of the Department of Agriculture. The forests that it manages benefit, effect, or interest a variety of persons and groups, ranging from lumber companies, to stockmen, to environmentalists, to campers and hikers to (yes) the armed forces, who may use a forest for training purposes. It is hard to imagine a practice that would equally satisfy all these concerned but very different interests and easy to imagine a practice satisfactory to lumbermen but upsetting to conservationists. The complexities of agency-clientele relations begin to open up.

The Department of the Interior has similar problems. Or rather, the National Park Service and Bureau of Land Management are likely to have similar problems. The National Park Service may be caught between the demands of what might be called wilderness campers and civilized or convenience campers. The BLM, an agency that manages millions of acres of public land that is in neither national forests nor parks, is likely to be caught between the demands of different types of users and also the demands of conservationists.

A different kind of clientele problem is illustrated by the Bureau of Mines, also a constituent of the Department of Interior. Among its other responsibilities are the enforcement of mine safety regulations. Here of course the interests of mine operators (management) and mine workers (labor) may be in conflict. Both groups can be construed as clients of the Bureau of Mines, but it is hard to imagine that the Bureau could make both sets equally happy. It must choose. One can look at virtually any of the Cabinet departments and their constituents and find these sorts of problems. In the Department of Health, Education, and Welfare, the regulations and decisions of the Food and Drug Administration very clearly affect the pharmaceutical industry, but they also affect those who buy medicine. Particular decisions favorable to the pharmaceutical industry may be antithetical to the interests of consumers. Although in the past consumers have not been well organized, they can be thought of as part of the FDA's clientele. Less obvious is the conflict between private education and public education that is presided over by the Office of Education. In transportation one finds competing modes of transportation—and also consumers. The same things are true of HUD.

If one looks at the independent regulatory agencies, similar problems are again found. The Interstate Commerce Commission counts among its clients the railroad industry, the trucking industry, and buses. As these compete with one another—at least trucking competes with railroad freight—it is entirely possible that decisions favorable to one carrier will go against another. In such a situation agency clientele relations can be complicated. And of course the consumer is also involved. Tariff increase requests granted by the ICC may favor a carrier but work a hardship on shippers. The action that develops support from one source creates hostility in another. Similar complications exist within the SEC, the FPA, the FCC, and other regulatory agencies. Not only are there different industries or different companies there are also consumers—members of the public—whose interests may conflict or appear to with those of industry.

The agency-client relationship can be explored well beyond

these fairly obvious examples. From one point of view agencies
of the government distribute benefits and burdens, or advantages
and disadvantages. One can ask what benefits are the clients
getting and what clients are getting them? How are the disadvantages or the burdens being distributed? What is the agency
getting or what is happening to it as a result? By distributing
benefits or simply by not distributing burdens (read by not enforcing a law or by enforcing it flexibly or by not issuing a new
regulation), an agency may avoid conflict with a politically powerful group and may indeed gain its support in budgetary battles.
The personal life of administrators may become more pleasant.
The way that an agency allocates the benefits and burdens at
its disposal may affect its clients, the agency-clientele relationship, and the agency. It should be emphasized that how the
benefits are allocated may not be an internal matter but of
some interest to congressmen, White House staffers, inquiring
journalists, and other interested parties. This interest itself
may affect the decisions and complicate agency-client relations.

It is worthwhile pushing the concepts of burden and
benefit further in order to indicate the variety of options open
to administrative agencies in their dealings with clienteles.
Taken together administrative agencies regulate, distribute, and
extract—to name only three activities.[2] Consider first regulation. Clients may be given substantial opportunity to participate
in the drafting of regulations that affect them, or they may
participate only formally or scarcely at all. Regulations themselves may be strict, even harsh, or they can be lax or simply
nonexistent. (That is, a particular client activity or facet of its
production may go unregulated. New automobiles did not always have price stickers on their windows; cigarettes did not
always have a warning on the package.)

But even this is not all. The enforcement of regulations
can move from strict through sporadic to virtually nil. And at
least in principle enforcement can vary with each client and
each regulation. The result of course is that clients may benefit

---

2. For further discussion along these lines see Theodore Lowi,
"American Business, Public Policy, Case Studies, and Political Theory," in
World Politics, Vol. XVI, No. 4, July 1964, pp. 677–715; Randall Ripley
(ed.) *Public Policies and Their Politics* (New York: W. W. Norton, 1966);
and Robert H. Salisbury, "The Analysis of Public Policy: A Search for
Theories and Roles," in Austin Ranney (ed.) *Political Science and Public
Policy* (Chicago: Markham Publishing Co., 1968), pp. 151–175.

enormously from the support, interest, and good will of administrative agencies; and they may work to get these. It is true also that agencies may benefit from the interest, support, and good will of their clients, especially if their clients are politically visible and influential. Mutual adjustments or accommodations may come about that permit the prudent enforcement of sensible or practical regulations. The point of all this is that regulatory agencies are in a position to distribute benefits and burdens, and how they do it may affect their relations with their clients.

A statement implied in the preceding paragraph is that agencies may not view all clients as equal. This point deserves to be made explicit. Latent clients—those for example not well organized or visible (this in the past has been true of consumers, though that appears to be rapidly changing) and thus unable to bring influence to bear—may not get much attention from an agency. Clients vary in the status of their members, in the resources they command, in their access both to the agency and to other points in the bureaucracy, to congressional committees, and to the political party machinery. A well-organized group or a company that has good access and commands resources is in a more advantageous position for influencing agency activity and agency decisions. A group that is not well put together or lacks resources and access may have to take what the agency gives. (Part of the politics of bureaucracy and an interesting part is the struggle of potential clients for access to and influence in the agencies that affect them.)

Some agencies are extractive. The Internal Revenue Service of the Treasury Department provides the clearest example, but not the only one. In some sense any agency that charges fees for the use of its services, facilities, or resources is performing an extractive function. And from another, very different perspective, the Selective Service System performed an extractive function. A little thought will suggest how clienteles want to be affected and how they can be affected. If one starts with the simple assumption that groups, firms, or individuals want to minimize their payments or protect themselves from hardship, it is a short step to the notion that they will seek to lower the amounts they pay to government agencies and may seek favorable tax treatment. They will try to pay as little as possible for what they get, whether it is irrigation water or grazing rights, or timber or whatever. (This is the equivalent of seeking to avoid onerous regulations.) Because the interests seeking low

payments may have access to and support in Congress and because to continue pleasantly an agency may want both the
support of users and congressmen it may agree to low payments,
indeed almost appear to propose them. Low payments may in
fact be so low that they are below cost and a particular interest
winds up being subsidized in part by the general taxpayers.
But taxpayers in general are largely unorganized, and the existence and extent of the subsidy may not be known or understood.
So it continues: an interest immediately benefitted is happy and
an agency is supported or at least avoids trouble.

Besides regulating and extracting, Government agencies
provide services and subsidies. Such agencies would appear sure
of support from their clienteles, but there are problems even
here. Subsidies may be low or high and easier or harder to
qualify for, as may services. Either may be bound or not in red
tape and be provided more or less quickly and efficiently. Conditions for eligibility may be few and flexible or the reverse.
The point is that a serving or subsidizing agency may not be
automatically supported by its clientele and indeed may be the
subject of some criticism.

There are a number of complicating points. The demand for
a free good is likely quickly to exhaust the supply, and thus it
may not be possible to fill demands from some members of a
clientele. Some members may then be dissatisfied. Alternatively,
conditions and restrictions may be set on the distribution of
services and subsidies, but this too may leave some members
of the clientele dissatisfied. Of course an agency may try to expand the supply of its resources so that it can respond to more
demands, but at some point the outsider who receives no benefit
but who pays taxes and is interested in economy may complain
and try to hold down costs.

Sooner or later an agency has to restrict its services, running
the risk of conflict with its clientele. Much depends, of course,
on who the clientele is and how demanding. If a clientele is not
large and has substantial influence its demands may be met at
a high level indefinitely. But if a clientele is of low status, such
as public assistance beneficiaries, and their demands are growing, there is likely to be constant complaint from outsiders. The
welfare agency must respond both to those who think it is not
doing enough or providing enough and those who think that too
much is being given away to too many. If the cost of services
or subsidies is well publicised then a service agency may be

caught between those who want (require) benefits and those who feel burdened by them. However, not all subsidies are widely known and some that are, are widely accepted. Veterans' pensions might be an example or, even more, the educational allowances that veterans receive. In this case the agency is not likely to be cross-pressured (not as likely), the benefitting clientele can be served, and a supportive relationship becomes almost automatic. (In this it should be clear that while generally it is in an agency's interest to serve its clientele, it is also in its interest to survive and thus it may be forced to compromise and cut back more than some of its beneficiaries think proper.)

Finally we can note that agencies procure and use a variety of material—supplies, equipment, services. The agencies' suppliers may be included in our consideration of clienteles. Though this may appear to stretch the definition of clientele it is clear that suppliers may benefit from an agency's activity and may have a clear interest in the growth of an agency's size, responsibilities, and budget. In simple terms, the bigger the agency the more it may buy. It is this source of support, this definition of clientele, that one would keep in mind when trying to identify the clientele of an organization like the Agency for International Development. It may give away a lot overseas, but it buys a good deal in this country, and its purchases benefit domestic interests. The same point multiplied dozens of times over is of course true for the armed forces.

Although separated for discussion purposes, it is of course not necessary that an agency only regulate or collect taxes or provide service or whatever. A single agency may combine all these functions. A single agency could serve different groups or clienteles in different ways or it could both regulate and subsidize the same clientele. A speculation that may be worth consideration goes as follows: If an agency could both service and regulate it might be able to build support and allies with its services and thus reduce the pressure to gain support by lax enforcement of regulations. But there may be problems here. Perhaps worth noting also are the consequences of organizing special agencies that only deal with one group or interest or clientele. This may make it all but impossible for the agency to do other than the bidding of that interest if it is to retain support. An agency that deals with several groups may be able to operate more flexibly and independently.

Client Tactics

It was made clear in the preceding section that clients may have much to gain from an agency—good service, high subsidies, understanding enforcement of regulations, and so on. But this is not automatic; a clientele must have access to the agency and be able to influence it. Conversely, agencies want to be able to influence their clienteles; they want their clientele to support them, to come to their assistance in conflicts, and perhaps to help in implementing programs. How does each party go about trying to get what it wants?

Most generally it is useful to keep in mind the word exchange.[3] Agency-client relationships may be understood as exchange (or trade) relationships, with each trading what it has for what it wants. Of course neither side can trade or exchange just anything; it must be something that is wanted by the other side. Money, service, low fees, and understanding enforcement are things an agency may have that are wanted by a clientele. The clientele may have political support, access to the right Congressional committees, information; the leadership may be able to enlist the attention and cooperation of members. In various circumstances such things may seem desirable to an agency. Even the implicit (but rarely if ever explicit) understanding that a future job awaits in private business may be attractive to an agency executive; even if only unconsciously it may affect his behavior towards an industry or firm.

But, as usual, there are difficulties. The agency may not have or may not be able to provide what a clientele wants. This makes exchange impossible. Or it may not take place because a clientele cannot provide what an agency wants; it may be unorganized, invisible, not politically influential. The agency may then seek support and friendship elsewhere, from quarters that provide what it seeks. In the end a regulatory agency becomes in effect a service agency, servicing or at least benefitting those it was set up to regulate. Further, it may happen that parties to an exchange become dissatisfied with the bargain that they have. Either party may come to think that it is giving more than it is

---

3. Among useful works elaborating the concept of exchange are George Homans, *Social Behavior: Its Elementary Forms* (New York: Harcourt, Brace and World, 1961) and Peter Blau, *Exchange and Power in Social Life* (New York: John Wiley and Sons, 1964).

getting and raise its demands. If the new demands are met, the relationship is likely to continue. But if they are not, then the relationship may be severed and a supportive relationship shift to neutrality or opposition. Just because the terms of a relationship may change, both parties may try to have some slack resources with which to meet altered demands. There may come a point when one party or the other thinks that the costs of the relationship are simply greater than the benefits. Then the relationship is likely to be over.

Exchange is a useful way to begin consideration of agency-client relationships (who is getting what), but of course it is not the only way. Any discussion of the tactics of influence and support can get much more concrete. To enhance their chances of being influential within the government, interest groups often try to get their own organizations within the executive branch. A glance at the organizational structure of the Executive Branch gives a fairly accurate though perhaps somewhat dated notion of the influential interests in the country. Major social and economic sectors have Cabinet departments. Special groups of some importance may be represented by independent agencies or have their own offices and bureaus. Of course organizations may be set up to serve not some particular group but to cope with some particular problems. But the problems may affect particularly a limited number of people.

Why do interest groups want their own organization? Because with their own organization they know where to go when they want something and they do not have to compete for attention. As it is easier for the American Legion to influence the Veteran's Administration than the Department of Health, Education and Welfare, there is a Veteran's Administration carrying out programs very similar to many of the programs of HEW. To be sure the VA predates the organization of HEW, but when HEW was created many social organizations were incorporated into it. The Veterans Administration was not. (As the American Legion loses numbers and influence it is possible that VA will be incorporated into HEW or the organization that takes its place.) From any group's point of view, having its own organization may make control (or exchange) easier. If an interest group does not have its own organization, creating one may be one of its goals; a reorganization may be proposed that would create an organization to give special attention to the interests of the concerned group. It is common for a group to propose giving its organization Cabinet rank or to suggest that its concerns deserve the attention of an organization located within the Executive Office of the President.

From an interest group's point of view it is not enough for an organization working on the interest group's problems to exist; it is also important that the interest group be influential within that organization. To this end, interest groups may try to exercise some control over staff appointments in agencies relevant to their interests. Of course they may be able to exercise little or no control over civil service positions, but they may be able to influence the selection of political appointees. If they cannot actually recommend who should get the job, they may be able to at least exercise a veto. The goal of course is an administrator and top staff who are sympathetic and responsive. To be sure, different clienteles may compete for influence, and it is not unheard of for one group to get the organization it wanted, only to find it sooner or later staffed with representatives of opposing groups.

An interest group may also ask an agency to appoint advisory committees made up of representatives of those affected by the agency's program. Public hearings on regulations proposed by an agency may permit interest groups to make their views known to administrators. More informal contacts (lobbying the bureaucracy) also occur. Some groups may make no headway in direct attempts to influence administrative agencies. When this happens a group may try to influence the administrative process by going through Congress or the courts. If an interest group can enlist on its side an influential Congressman or a committee with jurisdiction over its agency then it may get what it wants. A simple opinion or wish on the part of a Congressman may be all that is needed to move an administrative agency in the desired direction. If more is needed, there is always the possibility of legislation. If a group does not have access to the Congress there is always the possibility of litigation, with the hope that a court decision can alter administrative behavior.

Groups may of course try to influence agencies by informing their members of pending agency action, suggesting appropriate responses, and coordinating activities. If the leadership and headquarters staff of a professional organization or union or other interest can mobilize its membership to write an agency and congressman (who may in turn contact the agency), unfavorable action may be avoided. Groups may also try to influence agencies indirectly by shaping public opinion. Although scarcely appropriate in all situations, there are occasions when going to the public may appear to make sense. If a rate increase is felt to be necessary, for example by natural gas producers, the case may be taken to the Federal Power Commission but also spelled out in advertisements appearing in major papers across the land. To ward off official complaint and inquiry electrical utilities may through advertising suggest how much they are doing to increase capacity, hold down costs, and serve consumers better. If the railroads think they are likely to be disadvantaged by regulations allowing longer or wider trucks on highways, one can imagine articles appearing in national magazines with such titles as "Danger on the Highway," articles with no visible connection to the railroad industry. The drug industry, which has been the subject of considerable criticism in recent years, may appreciate and support articles and press reports about the expense and hazards of research and about spectacular recoveries attributable to the miracles of modern medicine. The grocery industry and American agriculture, concerned about public unrest with rapidly rising prices, may take some pains to explain why costs go up and how the effects of price increases on individuals can be minimized (substitute chicken for beef, and peanut butter for chicken, and beans for peanut butter). They may also argue that government regulations won't work and may indeed make matters worse.

The goal of such activities of course is to reduce public hostility and increase public understanding and sympathy. The hope is that public interest in and support for unfavorable agency action will be reduced and favorable agency action (allow the price increase, don't regulate) will be understood and approved. What an interest wants to avoid is a flow of mail to an agency (and to Congress) demanding action that would be hard on it.

In thinking of group action or group attempts to influence administrative agencies, a few additional observations should be made. So far we have thought only of clienteles or groups, but it will be useful to have in mind other related terms. Once such is trade association; Washington, D.C., is full of them. Examples range from the National Association of Manufacturers (NAM) to the Sporting Firearms Manufacturers Institute, to the Manufacturing Chemists Association, to the Asbestos Information

Association. These are organizations that represent in Washington and in the media the interests of particular groups of related companies. They can be expected to speak up whenever legislation or administrative regulations affecting their members have been proposed and are being considered. If the Labor Department is considering setting more stringent standards for employee safety and is beginning to enforce more stringently existing standards under the Occupational Health and Safety Act of 1970 the NAM can be expected to ask questions and point to costs and the hardships that will be incurred. Unions, among other groups, are likely to be pointing to the necessity for action. Final action may be affected by how well each side advocates its views. In some respects our policy-making process is an adversary process. The values or positions not well represented by alert, articulate spokesmen may get the short end.

Lobbyist is of course another term to have in mind. It may be most common to view a lobbyist as someone—a former congressman, a well-connected lawyer, a one-time journalist or public relations man—who knows his way around Congress and advocates one cause or another. There is something in this view, but it is important to remember that lobbyists cover not only Capitol Hill but also the bureaucracy, and if they work only the bureaucracy they will not be required to register and report their expenditures. Bureaucratic lobbying is, if not hidden lobbying, at least much less visible lobbying. Some lobbyists (or legislative aids or staff assistants—probably no one is officially titled lobbyist) work only for a particular organization and do it on a full-time basis. The AFL-CIO, the American Medical Association, the NAM, or the National Rifle Association have full time staff. But smaller groups and interests without the resources or need for full-time staff may hire representatives who represent other clients as well. Washington has firms of lobbyists for hire, though they are likely to be officially either public relations or law firms. Washington has many law firms that do a substantial amount of business representing clients in the administrative agencies.[4]

For all its lobbying, advertising, and other activities a clientele may not get what it wants; in the end it may have to live with what it tried to ward off or water down. The reasons

---

4. A readable book full of anecdotes and war stories is Joseph C. Goulden, *The Superlawyers* (New York: Weybright and Talley, 1972).

are many. We have just mentioned the adversary process; in any conflict the other side may have better data, more skill, more money, or more votes. A group may not be able to mobilize its own members on a particular issue, or worse, the group may appear in public to be divided. The group itself may be made up of low-status members without political resources (contrast the National Welfare Rights Organization and the American Bar Association), or it may be fighting a strong tide (automobile safety standards in the wake of Ralph Nader's writing.) Public policy is by no means always what a particular group wants, but it is hard to understand the public policy process or the content of public policy without looking at agencies and the clienteles associated with them.

Agency Tactics

The agencies of the executive branch operate more or less in the open, subject to public view. What they do is affected by the views of their clienteles and public opinion. In the words of V. O. Key, Jr.

> Government may be regarded as operating within a context of public opinion that conditions its actions. The context is not a rigid matrix that fixes a precise form for government action. Nor is it unchangeable. It consists of opinions irregularly distributed among the people and of varying intensity, of attitudes of differing convertibility into votes, and of sentiments not always readily capable of appraisal. Yet that context, as it is perceived by those responsible for action conditions many of the acts of those who must make what we call "opinion related decisions." The opinion context may affect the substance of action, the form of action, or the matter of action.[5]

Key's phrase, "opinions irregularly distributed among the people," is particularly important; most of the population knows very little about executive-branch agencies. There is thus no meaningful context of public opinion for much executive branch action. But particular segments of the population interested in the work of a particular agency (read clienteles) may have both information and opinions that affect agency action.

---

5. V. O. Key, Jr., *Public Opinion and American Democracy* (New York: Alfred A. Knopf, 1964), p. 423.

Government agencies may be affected by outside opinion; they may in turn try to alter it by building a favorable impression of themselves and their programs. It is in an agency's interest to be viewed as working in the public interest (whatever that may mean) and carrying out its program efficiently, economically, and effectively.[6] And it is certainly in its interest not to have the reverse image. In testimony before Congress, in public speeches, in reports and news releases, officials of agencies try to emphasize the good the agency is doing and to explain or ignore alleged or real deficiencies. To gain support, agencies may certainly provide service, regulate cautiously (or strictly, depending on the circumstances) act responsively. But as important, agencies may go to some effort to report on what they do; they can be expected to explain, defend, justify, and interpret. In other words they carry on public relations (or public information and education) activities. High agency officials speak before trade association meetings and conventions of all sorts. Articles appear in magazines under the names of officials and letters to the editor in such publications as *The New York Times* and the *Wall Street Journal* point out unfavorable errors in other articles, clarify points, and offer explanations. An agency may issue press releases, hold press conferences, and cooperate with individual writers seeking stories. Law enforcement agencies and the military services have been particularly famous for their image-building activities on television and movie screens. (Obviously, not all agencies are equally blessed with dramatic possibilities; the Bureau of Commercial Fisheries will probably never become a household agency.) With a view to their image, agencies may also withhold information. Much secrecy can be justified on grounds of military necessity and national security, and more can be explained on grounds of individual privacy and the demands of corporate competition, but some inevitably can be understood as simply organizational image protection.

In addition to substantive action and active public relations agencies may do other things to maintain clientele interest and support. Most importantly they may build clienteles into the planning and administration of programs. For example, agencies can appoint advisory committees with members drawn from the major interests served. To be sure groups may seek such com-

---

6. See Francis E. Rourke, *Secrecy and Publicity* (Baltimore: Johns Hopkins Press, 1961).

mittees in an attempt to influence agency action, but an agency may initiate such a group with the hope of gaining support and perhaps co-opting the interests involved. Agencies may even encourage the formation of private groups with helpful views that can speak and act in ways not open to officials who have to maintain at least an appearance of neutrality.

The Public Interest

After this discussion of clientele groups and special interests, some attention to the term "public interest" surely seems in order.[7] Do public agencies work in the public interest, or do they mainly exist to benefit particular groups? Can particular courses of action be identified as being in the public interest? What is the public interest? Can it be objectively determined, or only subjectively defined? The quick answer is that there is not a public interest or a national interest.

It is impossible in many and probably in all situations to define *the* public interest or *a* public interest, and many government programs and much agency activity is carried out in the interest of and for the benefit of particular or special interests. This is a point long since agreed upon by many political scientists and other students of politics, but many citizens may not be persuaded.[8] Even if they agree that an agency is not presently acting in the public interest, they may think that if it altered course it would be. But is this true? Probably not.

If a regulatory agency enforces particular regulations in a

---

7. Three major books on the public interest are Glendon Schubert, *The Public Interest* (Glencoe: The Free Press, 1960); Carl J. Friedrich (ed.) *The Public Interest, Nomos V* (New York: Atherton, 1962); and Richard Flathman, *The Public Interest* (New York: John Wiley and Sons, 1966).

8. The difficulties inherent in the term "public interest" have been emphasized by Anthony Downs: ". . . the term public interest is constantly used by politicians, lobbyists, political theorists, and voters, but any detailed inquiry about its exact meaning plunges the inquirer into a welter of platitudes, generalities, and philosophic arguments. It soon becomes apparent that no general agreement exists about whether the term has any meaning at all, or if it has, what the meaning is, which specific actions are in the public interest and which are not, and how to distinguish between them." Anthony Downs, "The Public Interest: Its Meaning in a Democracy," *Social Research*, 29 (Spring 1962), pp. 1–2. This is quoted in Virginia Held, *The Public Interest* (New York, Basic Books, 1970).

fairly lax manner a particular group or industry may be benefitted, though this may appear not to be in the public interest. Under pressure from employees or consumers or other groups the agency may tighten up and begin to enforce its regulations. Is this in the public interest? Many would say no; that the agency was now acting only in the interest of others. One could consider a host of subsidy programs, particular provisions of tax law, or the existence of particular services—and ask of each whether it is in the public interest or in the interest of some particular group or clientele. In the end it seems clear that the meaning of public interest is flexible. It is not unusual to find that programs we favor are in the public interest and other programs are not.

Despite its flexible meaning the term public interest is in common use. The reasons are not far to seek. It simplifies the world to assume that public officials and public agencies work in the public interest. More important, beneficiaries and potential beneficiaries of government programs and agency action may find it easier to promote and sustain a program if they can attach to it a symbol with positive connotations, like the "public interest." Probably every subsidy program of the federal government would be defended by its beneficiaries as being in the public interest, though those not benefitting might have another view. Agencies too, though their services may benefit mainly or even exclusively particular groups, may argue that what they do is in the public interest. The public interest is a cloak that special interests draw around them.

Perhaps the impossibility of defining a public interest will be clearer if you stop briefly to consider the multiplicity of interests in the country, and the conflicts among them. To provide service to one group may mean not providing it to another. Or providing service to one group may be strongly opposed by another. The problem in these situations of course is how to choose. It might be comforting if there were some single public interest that could be first identified, then followed. But such seems unlikely at a minimum. What seems closer to reality is that the views and values of some interests (and not others) are identified and followed, perhaps inaccurately and often with some compromise. The outcome may be defined as being in the public interest for reasons of acceptance, stability, support, and image, but saying does not make it so. The public interest is a verbal symbol, accepted rhetoric, that frequently conceals the real distribution of both benefits and burdens. It may be associated with a proposed course of action to gather support for it, or it may be used to defend the status quo. Virtually anything can be defended as being in the public interest, and probably has been. But the political analyst is not misled by rhetoric. Rather he focuses on the public agency-private interest relationship and tries to discover how benefits and burdens are distributed; he tries to discover what is being done for whom and why.

PART IV BUREAUCRATIC BEHAVIOR: ROUTINES AND RHETORIC

The last major section of this book deals with several aspects of policy-making and implementation that have not yet been explicitly considered. Naturally, it focuses most attention on the roles of officials and bureaucratic organizations, but interaction with other participants in the policy process will be frequently considered. The section begins with a chapter on planning and program development, a subject that received brief attention in an early chapter but one which warrants further attention now. A second chapter is concerned with the allocation of resources. It focuses mainly on money and budgeting and deals both with the politics of budgeting and the economics of budgeting. It attempts to show the relationship between these two sides of the budgetary process. This chapter also considers the connections between budgeting and program planning and development. A third chapter deals with program evaluation and the use of social research in evaluation budgeting and program planning. Although it might have been possible to build parts of this chapter into preceding chapters, this topic is so timely and so important that separate attention seems worthwhile. A fourth chapter in this part deals with organization and reorganization; in other words, it deals with organization design. Alternative organization structures and the relations between structure and program are among the topics discussed.

12 Program Planning and Program Development

The Meaning of Planning

"Planning" is a word that appears frequently in the literature of public policy and administration. It appears to have many meanings and many uses and can be associated with numbers of activities with various goals.[1] Because it is both a common and an ambiguous word (concept), it deserves careful and cautious attention, yet we can begin with some common-sense notions. Planning implies preparation for the future. "To Plan", according to a dictionary, means "to devise or project a method or course of action." And this of course is what much planning in public agencies is all about, future courses of action. Or is it? Some observers might argue that much planning that goes on in government agencies has little to do with future courses of action and more to do with legal requirements for planning or the need to appear administratively up to date. Planning may be real preparation (or at least a real attempt), or it may be *pro forma*, symbolic. Plans may be what planners prepare and decision makers ignore. Planning can mean the detailed state-

---

1. See Herman Mertins, Jr., "A Study in Transitions," in *Public Administration Review*, Vol. 31, No. 3 (1971), pp. 254–255. This issue of PAR is devoted to a "Symposium on Changing Styles of Planning in Post Industrial America" and contains a number of articles worth pursuing. A major paper is by Bertram M. Gross, "Planning in an Era of Social Revolution," pp. 259–297.

ment of ideals and values with little hope of implementation. A plan may be narrow, short-range, and feasible. On the other hand, planning may result in a document that is much debated but never carried out. In a sense, perhaps, plans represent alternative futures and ways of getting there that are more or less detailed, more or less different from the present, more or less likely, possible, feasible, workable—and of course more or less costly. Planning is simply the process of preparing the plan.

A little thought will suggest a variety of possible contexts for planning. Think first of the variety of public-policy areas and immediately one can think of health planning, land use planning, welfare planning, resource planning, transportation planning, housing planning, education planning, to say nothing of defense planning, and so on and on. And indeed if one picks up texts or books in any of these fields one is likely to find a chapter devoted specifically to the topic of planning. Policy planning can of course be more or less general. Human resources planning might involve an attempt to develop a coordinated or consistent plan for health, education, welfare, manpower training, and maybe even population. Alternatively it is easy to think about a plan dealing simply with the course of manpower training over the next five years. Even narrower or more specific planning is possible.

Rather than, or in addition to, a policy focus, planning may have an organizational context. Cabinet departments, their constituent units, and independent agencies may all plan their future, though it is not clear that they do. That is, they may think about their likely future workloads, programs, size, organizational structure, manpower, budget, space, and how all these relate to one another. What changes appear likely to come and which others are required or desirable? In principle, such organization plans may be coordinated with one another, but given the independence and autonomy that bureaucratic organizations commonly seek and find, coordination is not likely.

Planning may also go on or appear to within specific areas of administrative activity. Thus one can speak of financial planning—what will the financial needs of the organization be over the course of the next several years? Personnel or manpower planning is another possibility. Such a plan would attempt to forecast or estimate or project manpower needs and might also specify the steps necessary to meet the quantitative and qualitative goals. In effect, of course, manpower plans and financial plans can be viewed as sub-plans related to a more general organizational or program plan. To make the point another way, a program plan will have manpower and financial implications that may be detailed in the manpower and financial plans. Building or space plans are also possible (if the organization grows what will the space requirements be).

Planning may have geographic focus. In principle the scope of planning can range from a neighborhood to a nation. Today neighborhoods or communities may have an interest in planning the course of their future development. City planning with an emphasis on land use has a reasonably long though not notably successful history in the United States. Today there is increasing interest in regional or statewide planning for particular policy areas—as in regional health planning (again, not notably successful)—and there has also been interest in metropolitan area planning and in river basin planning.

Clearly, planning can vary substantially in its comprehensiveness. A comprehensive plan for a city or region might attempt to include sections encompassing proposed developments or changes over a wide range of public activity. Or a plan can simply deal with the provision of health facilities in a particular region over the course of the next 10 or 25 years. Perhaps clear enough in the preceding discussion but also worth noting is that planning can vary in time span. Plans may be for the immediate future and planning may be long range, perhaps for a quarter century or even more.

Finally, in thinking about planning one should be aware of such terms (activities) as contingency planning, advocacy planning, and development planning. Contingency planning refers to the preparation of multiple plans, each of which may be appropriate for a particular set of conditions. In effect the contingency plan answers the question, what would we do if . . .? Advocacy planning is activist in nature; the aim is more or less rapid social change aimed at altering particular social conditions. Advocate planners, rather than becoming the staff of a bureaucracy, may work with particular social groups and indeed oppose positions taken by the bureaucracy. Development planning, a term used commonly in books and articles dealing with the developing countries, refers to plans focused on the economic development of the country in question.

We see now that the word plan may be attached to a variety of documents of varying size and scope, but we have not yet focused specifically on a main subject of this chapter, program planning. Program planning simply refers to work within an organizational context aimed at forecasting future conditions (changes in workload, effective demand for service, available revenue, probable developments in technology) and designing appropriate responses. Though it may be described simply and succinctly, program planning is by no means easy or always fruitful, as the following section will suggest.

Program Planning

Program planning is a phrase that covers a number of activities—these few pages can only give the barest sketch of the subject and a somewhat idealized one at that. No one should assume that everything described here actually goes on in every organization. Further sections point out many of the conditions that get in the way of planning. Here it suffices to emphasize that the simple model suggested here is subject to modification in every organization.

Program planning begins with an assessment and evaluation of the status quo. (Inadequate, inaccurate, or absent assessment may have unfortunate consequences for the quality of any planning that goes on.) Where are we now? What are we doing or giving, or delivering to whom? With what effect? In other words, with the present resources and organizational structure, what is being accomplished? This first step (more about evaluation later) is essential for program planning. Program planning takes the results of assessment and evaluation and moves forward into the future, specifying goals and objectives to be reached by particular dates. But how? What does this mean? Program planning has a number of possible components that we should consider separately.

A planner/analyst might begin with present problems or dissatisfactions and attempt to suggest alterations or additions to present programs that would cope with the problems or reduce the level of dissatisfaction. Probably a good deal of planning goes on in this reactive, relatively short-range pragmatic way. But more, at least in principle, can be done. The planner could gather data on the population served by a particular program and ask whether that population ought to be expanded or altered in the future, and if so suggest modifications in program (and legislation). The planner may consider the effect that population or economic or other changes will have on the workload or the mission of his organization. Is the population going to grow? Will the age distribution change? Will the socio-economic status of the population change? The point again is the anticipation of changes in order to plan or develop or prepare responses.[2]

What revenue resources are likely to be necessary in the future? Available? Analysts and planners do not set tax rates, but if they see shortages coming they can give early warning to other decision-makers. In addition, if some attempt is made to come up with accurate revenue projections there may be less chance of designing completely unrealistic or impossible programs and a greater likelihood of designing programs congruent with available funds. Obviously, revenue estimating is not unrelated to consideration of population trends and more general economic trends. One special danger in revenue estimating should be singled out for special mention and caution. It occasionally happens that some program area will grow very rapidly over a short period of time—space did, health research did, funding for higher education did, and recently funding for law enforcement has been. It is imprudent to assume that a high rate of growth will continue indefinitely. It won't. A decent regard for the inevitable suggests that any planner or analyst ought at least to plan for the consequences of leveling off and recession, even while his organization is growing rapidly.

What manpower resources will be available and what are the manpower consequences of various levels of activity or different emphases in program? These are important questions for a planner. And this question suggests that manpower planning has two dimensions or two approaches. One asks, what kinds of service will available manpower resources allow us to provide. This question can of course have a time dimension (over the next one year, two years, five—what will the manpower resources be?). Different packages of services can often be put together with the same manpower resources. But the main point is that available manpower imposes limits on what an agency can do. Of course, more money (can more money be obtained?) might be used to expand the supply of manpower,

---

2. It must be emphasized that planners designing responses may not know what will work. The social welfare field is littered with programs and plans that did not work the way their designers said they would.

but not always overnight. It takes many years to train a doctor or a scientist. On the other dimension, the planner must ask what the manpower implications of his program plans are, so that if his projected program for five years in the future assumes a growing level of manpower steps can be taken in timely fashion to assure its availability. It might also be noted that different sorts of manpower may be substituted for one another, and within limits machinery may be substituted for men. Planners must be aware of such complexities.

Planners working within a particular organization must be aware of what other organizations in their policy space are doing and planning. (They often aren't, and to be fully aware might be impossible. Still, effort in this direction is prudent.) If military planners assume an airlift capability in their estimates of future strength and location, then Air Force planners ought to plan for the provision of troop-carrying capacity. If the Bureau of Land Management, the National Park Service, and the Forest Service all devote resources to campsite development, the total result may be overcapacity and misused resources. If each assumes that more campsites will be provided by the others, the result is likely to be campers turned away. A local example may emphasize the point. If a school district assumes that library and reference services will be provided by the county library and the county library assumes student needs will be met by the school district, the likely result is that students will be poorly served both by the school and the library. The illustrations could be extended, but the simple point is that if planners work with erroneous information and assumptions (and they often do), their own plans may be faulty.

Planners might also do well to look into the technological future. Obviously technological forecasting, like forecasting in other fields, is uncertain, but it is also important. Changes in technology can bring new problems that an organization will have to cope with. Technology may also alter the way in which an organization organizes and delivers service. Both these dimensions of technology suggest that program planners must be aware of technological developments.

After collection, analyses, and syntheses of data a single course of action may not be clear, and within the limits of probably available resources alternative courses of actions may be possible. These various alternatives may each be elaborated in more or less detail as an aid to discussion and decision-making. It may also be that a relatively high but not very likely level of revenue could lead to one course of action and a lower but more likely level of revenue could lead to a different course. Such a situation can be made explicit with probabilities estimated. More generally, the planner or analyst may put together packages of assumptions with different probabilities—one package would include estimates of the most probable revenue level in two years, available manpower, state of technology, and an appropriate program or programs. Other packages of assumptions with higher or lower probabilities could also be prepared with their related programs.

Obviously a single planner or even a staff of planners can not consider all possible future states and possible courses of action for the organization. What I mean to emphasize is that an organizational planner should think about probabilities, possibilities, and alternative courses of action. What I mean to emphasize is contingent and flexible planning. And I certainly do not mean to suggest that plans are fixed or permanent. (That is the trouble with making a plan into a document. Putting it on paper seems to fix it.) Rather, program plans should be subject to continuous revision, with planning regarded as a process aimed at constantly modifying and updating program plans.

Obstacles to Planning

How to go about planning, or at least what planning means, is clear enough in principle. But there are a number of difficulties that may hinder if not altogether prevent planning or may make any planning activity and the resulting plans essentially meaningless. The most obvious difficulty is that planning requires resources and may not appear to offer a quick pay-off or return. Any pay-off at all may be problematic, and there are always daily pressures. The result is that planning is likely to be slighted in favor of daily operations. Of course, by resources I do not mean only money, but also men and time. An organization may not have enough men to free any up for thinking much beyond tomorrow, and in any event the men it has may have neither the analytic skills or imaginations to make their planning more than simply formal. An organization may not have the resources (or the leadership may not have the interest) to establish a separate unit responsible for planning. Yet if planning is just added to the responsibilities of another unit it may get short shrift from men who have other things to do. Even if a planning unit exists it may be far down in the hierarchy and its head unable to deal directly with the policy-making executives. Even if it plans ably it may plan for nought. Or its plans may not be taken seriously by those responsible for allocating funds: again planning may be for nothing.

All these are internal, organizational, or perhaps political problems. They are not unimportant, but even if on paper an organization, bureau, or department appears to be well staffed and organized for planning there may still be problems. Most generally the plans made by a particular organization may be or become irrelevant because the assumptions about the future on which a plan is based may turn out to be faulty. The population may grow faster or slower than an organization thought it would, and it may be overbuilt or underbuilt. An organization may assume growth in revenue and plan accordingly, and the revenue not materialize. (If the organization has hired staff and made commitments based on optimistic but erroneous assumptions it may be in serious trouble.) Estimates of future demand or workload may be way off: demand for health service may increase, demand for higher education decrease or level off. The state of technology may change more rapidly than forecast. The point is that any plan is perforce based on estimates of future conditions, and these may turn out to be wrong. It is worth noting that estimates about next year have a better chance of being accurate than estimates for the next five—and 25-year plans are very hard indeed to take seriously. The incentive to concentrate on short-term planning is obvious.

A related point is worth noting: estimates of the future may be inaccurate because data about the present is inaccurate or simply absent. A great deal has been written lately about the sorry state of social indicators in the United States, and for many parts of the world accurate data about tthe status quo is very hard to come by.[3] If one has to plan for an unknown future

---

3. For work on social indicators see Raymond A. Bauer (ed.), *Social Indicators* (Cambridge: M.I.T. Press, 1967); Eleanor B. Sheldon and Wilbert E. Moore (eds.), *Indicators of Social Change: Concepts and Measurement* (New York: Russell Sage Foundation, 1968); Bertram M. Gross (ed.), *Social Intelligence for America's Future* (Boston: Allyn and Bacon, 1969); *Federal Statistics*, Report of the President's Commission on Federal Statistics (Washington: U.S.G.P.O., 1971).

by starting from an unknown present the difficulties are compounded. Any plan developed in such a situation is likely to be virtually all symbol and little substance and have little effect on policy as it in fact develops. A lack of data is not the only problem. As serious in many fields is simple ignorance.[4] In field after field of public policy we do not know what works and what doesn't, what will and what won't. Nor can we predict what the consequences of new proposals will be, except that they probably won't be what was predicted.

To these difficulties can be added others. Plans must be implemented by others who may not share the goals of the planner and who indeed may not even be sure what goals the planner had in mind.[5] Implementors may not have the skills the planner assumed, and they may themselves have goals and values that the planner did not assume. Looking at such difficulties one observer recently concluded:

> Most public programs fail to produce results that meet the reasonable expectations of their planners. They fail because planners and policy makers cannot determine in advance the application of a given policy in all situations; discretion must be left to those who carry out the policy.[6]

In addition, the plans of any organization must be implemented in a context of other organizations and institutions. This is by now banal. But the plan of organization x can be contradicted by the plans of organizations y or z. Plans developed in an administrative context may be ignored or thoroughly changed by a legislature. And of course other countries may not cooperate.

---

4. The extent of our ignorance in the areas of social policy has been emphasized in a number of places recently. See particularly Alice M. Rivlin, *Systematic Thinking for Social Action* (Washington: Brookings Institution, 1971) and Charles M. Schultze, *et al.*, *Setting National Priorities: The 1973 Budget* (Washington: Brookings Institution, 1972, pp. 452 ff. A quotation from Schultze is to the point, ". . . it has become clear that in many of the new areas of federal concern, no one really knew what would work."

5. Two organizing concepts fashionable in the late 1960's and early 1970's—decentralization and citizen participation (or employee participation)—can wreak havoc with central plans.

6. Robert A. Levine, *Public Planning* (New York: Basic Books, 1972), p. 162.

(Why should they?) Plans for defense against attack from the north can be wiped out if an attack comes instead from the south. Opponents may not respond to signals or strategies the way planners assumed (hoped) they would. Plans to limit imports and increase exports can be foiled by other countries that limit their own imports. These points are obvious, but they are important. They suggest there are limits to the value of planning and indicate why resources spent on planning are resources committed with some uncertainty about pay-off. The further the future, the more uncertain the pay-off. Is it any wonder that current operations may drive out planning?[7]

Reasons for Planning

With all the difficulties planning does go on, plans are made. One might be justified in asking why? Different planners and executives may have various motivations and their projects (plans) may have many rationales. It may be instructive to consider some of the possibilities.

Possible rationales for planning and for plans (not mutually exclusive) include:

> To draw attention to problems and criticise the status quo.
> To stimulate discussion and debate about alternatives.
> To propose specific courses of action.

---

7. This pessimism must be qualified. Planning can work. Putting men on the moon certainly represents, among other things, a triumph of planning. Why plans were achieved in this context and have frequently *not* been achieved in social-policy contexts was once made clear by an Administrator of NASA, Thomas Paine: "NASA can define specific, stated, measurable goals, articulate them, and demonstrate obvious success to its public. Cities have at best very general objectives, many of which are undefined and unmeasurable, some of which cannot be stated in any operable way, and are subjects of passionate public dispute. More importantly, NASA's end products respond to, and are tested against, natural laws which are rational, systematic, codified, and well understood by its professionals. When they are not understood, the power of modern science is called in to rectify the situation. Cities, on the other hand, have their report card marked against wobbly success standards involving prejudice, special interest, wishful thinking, conflicting values, loose rhetoric, prophecy and revelation, or in the current vernacular SOUL. A social theory to guide urban societies is non-existent—or worse." Quoted in Stephen K. Bailey, "Educational Planning: Purposes and Power," *Public Administration Review*, Vol. 31, No. 3 (1971), p. 346.

To meet requirements for federal funding.

To present the appearance of rational administration.

To present the appearance of a productive planning department.

To use resources economically and avoid waste, improve coordination.

To satisfy superiors.

To keep up with other organizations that have plans.

To publicise an organization's activities and impress outsiders.

Clearly there are a number of possibilities, and the imaginative reader may be able to lengthen this list. With just a little effort one can imagine preparing a plan in order to use up money at the end of a fiscal year. (With this list of reasons we begin to see why plans may never get implemented but only gather dust on library shelves or take up space in filing cabinets.)

It is possible to consider the reasons for planning and the substance of plans from other perspectives that may shed further light on the complexity of the process and the many implementation difficulties. A plan may have both public and private reasons. For example, a plan forecasting future environmental changes and proposing an environmental policy may be the result of a specific legislative requirement. This is the public reason for its existence. Yet the substance of the plan may be best understood by trying to find out whose support the planning agency wants to maintain or gain.

A form-substance dichotomy may lead to the speculation that plans in form may not be plans in substance, and the speculation is worth taking seriously and briefly pursuing. Plans may for a variety of reasons be required by either a legislative or administrative body, and if they are required they will in all probability be produced. But the substance may be absent. Forecasts may be inaccurate to the point of being guesses, proposed programs may be either unrealistic or unimaginative or both, and problems of implementation and coordination with other agencies may be ignored. The plan may not even be intended to effect future agency performance or legislative program. Yet it exists and can be pointed to, produced in accordance with requirements.

Symbol and substance are another pair of words to have in mind when thinking about plans and planning. Plans may be symbols, intended to illustrate values, build an image, assure observers of concern. Yet they may not be intended to change reailty, but rather to give the impression of change. What do plans symbolize? Surely they symbolize concern for the future and interest in controlling it. Plans may symbolize rational administrative values and an interest in efficiency and economy, and this apart from substance. An environmental plan may in addition symbolize worry about pollution and concern for protecting the environment. Of course real effects may be seriously intended and the language of the plan consistent with them, but seriousness cannot be assumed. Yet even this point deserves qualification. It is easy to imagine that planners themselves, professionally trained in schools of planning or in departments of economics, may be serious in what they do while the officials for whom they work may not be. Plans may be used in ways other than the planners hoped or intended.

Means-end is another dichotomy that comes to mind when thinking of planning. A plan may be both or either. It may mean different things to different people. A regional health plan may be used by some as simply a means to stimulate thought and discussion about the present and possible future location of health facilities in a region, with no thought that the plan is a rigid blueprint. It is not an end, but simply a means to perhaps more informed decision making. Yet the same plan to others may be an end. For some the production of the document itself may be an end, and worry ceases when the printer gets it. More seriously, for others implementation of the steps described may be a major goal with dissatisfaction and disappointment resulting if discussion is the only outcome of the plan.

To these various ways of interpreting plans we may add more. A plan may be viewed as an ideological document, an economic document, a political document, or a professional or administrative document. Of course these terms are not mutually exclusive, but their different emphases should be kept in mind. A plan may be the product of civil-servant planners working in a particular organization, and though technically proficient they may lack political support. By the same token a plan or maybe more simply a program proposal may have wide support but be so technically deficient that it completely misses intended targets. The products of advocate planners may be challenging and clear, but politically unrealistic because based on values not widely shared.

Perhaps the phrase to remember is "the politics of planning." It sums up much of the preceding discussion and suggests the balancing, negotiation, and conflict that are part of the process of producing a plan. Within an organization different interests must frequently be taken into account and different factions mollified. A plan, like a political ticket, may have to be balanced, if implementation is the goal. Once prepared a plan will in all likelihood require legislative implementation and funding. Plans are not self-executing. Once again there may be conflict, negotiation, compromise. There is thus both an internal and an external politics of planning, and it is as important to keep this dimension of planning in mind as it is the more analytical aspects.

Program Development

Despite the many obstacles to program planning and indeed in the absence of program planning many programs are developed and carried out. How? There is no single answer, of course. The programs carried out by the many federal government organizations have developed over time in many different ways for many different reasons. There is no single or best model of program development, and individual case studies may be misleading. At the same time some order must be given to the process of program development—if only for the purposes of exposition—and with the caution that the order imposed may be more or less artificial, arbitrary, unrealistic.

At the start we can divide program development into several phases—initiation and invention, consideration and deliberation, modification and choice, implementation and evaluation. Though these steps are fairly familiar, it is hard to imagine policy development not proceeding generally in this fashion. But within these very general steps there is much opportunity for variation and innovation. To illustrate we can briefly consider each one in turn, recalling what we know already of American government, politics, and public policy.

Initiation and invention may go on in many places and in different policy systems; the initiation of new programs (and practices and procedures) may begin at different points. A program may have its beginning in a Congressional office, in the White House, in some government department or bureau, in the offices and meetings of some organized group, or in the report of a Presidential Commission. In any case initiation of a new program may result from dissatisfaction with a current program. (For this reason reaction may be a better word than initiation.) Invention of course need not be involved. Agencies look at each other, state agencies, foreign agencies, and business organizations and commonly adopt and modify for their own use what is being done elsewhere. (The agency that is insulated or isolated and is not searching may stay the same way a long time.)

Of course few changes are adopted simply and quickly. Particularly if other interests are at stake program adoption is likely to be preceded by much debate and discussion, bargaining and negotiation. Politics is part of the program development process. Programs are developed in a political environment, and often substantial amounts of time (years) elapse between initiation and final decision. The impact of politics and the time required from start to finish are often underestimated by outside experts and presidential appointees new to Washington. And while it may be true that small plans cannot stir men's souls, it is also true that it is hard to get broad agreement quickly on broad new programs, unless of course they are intended to cope with a clear and urgent crisis. In that event a program may be adopted quickly, flaws and all.

Consideration and deliberation go on in many arenas, and representatives of each communicate with others. Although minor modifications in an existing program may receive careful attention only in the department most immediately concerned (and therefore major changes may be labeled minor in order to ward off attention), a broad program may be debated throughout the policy-making system, and as a result of the deliberation each participant may arrive at a position on the measure. This is clearest in the case of the conference committee that must meet when House and Senate versions of a bill differ, but meetings that serve equivalent purposes are held when departments or a department and the White House or a department and the OMB cannot see eye-to-eye on an issue. Until agreement is reached (perhaps on a compromise rather different from any original suggestion) the program in question does not move forward. When there is agreement (and if necessary a bill is signed) a new program goes into effect. Implementation of course is not automatic and a major part of program development in this implementation phase. As surely here as in the early stages of discussion a program can be developed or allowed to wither. In fact, it is suggestive to assert that programs develop through implementation, just as muscles develop through use.

With the implementation may come (they are not always present) evaluation and modification, and the program development process starts again. Evaluation need not be systematic (it rarely is), and it may not even be present. There may be attempts to provide feedback on the part of consumers and those attempts may be rebuffed. But still in principle evaluation and modification are the final part of the program development process. Or perhaps they are the first stage of a new program.

To this sketch of program development should be added other ideas. Program development is clearly a political activity,[8] but it is also more than that. Today experts are commonly (perhaps increasingly) involved in providing data, analyses, and forecasts. And just because they do they may effect the outcomes of program debates, though the outcomes may not be what they recommended. Program development is perhaps becoming, albeit slowly, professionalized. Program development today may be viewed as problem solving and there is perhaps increasing (though hardly widespread yet) interest in systematic experiment as a way of studying the effect of a program before it is adopted on a wide scale.[9] In a view gaining some currency today program development resembles hypothesis testing: we keep what works and throw out what doesn't. But for all the rational overlay (and it may be getting thicker), at bottom the development of public programs is political. And, further, one must remember such words as routine, habitual, inflexible. Not only may a program be carried out as a matter of routine, long after its original rationale has lost any force—even the process of developing programs in an agency may become routine, just as budgeting and personal classification may be routines. If this happens then new techniques for searching, for assessing alternatives, and for making decisions may be ignored while familiar routines for program development are retained.

---

8. For a recent clear statement of this see Arnold Meltsner, "Political Feasibility and Policy Analysis," *Public Administration Review*, Vol. 32, No. 6 (1972), pp. 859–867.

9. See Peter H. Rossi and Walter Williams (eds.), *Evaluating Social Programs* (New York: Seminar Press, 1972).

13 Budgeting in Government

What the government does and how much it spends are closely related; programs and budgets are inextricably linked. The plans of a President and the programs of executive branch agencies are nothing without funds. A civil-rights law with no organization to enforce it—and this takes money—is law only on the books. Social welfare programs are nothing without money; they are merely paper programs. To build public housing, to preserve natural resources, to provide a transportation system—all these activities take money. It is the President's budget that allocates funds among the many and varied programs of the federal government. The budget can be viewed as an expression of priorities, preferences, and values; it converts hopes and symbols into realities. Lip service may be given by Congressmen and Presidents to many things; the budget shows what they are really willing to support.

The Budget Cycle

Each year in January the President of the United States sends his budget and his budget message to the Congress. Although the details of budget preparation may vary from year to year the budget message represents the culmination of many months of work in the executive branch, months of evaluation, calculation, and negotiation. And because a budget *must* be presented every year, budget preparation represents one of the

246

major routines of government. Every year officials must decide how much money to ask for and how to allocate it among various projects and programs. Other officials both in the executive branch and the Congress must decide how much to grant. How such decisions are made is an important subject, but before taking it up we should have in mind the basic framework of the budget process. (See chart on the following pages.)

In the early spring some 10 months before the submission of a budget to the Congress, work begins. The Council of Economic Advisors, the Treasury, and the Office of Management and Budget develop the economic forecasts necessary for choosing overall spending and tax policies. Policies appropriate for a slowing economy may be inappropriate if the goal is to control a high rate of inflation. In the first case, for example, both a high rate of spending and tax cuts (and thus a substantial deficit) may be in order; in the second case, opposite policies may be what are required.[1] Forecasts concerning the condition of different sectors of the economy (agriculture and manufacturing, for example) and of different regions of the country may also be useful in determining where and what to spend. In addition to economic forecasts, revenue estimates must also be made so that budget officials will have some idea of the amount of money likely to be available.

Also in the spring estimates will be requested from major agencies concerning their spending requirements for the coming fiscal year. This information, together with the economic and revenue information available, will lead to the establishment of planning figures, which are sent to all agencies. These are somewhat less than absolute ceilings, but more than simply flexible guidelines. With these figures agencies go to work preparing their budgets, working throughout the summer with department and OMB officials. (Bureaus and other constituents of departments develop budgets that become part of the department

---

1. There are a number of basic economics texts available that treat government spending and fiscal policy in some detail. Brief readable discussions can be found in Marshall Robinson *et al., An Introduction to Economic Reasoning* (Garden City: Anchor Books, 1967, 4th rev. ed.); Robert L. Heilbroner and Peter L. Bernstein, *A Primer on Government Spending* (New York: Vintage Books, 1963); David J. Ott and Attiat F. Ott, *Federal Budget Policy* (Washington: Brookings Institution, 1969, rev. ed.); Willis L. Peterson, *Principles of Economics: Macro* (Homewood: Richard D. Irwin, 1971).

FORMULATION OF EXECUTIVE BUDGET

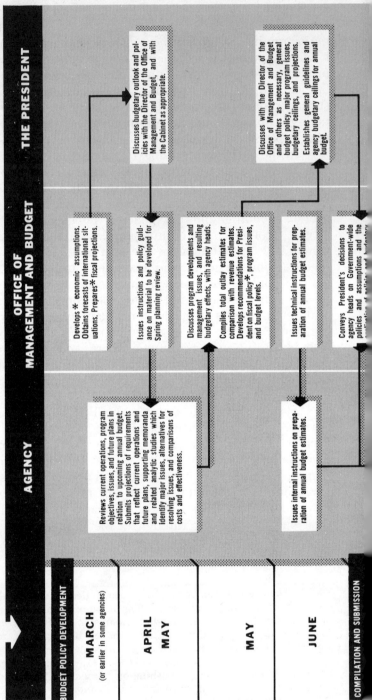

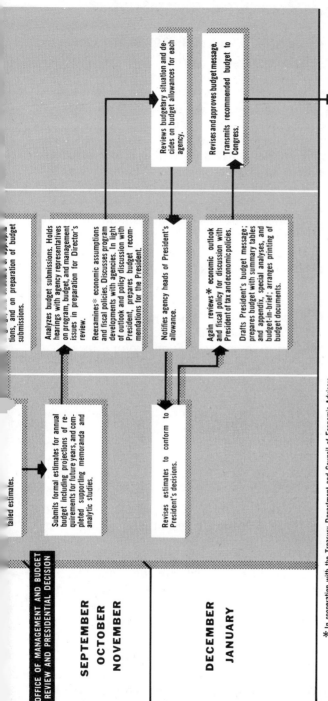

tions, and on preparation of budget submissions.

OFFICE OF MANAGEMENT AND BUDGET REVIEW AND PRESIDENTIAL DECISION

tailed estimates.

Submits formal estimates for annual budget including projections of requirements for future years, and completed supporting memoranda and analytic studies.

Analyzes budget submissions. Holds hearings with agency representatives on program, budget, and management issues in preparation for Director's review.

Reexamines* economic assumptions and fiscal policies. Discusses program developments with agencies. In light of outlook and policy discussion with President, prepares budget recommendations for the President.

Reviews budgetary situation and decides on budget allowances for each agency.

Notifies agency heads of President's allowance.

Revises estimates to conform to President's decisions.

Again reviews* economic outlook and fiscal policy for discussion with President of tax and economic policies.

Drafts President's budget message; prepares budget with summary tables and appendix, special analyses, and budget-in-brief; arranges printing of budget documents.

Revises and approves budget message. Transmits recommended budget to Congress.

SEPTEMBER
OCTOBER
NOVEMBER

DECEMBER
JANUARY

* In cooperation with the Treasury Department and Council of Economic Advisers

TRANSMISSION OF BUDGET TO CONGRESS
MID-JANUARY

EXECUTIVE OFFICE OF THE PRESIDENT/OFFICE OF MANAGEMENT AND BUDGET

GPO : 1972 O - 490-485

DECEMBER 1972

budget.) During the late 1960's and early 1970's the Office of Management and Budget required as part of a budget detailed statements of goals and objectives, program and financial plans, and explicit analyses of possible alternatives, but recently has backed away from many of these requirements. Still, agency staff will be expected to justify what they request.

During the fall the budget begins to take shape and final reviews are conducted at the OMB and White House. During November and December in particular agency budgets are reviewed by the Director of OMB, and agency heads have a last chance to appeal cuts in their budget. On occasion they may appeal directly to the President, but this may depend on apparent presidential wishes. If he says that the Director's decisions are his, then there is not much agency heads can do until they testify before Congressional committees.

In the last part of December and first part of January the budget goes to the printer to be ready for delivery to the Congress in the latter part of January—though there may be a slippage of a few days or weeks. After the budget message is delivered and the budget sent to Congress, appropriations committees take over, first in the House and then in the Senate. More precisely, subcommittees of these committees take over and the government budget is divided among several subcommittees. As the House completes work on an appropriations bill (in fiscal year 1971 there were 14 such bills; the Congress *does not* act on the budget as a whole) it moves to the Senate, perhaps to a conference committee, and then to the President. The fiscal year, that is, the budget year, starts on July 1, but frequently by that date Congress has not completed its consideration of all appropriations bills.[2] Agencies may thus be left without funds, but can operate on the basis of continuing resolutions giving them authority to spend at the previous year's level.

With this brief review in mind, several points about the budget process can be made. First, officials are commonly dealing with three budgets at once, though at different stages. There is

---

2. For data from 1964 to 1971 see *The Federal Fiscal Year As It Relates to the Congressional Budget Process,* Hearings Before the Joint Committee on Congressional Operations, 92nd Congress, 1st Session, (Washington: U.S.G.P.O., 1972), pp. 47–49. In fiscal 1971 not one of 14 appropriations bills was passed prior to the start of the year. In that year the Department of Defense had its budget approved 185 days *after* the start of the fiscal year.

the current budget, and one must think about how it is being spent and whether it will be enough. Inaccurate forecasts or changed circumstances may make it necessary to go back to Congress in mid-year and ask for more money, in other words, to request a supplemental appropriation. Second, there is the budget pending before Congress for the coming fiscal year. Testimony must be prepared, negotiations conducted, and fingers crossed. At the same time, even though Congress has not completed action on the pending budget, planning for the budget to be submitted next year must go forward. As this is written, it appears that the HEW budget for fiscal 1973 will not be approved until February 1973, some 7 months late, but in January 1973 the budget for fiscal 1974 must be presented. Obviously, the budget process contains much uncertainty and must be continually modified as decisions are made and more information becomes available.

A second important point is that no new President can have a quick impact on the budget. He is inaugurated in the middle of a fiscal year, and the first budget that a new President submits (only weeks after he takes office) is almost entirely the work of the prior administration. Planning for the second budget must begin as soon as he takes office and well before he has taken hold. A new President's impact on it is likely to be marginal at best. The third budget that a President submits may be viewed as his own. But, the third major point, much in any budget is there because of the actions of preceding Presidents and Congresses. Much in the budget is more or less uncontrollable, and any President can have only some impact on the fringes. Over the space of eight years, of course, a President (and Congress) can have noticeable impact. And in the short run a President can have substantial impact on government spending for some programs by simply impounding funds that have been appropriated though he cannot impound just anything or with impunity.[3] It is accurate to describe much of the budget as uncontrollable.

A final point to keep in mind is that there are ways around the annual appropriations process. In his book on *Congressional Control of Federal Spending*, Robert Wallace lists ten different

---

3. A useful volume on impoundment is *Executive Impoundment of Appropriated Funds*, Hearings Before the Subcommittee on Separation of Powers of the Committee on the Judiciary, 92nd Congress, 1st Session (Washington: U.S.G.P.O., 1972). In 1973 many of President Nixon's impoundments were successfully challenged in the courts.

types of spending authority; the first of these and by far the most common is ordinary current appropriations, but there are a variety of other possibilities.[4] A very large piece of the budget, social security, is not subject to annual appropriations, and numbers of smaller pieces also get around this hurdle. Some government spending is guaranteed by law—for example, veterans' pensions, civil service pay, military pay rates—and unless the law is changed an appropriations committee has no choice but to appropriate the required funds.

Politics and Budgets

It is useful to remember the title of Professor Lasswell's classic book, *Politics: Who Gets What, When, How?* Budgetary decisions clearly are decisions about who gets what. Just as certainly they are infused with politics. What does this mean? It means that budgets are the result of bargaining and negotiations, and that any annual budget represents in some sense a compromise between what an agency started out to get and what other decision-makers thought it ought to have.

It is important to know who the principals are in this politics of budgeting. First are the bureaus and departments and the independent agencies, the units that make the initial requests and who finally spend the money. Then come the Office of Management and Budget and the President; they evaluate requests and make recommendations. The Office of Management and Budget makes recommendations to the President, the President makes recommendations to the Congress. The House and Senate Appropriations Committees are the third set of participants.

Each of these participants has different interests and faces different problems in the budgeting process. Bureaus, departments, and independent agencies have to decide initially how much money they want. Departments must review bureau budgets and prepare departmental budgets. They, therefore, must allocate funds among their bureaus. The Office of Management and Budget must formulate initial guidelines, and make final recommendations to the President. In each case its problem is to decide how much each organization should get. The President

---

4. Robert Ash Wallace, *Congressional Control of Federal Spending* (Detroit: Wayne State University Press, 1960), p. 21.

in turn must decide how much to ask from Congress. Like the Office of Management and Budget and the President, the Congress—more especially the House and Senate Appropriations Committees—must decide how much to give each agency. They must decide whether to accept the President's recommendations or to change them. The Senate must decide how to react to the action of the House.

This list of questions gives some notion of the questions that the participants in the budgeting process face. How do they arrive at their decisions? Aaron Wildavsky's *Politics of the Budgetary Process* provides a valuable discussion; and the paragraphs that follow lean heavily on this source.[5]

Agencies usually try to increase their budgets. They are not always successful, and some may not even try; but agencies each year are likely to ask for somewhat more than the year before. If an agency is to keep the confidence of the appropriations subcommittee that deals with it, its requests for funds must appear reasonable in the light of past increases. Agency officials know that increases are likely to be scrutinized, and a noticeably larger increase will receive a thorough going-over. However, neither is an agency likely to ask for a bare-bones budget with no slack in it. Administrators do not like to admit budget padding, but it is certainly true that the programs in a budget may vary in importance; if cuts have to be made, some programs can be cut more easily than others. Even though Congress (and some citizens) may have a different opinion, from the administrator's point of view it makes sense to build slack into a budget. It not only protects him from the consequences of Congressional action, but it also provides him with operating flexibility throughout a fiscal year.

An agency is likely to decide how much to ask for by looking to its past. With the amount it received last year as the base, it will probably try for as big an increase as it obtained then. Yet the past is not all that an agency attends to in deciding how much to request. An agency receives guidelines from the Office of Management and Budget, and certainly these are considered, though perhaps not followed. Officials of the administration may make public speeches indicating interest in one or another area of public policy, and these expressions of interest may be taken

5. Aaron Wildavsky, *The Politics of the Budgetary Process* (Boston: Little, Brown and Co., 1964).

as hints of support by agency officials when a budget is drawn up. If the President shows interest in oceanography and a willingness to support it, this cue is not likely to pass unnoticed in the National Oceanic and Atmospheric Administration or in the Office of Naval Research. If an influential congressman indicates a willingness to support a particular activity, this fact may be reflected in an agency budget.

No matter how conscientious an agency, when a budget comes under the scrutiny of the Office of Management and Budget, it is likely to be cut. Surely OMB does not cut indiscriminately (though it has been charged with cutting arbitrarily), and sometimes it may not cut at all, but it does cut frequently. Any particular action depends heavily on the guidance the office receives from the President. Just as the agencies search for clues that might indicate presidential support, so does the OMB. Is the President interested in education, in health, in law and order, in traffic safety? Then programs in these areas may be generously funded. Is the President disinterested in antitrust activity or the shipping industry? Then programs in these areas may receive critical scruntiny.

But the Office of Management and Budget does not look only to the President for guidance. It is also likely to be influenced by the past actions of the Congress and indeed may model its decisions along the lines of past Congressional decisions. Has Congress been generous with the Law Enforcement Assistance Administration? Then OMB may be generous also if only because it does not want to diminish its influence (tarnish its image) by being reversed. Has Congress been harsh with AID in past years? Then OMB may also be critical. There is little point in recommending funds that will almost surely not be obtained.

Besides such political considerations, OMB considers other and more measurable factors. An agency's present and potential workload and associated costs may be considered, especially if the workload is readily quantifiable. Agency cost-benefit analyses may be reviewed to see if they support what the agency is requesting. And of course the availability of funds and the presence of competing demands may have some effect on what is recommended. The demands of Vietnam made severe inroads on the budgets of many domestic agencies. A desire to control inflation may place severe upper limits on government spending.

When budgets for all the agencies are finally drawn together into the President's budget, they go to the Congress. The

President's budget goes first to the House Appropriations Committee, where it is divided among a number of specialized subcommittees that consider it in public hearings and closed sessions. To the hearings come administration officials who must justify their requests. Generally they find that the attitude of the subcommittee members is skeptical. The members of the appropriations committee in the House are usually intent on cutting the President's budget. (This may mean for any agency that its budget will be cut twice—once by the Office of Management and Budget and once more by the House Appropriations Committee.) In many instances the only real question is how large the cuts will be, but it is hard to predict what the committee and its subcommittees will do. Cuts may be arbitrary and unpredictable. At times cuts will be simply symbolic assertions of committee authority. Sometimes a budget may not be cut at all, and sometimes more money may be added, particularly to a program that has more congressional than presidential sympathy.

Much scholarly attention has been paid to the hearings held by the House appropriations subcommittees, and some comment on them may be worthwhile. In brief, administrative officials view the hearings as grueling and inherently unpredictable affairs. Interviews with bureau officials bear this out:

> There is not a bureau head here whose blood pressure doesn't go up before the House Appropriation Budget Hearings—even the oldest one. It's an ordeal. You don't know what questions they might ask or what case they might bring up.[6]
>
> Sometimes a Congressman will reach in his pocket and pull out a letter from a constituent or another Congressman, and we won't know what's coming next. Sometimes these questions don't even pertain to our estimates. And its like the man who carried his bass viol across town and never got a chance to play.[7]

Attempting to protect themselves as much as possible from adverse committee action, administrative officials may do a number of things. Certainly they may try to build a generally supportive political environment; in particular they may seek the backing

---

6. Quoted in Richard F. Fenno, Jr., *The Power of the Purse* (Boston: Little, Brown and Co., 1966), p. 283.
7. Fenno, *Power of the Purse*, p. 284.

of organized interest groups. But they also take care to keep their relations with their particular subcommittee in good repair. By emphasizing communication and consultation and by being frank and open, agencies try to establish a relationship of trust and confidence with their subcommittee. In addition they take appropriations hearings very seriously, preparing for them carefully and being cautious and deferential during the hearings.

> We have dress rehearsals here. I play the subcommittee chairman and we practice. I try to know what's going through the minds. . . . I conceive of myself as a football coach. I train them down here; but up on the Hill I just go and sit on the sidelines.[8]
>
> The bureau heads come in to talk it over, or we'll go to lunch. Then I'll say that I'm going to hold a departmental hearing strictly within the family and throw all the questions I can think of at them to see what they do with them. I throw the questions I know the Committee will ask.[9]
>
> For heaven's sake, rehearse. We sit around here and the division chiefs fire all the questions they can think of and I answer them. I make my whole presentation . . . you need to get a grasp of what they're going to say so you don't fumble around when the time comes. It's like boning up for a Ph.D. exam. I always know what they're going to ask and I don't think a single question has been asked that I didn't think about in advance in recent years. Ninety-five per cent of it is wasted. But that one nugget that you rehearse may make all the difference in the world.[10]

In the hearing, openness and honesty are the order of the day, and administrators say it does not pay to argue.

> The most important thing in a Committee hearing is creating an atmosphere of confidence—so that you have confidence in the Committee and they have confidence in you. I tell my people to be perfectly honest and to have a full free and frank discussion with the Committee, even if it hurts you a little bit. That will mean more than anything else in getting your money. Nobody likes to admit things

---

8. Fenno, *Power of the Purse,* p. 293.
9. Fenno, *Power of the Purse,* p. 293.
10. Fenno, *Power of the Purse,* p. 294.

and cast reflections on his own shop, but don't try to fool the congressmen. You can't. They have a fifth sense when someone is not talking freely and frankly. If you have a perfectly open discussion, they'll have more confidence in you, and your appropriations troubles will be minimized.[11] I like to go at things directly. I'm the kind of guy who likes to argue. But you shouldn't argue with congressmen. I learned that a long time ago.[12]

After hearings are completed the committee in closed session makes its decisions, and many agencies, try though they did, find that they received less than they requested. Ordinarily the recommendations of the subcommittees are accepted by the Appropriations Committee and also by the House. After House action, appropriations bills are sent to the Senate for consideration. Not without reason, the Senate Appropriations Committee is considered (and considers itself) the Congressional court of appeals or the court of last resort. Administrators hope that the Senate committee will restore at least some of the funds taken away by the House, and in many cases the committee obliges. A quotation from *The Politics of The Budgetary Process* is to the point.

> A member of the Senate Appropriations Committee is likely to conceive of his proper role as the responsible legislator who sees to it that the irrepressible lower House does not do too much damage either to constituency or to national interests. Though members of the House Appropriations Committee tend to view their opposite members in the Senate as frivolous dilettantes who swap favors and do not care what happens to the public purse, Senators tend to reverse the compliment by regarding their brethren in the other chamber as jealous and power-hungry types who do not care what happens to "essential" programs so long as they can show that they have made cuts.[13]

After Senate action, appropriations bills often must go to a conference committee to have differences between Senate and House versions resolved. When they are resolved and the same

11. Fenno, *Power of the Purse*, p. 298.
12. Fenno, *Power of the Purse*, p. 301.
13. Wildavsky, *Politics of the Budgetary Process*, p. 51.

measure is passed by both House and Senate, it goes to the President for signature.

Even from such a brief sketch of the politics of budgeting, it is clear that budgeting is hardly a rational analytical process. Rather, it seems some sort of political game with many players. each vying for different prizes. Agencies want as much money as they can get for their programs. The Office of Management and Budget wants to protect the President and tries to put together a budget that is responsive to his desires and stands a chance of getting through Congress. The House Appropriations Committee wants to economize, and the Senate Appropriations Committee wants to right the wrongs of the House Appropriations Committee.

Program Analysis and Resource Allocation

In the last dozen years economists, systems analysts, and others have devoted a great deal of thinking and writing to the goal of making government budgeting more analytical and more economical. During the sixties budget reform was much in the air in Washington. But the results of all the effort have been slim and great amounts of ink and paper, time and energy have gone for nothing. The advocates of Planning, Programming, and Budgeting (PPB) have backed off from their initial enthusiasm and claims, and new budgeting techniques are no longer the fashionable topic that they were just a few years ago. But the history of budget reform over the last few years provides an informative illustration of the difficulty of introducing change into the bureaucracy.

At the beginning of the 1960's a number of criticisms of government budgeting as it was then carried out began to receive a good deal of attention, though the criticisms themselves were hardly new. One criticism was that there was no clear connection between a budget and what a government agency was doing. Budgets were organized by agency and by input (so much for personnel, so much for space, so much for transportation, so much for supplies), but it was hard if not impossible to see how much different activities cost. Another major criticism was that goals and objectives were not clearly stated and budget decisions frequently involved little systematic analysis of the costs and benefits of alternative ways of reaching the same or comparable goals. In addition, there was little evaluation of on-going programs to see what was being obtained for funds expended. Consideration of the budget was on an agency-by-agency basis, even though several agencies might be doing either complementary or contradictory things. For example, funds spent on natural resources in the Department of Interior were considered apart from funds devoted to natural resources in the Department of Agriculture. Another criticism was that budgeting was on an annual basis with little or no systematic thought given to the future financial implications of currently proposed projects.

The effort to correct these apparent deficiencies began in the Defense Department in 1961. A year earlier Charles J. Hitch and Roland McKean had published a book, *The Economics of Defense in the Nuclear Age*,[14] describing how in their view the Defense Department budget should be put together. When Robert McNamara became Secretary of Defense he appointed Hitch Assistant Secretary (Comptroller). The ideas that Hitch propounded in his book began to be introduced in the Defense Department. Funds began to be explicitly allocated to the various programs or missions of the armed forces—such as strategic forces, general purpose forces, reserves, research and development, support, and so on—rather than only to personnel, construction, procurement, operation and maintenance, and the like. A second feature of the new defense budgeting system was that more attention was given explicitly to the analysis of alternative ways of achieving the same goal. Secretary McNamara required the military departments to be explicit about what they wanted to accomplish and to justify the route they had chosen to reach their objectives. The form of analysis he most emphasized has been called many things—cost-benefit analysis, cost-effectiveness analysis, cost-utility analysis. Such analyses involve the systematic comparison of the costs and benefits of alternative means of accomplishing the same objective. The cost-benefit analyst arrays in front of himself a number of ways to accomplish the task he is concerned with—a variety of fighter bombers to provide close support for ground troops, approaches to the problems of unemployed urban youth, or ways to transport people in urban areas. The analyst then must find out which alternative will provide the most benefit for the least cost. He may start with a given number of dollars and see which alternative

---

14. Charles J. Hitch and Roland N. McKean, *The Economics of Defense in the Nuclear Age* (Cambridge: Harvard University Press, 1960).

will give him the most return for his money. Or he may start with a particular goal and see what alternative will reach that goal with the fewest dollars.

A third component of the budgeting system that was introduced into the Department of Defense was long-range financial planning. Budget officers were required to think ahead five years and make clear what they thought their requirements would be during that period. Their current requests could then be assessed not only in the light of what they had spent in the past but what they anticipated spending in the future. Budget officers were required to be explicit about the future cost implications of current outlays. If a research and development laboratory is built this year, it will have to be staffed and maintained in future years. How much will this cost? If a contract is let this year to design a new reconnaissance plane, how much will building it cost? These questions began to be asked in the early 1960's.

The new budgeting system in the Department of Defense came to be known, as most things are in Washington, by a set of initials—PPBS, for Planning, Programming, Budgetary System. From the Defense Department, PPBS spread over the rest of the federal agencies and came to be known as PPB. In 1965 President Johnson ordered all departments and agencies to begin using the practices pioneered in the Defense Department. He expected them to be explicit about their objectives, to systematically analyze the costs and benefits of alternative ways of reaching objectives, and to develop financial plans for multi-year periods. In May 1966 departments and agencies began implementing PPB in their submissions to the then Bureau of the Budget.[15] Quickly a host of problems, only some of which had been anticipated, became apparent. An immediate problem was the definition of program. Programs consist of activities, and the budget analyst has to decide which activities to group with one another. Although the problems may not be clear, defining programs is by no means an easy task, as Aaron Wildavsky has made clear.

> The difficulties with the program concept are illustrated in the space program. A first glance suggests that space projects are ideally suited for program budgeting because they appear as physical systems designed to accomplish

---

15. For a description of the early days see Virginia Held, "PPBS Comes to Washington," *Public Interest,* Summer 1966, pp. 102–115.

different missions. Actually, there is a remarkable degree of interdependence between different missions and objectives—pride, scientific research, space exploration, military uses, etc.—so that it is impossible to apportion costs on a proper basis. Consider the problem of a rocket developed for one mission and useful for others. To apportion costs to each new mission is purely arbitrary. To allocate the cost to the first mission and regard the rocket as a free good ·for all subsequent missions is ludicrous. The only remotely reasonable alternative—making a separate program out of the rocket itself—does violence to the concept of programs as end projects. The difficulty is compounded because the facilities that have multiple uses like boosters and tracking networks tend to be very expensive compared to the items that are specific to a particular mission. Simple concepts of program evaporate upon inspection.[16]

Another problem was a lack of data that prevented the analysis and evaluation of programs. Elizabeth Drew made the problem clear in 1967.

Those who picture Washington as one mass of files and computers containing more information than they would like will be comforted by the experiences of program planners in attempting to evaluate on-going programs. Whatever the files and computers do contain, there is precious little in them about how many and whom the programs are reaching, and whether they are doing what they are supposed to do. If the purpose of an adult basic education program is to teach people how to read and write, the Office of Education might reasonably be expected to know how many people thereby actually learned how to read and write, but it does not. The higher education study was delayed because there simply was too little information about who was receiving federal scholarships, or what happened to all those who had been receiving National Defense Education Act loans since 1958. Did they finish college? Did it affect their subsequent careers? No answers. The Public Health Service might be expected to know

---

16. Aaron Wildavsky, "The Political Economy of Efficiency: Cost Benefit Analysis, System Analysis, and Program Budgeting," *Public Administration Review*, 26 (1966), p. 303.

whether its various health services are in fact making people healthier, but it does not. The study of disease control was to have encompassed more diseases, but so little was known about the effective treatment of alcoholism and heart disease that these components had to be dropped. Those working on the income maintenance study found that the Welfare Administration could not tell them very much about the public assistance caseload—who was on welfare, where did they come from, why were they on it, what they needed in order to get off.[17]

It should be emphasized immediately that a shortage of data is by no means a simple problem to solve. The right data needs to be collected, data costs money to collect, data get out of date, it may be carelessly collected, or it may be improperly or just unimaginatively analyzed. Data collection and analysis can be threatening to some managers and resisted. If the results of analysis are negative with regard to the benefits of a program, the analysis is at least as likely to questioned and disregarded as the program. Although an absence of impact data may on occasion be a simple oversight, it may also be intentional and then be difficult to remedy meaningfully.

There were other problems with PPBS. Presumably cost benefit analysis requires the measurement of both costs and benefits—and neither may be easily or adequately measured. It is easy to measure direct dollar costs, but the concept of cost may include a host of other considerations—indirect costs, political costs, social costs, opportunity costs, and future costs. (The total cost of a project to be completed in the future is not a simple figure to estimate if the project is large and complex.) Given the elusiveness of the figures it is tempting to weigh most heavily direct dollar costs, and it is also possible for advocates to underestimate costs and critics to overestimate them. If costs are difficult to measure, benefits are often all but impossible. Is a scenic right-of-way more beneficial than a dull one, or a handsomely designed building better than a plain drab one with the same square footage? How can one measure the benefits to be derived from medical research or indeed the benefits to be gained from providing college scholarships to needy students? The point is that an intuitively plausible concept—cost benefit analysis—

17. Elizabeth Drew, "HEW Grapples with PPBS," *Public Interest*, Summer 1967, p. 11.

may be useful in some situations, and absolutely useless in others.

This by no means exhausts the problems and criticisms of PPBS. One of the characteristics of PPBS was its emphasis on the explicit statement of objectives. Yet, it was asked by many, can agencies afford to be explicit, if being explicit is likely to hinder their chances of getting what they want and doing what they want to? If an objective is likely to be controversial, can an agency be expected to be clear about it? Perhaps not being explicit is a way of avoiding conflict and even accomplishing objectives. Another difficulty was presented by the emphasis on multi-year planning. Like cost benefit analysis it may be intuitively plausible, but annual appropriations are the most common. Congressmen are elected every two years, Presidents are elected every four years and subcabinet officials frequently stay in office no more than two years. With this kind of change can multi-year planning be much more than an interesting but resource consuming exercise?

Despite these several problems the Bureau of the Budget pressed the implementation of PPBS. Agencies were expected to prepare and submit program memoranda, program and financial plans, and special analytic studies. In the summer of 1967 the Bureau of the Budget sent to all agencies a bulletin describing the required content and format for these documents.[18] The Program memoranda were supposed to "succinctly present the agency head's major program recommendations to the President within a framework of agency objectives, identify the alternatives considered, and support the decisions taken on a basis of their contribution to the achievement of these objectives." The Program and Financial Plan was supposed to present in tabular form a complete summary of agency programs in terms of costs and outputs. And the Special Studies were supposed to present in detail the analysis underlying the decisions described in the Program Memoranda. "Special Studies will, in general, formulate and review program objectives in terms useful for making program comparisons; they will review in terms of costs and benefits the effectiveness of prior efforts, compare alternative mixes of programs, balance increments in costs against increments in effectiveness at various program levels with attention to diminishing

---

18. Bureau of the Budget Bulletin 68-2, July 18, 1967, reprinted in James W. Davis, Jr., *Politics, Programs, and Budgets* (Englewood Cliffs: Prentice-Hall, 1969), pp. 178–186.

returns and limitations of physical resources, and assess the incidence of benefits and costs as well as their totals."

Obviously all this was quite an order, and it quickly became
even clearer than it had been that PPBS was going to be difficult
if not impossible to implement. It became clear that just trying
to implement it (or just appearing to try) would take much
effort and result in a flood of paper. It became clear that it was
impossible to measure all the benefits and costs of everything.
It became increasingly apparent that techniques that had apparently worked in the Defense Department could not be easily
transferred to all other departments. And there was a huge manpower shortage, both qualitative and quantitative. In the agencies there was a shortage of employees capable of doing analysis
and in the Bureau of the Budget there were not enough people
to review analyses. There was even disagreement on the meaning of PPB and its requirements, disagreement not only among
agencies but even within the Bureau of the Budget. It indeed
was not clear that the Bureau knew what it was trying to do or
that it knew what it wanted departments and agencies to do. In
1968 one student of the topic could write:

> The spread of the new budgeting system in the United
> States has been accompanied by mounting confusion. As
> with any significant innovation, it has been met by both
> inertia and hard-fought resistance—particularly among
> old-time budget personnel. This has led to ritualization,
> over-formalization, and over-documentation. Indeed, the
> flood of PPB paper work, clogging the channels of govern-
> ment communications, has in some cases threatened the
> very capability for rational action that it was supposed to
> enhance.[19]

In the same year a review of the use of PPB in a number of
major federal agencies could conclude that "the planning, programming, and budgeting functions are not performed much
differently in most agencies than they were before the introduction of PPBS."[20] Some commentators began to wonder how PPBS
would show up if cost benefit analysis were applied to it.

---

19. Bertram M. Gross, "The New Systems Budgeting," *Public Administration Review*, 29 (1969), p. 115.

20. Edwin L. Harper *et al.*, "Implementation and Use of PPB in Six-
teen Federal Agencies," *Public Administration Review*, 29 (1969), p. 624.

The observations of an official of the Bureau of the Budget are particularly instructive. With regard to the Program Memoranda, Jack Carlson wrote, "Many of the PM's tend to be descriptive, verbose, nonanalytic accounts of existing and proposed programs, together with an impassioned plea for funding at the full request."[21] With regard to Program and Financial Plans Carlson was even more negative.

> In the beginning, the agencies were asked for planning figures on how much and in what way they would spend money in the future; the result was a series of lengthy wishlists of what the agencies would like to spend on their programs if no fiscal constraints were imposed. Some agencies showed program increases in all areas of more than 25 per cent per year while other agencies showed small increases reflecting a level they thought politically feasible. The lack of consistent constraints on the future availability of public resources made this exercise almost useless.[22]

Carlson was not quite so critical of special analytic studies, but did note that agencies commonly concentrated their scarce analytical talent on minor issues or issues with small dollar consequences.

The flood of criticism that greeted the implementation of PPB resulted in modification and efforts to improve it. Rather than asking that everything be analyzed, the Bureau of the Budget limited its requests, thus encouraging agencies to focus their attention. And effort was also made to upgrade and enlarge budget and analysis staffs. Advocates of PPB began to back away from the extravagant claims that had been made for PPB in 1965 and 1966. Some might say that PPB had been tried and found wanting; others might say that it had not really been tried. In any case, PPB, described once as the "happening" of the decade in public administration,[23] was allowed to recede from

---

21. Jack W. Carlson, "The Status and Next Steps for Planning, Programming and Budgeting," in Robert H. Haveman and Julius Margolis (eds.), *Public Expenditures and Policy Analysis* (Chicago: Markham Publishing Co., 1970), p. 376.

22. Carlson, p. 377.

23. See the foreword by Dwight Waldo to a symposium issue of *Public Administration Review* devoted to PPB, 29 (1969), p. 111.

view. In the summer of 1971 the Director of the Office of Management and Budget sent a memorandum to all agency heads making this explicit.

> Agencies are no longer required to submit with their budget submissions the multi-year program and financing plans, program memoranda and special analytical studies as formerly specified. . . .[24]

It was clear further in the message that some parts of PPB would continue to be used selectively. The Office of Management and Budget would still require benefit cost analyses when new programs were proposed and might also require studies of future costs for new programs. But PPB as it was described and advocated in the 1960's had passed away.

The advocates of PPB had assumed too much, promised too much, and demanded too much. One gets the impression that many advocates of PPB were ignorant of the substance of many policy areas, and even more ignorant of the way bureaucrats and bureaucratic organizations operate. Analysts were at once confident and naive. A retrospective comment by a former member of Robert McNamara's staff is illustrative.

> In 1957 I packed my bag of recently acquired professional tools and flew off to the RAND Corporation, with the blessed optimism of youth, to solve the problems of the world. This was an exciting period at RAND, where there was stimulating research environment and a superb community of professional colleagues. Most of us felt that we were beginning to understand how to analyze public policy problems and how to improve the management of the public sector. Some of the products of this period are the techniques that have come to be known as systems analysis and program budgeting. The then unrecognized assumption of this work and these techniques was that public officials, given the correct information and sufficient authority, would do the right thing.
> Along with a few other RAND colleagues, I then joined the

---

24. Quoted in Leonard Merewitz and Stephen Sosnick, *The Budget's New Clothes* (Chicago: Markham Publishing Co., 1972), pp. 301–303. For a recent discussion of the fate of PPB see Allen Schick, "A Death in the Bureaucracy: The Demise of Federal PPB," *Public Administration Review*, Vol. 33, No. 2 (1973), pp. 146–156.

staff of Secretary of Defense Robert McNamara early in the Kennedy Administration. This staff should have provided the perfect testing ground for these new techniques —a department that had a tradition of planning, a Secretary that was receptive to analysis and had the energy to translate the support of the President into effective command of the department, and the motivation of working on very important problems. Although I should have known better, I only slowly developed a sense of unease that something was wrong with the premise of the information-analysis-directive approach to the management of the public sector. Briefly this approach fails to account for the institutions of bureaucracy and representative government. By 1964 I came to recognize that there is nothing inherent in the nature of bureaus and our political institutions that leads public officials to know, seek out, or act in the public interest. Cynics and a few political scientists could have told me this earlier—but without effect, prior to my personal experience in the bureaucracy.[25]

But if PPBS (or PPB) has passed from the scene budget reform and the ability of the President to control the bureaucracy are still live issues, and probably always will be. In April 1973 President Nixon sent a memorandum to twenty one government agencies (precisely the number that had received President Johnson's 1966 PPBS memorandum) calling on them to focus on *results* and explicitly formulate (in ways that facilitated the measurement of progress) major agency goals. "Your listed objectives should include new policy initiatives, major operational achievements and improvements which can be made in current programs, giving particular attention to objectives which you consider to be of Presidential level importance."[26] Agencies were given specific deadlines for submission of their objectives to the Office of Management and Budget which would in turn review them for consistency with the President's goals.

Some agencies had little difficulty complying and indeed had already been practicing something like the presidentially di-

---

25. William A. Niskanen, Jr., *Bureaucracy and Representative Government* (Chicago: Aldine-Atherton, 1971), pp. v–vi.

26. The quotation is from a report in the *National Journal*, Vol. 5, No. 22 (1973), p. 785. For recent discussion of Management by Objectives see this issue and Vol. 5, No. 33, pp. 1201–1210.

rected "Management by Objectives." But, no doubt predictably, there were problems, questions, and criticisms. Some officials observed that it was impossible to set meaningful goals, at least in some agencies, that allowed the measurement of progress. How can one measure progress toward the goals of the State Department? Or how can one measure progress toward eradicating cancer or heart disease? Some officials feared a flood of paperwork. There was concern that the new requirements represented a further attempt to extend Presidential influence and control into and over the bureaucracy and some officials both in the agencies and in OMB feared that power might flow from program specialists to professional managers who did not understand particular programs. In short, there was less than complete enthusiasm. The statements of objectives that came from agencies ranged from clear and useful to vague and general.

What the latest set of guidelines will accomplish is still an open question, and any attempt at forecasting is risky. But certainly there is a strong possibility that "Management by Objectives" will not have much impact on what is being done, or how, that it will not last much longer, at least as an explicit style, than the administration which introduced it. Many of the criticisms brought to bear on PPBS may be applied also to MBO and one press headline is at least provocative: "Yesterday's Panacea PPB is Out; Today MBO Is In."[27] It is worth noting further that Congress never wholeheartedly supported PPB, and it is not clear Congress has any interest at all in MBO. Insofar as it represents an attempt to strengthen the President any Congress could be expected to be skeptical and a Congress of the opposite party hostile. And finally, it is simply very hard if not impossible to change the traditions, routines, and rigidities of the budget process. Attempts to make the budget process more "analytic" and more "rational" are likely to continue, but success is not likely. Presidents will continue to try to control the bureaucracy, but are likely to continue to fall short.

A Note on Government Spending

Any detailed discussion of the current budget would be out of date within the year and is surely out of place. But before closing this chapter on government budgeting, it does seem im-

---

27. See *National Journal,* Vol. 5, No. 22, p. 788.

portant to consider current and likely future spending levels in general terms.[28] In January 1973 the President requested over 268 billion dollars for fiscal 1974, and the budget is likely to go even higher in future years. Inflation will affect what the government buys, work loads will go up, in many programs the number of beneficiaries will increase. Thanks to these and other reasons the federal budget by 1977 may be as much as 335 billion dollars and perhaps a good deal higher.

Defense does not constitute the largest part of the budget. Indeed, from 1963 to 1973 defense and defense-related expenditures had dropped from 53 percent of the budget to 34 percent, while civilian outlays were climbing to 66 percent from 44 percent. This growth in civilian parts of the budget (and continued growth) can be traced to rapidly rising social security benefits, to the start and growth of a number of social welfare programs, and to various revenue-sharing programs.

In recent years there has been substantial criticism of the budget. The two most common criticisms are that defense spending is too high and that too little is being spent for such purposes as urban improvement, social welfare, and environmental protection. The criticisms are likely to have some effect, though doubtless not as much as the most vocal critics might wish. After the criticism and complaint what is likely to happen is that defense spending will grow, but slowly, and Congress will add funds to those proposed by the President for domestic spending. In the end the total federal budget will reach new heights each year.

Given the all but inevitable growth in the budget it is essential to consider the revenue side of the ledger. Naturally consideration of the future involves assumptions that may prove inaccurate and forecasts based on them may be erroneous. But with this caution the future looks bleak and money tight. Since 1963 income taxes have been cut several times and excise taxes have been lowered. Social security taxes have gone up, but the

---

28. The discussion in this section relies heavily on Chapters 12 and 13 in Charles L. Schultze *et al.*, *Setting National Priorities: the 1973 Budget* (Washington: The Brookings Institution, 1972). See also Murray L. Weidenbaum and Dan Larkins, *The Federal Budget for 1973* (Washington: American Enterprise Institute for Public Policy Research, 1972), and Juan Cameron, "The Bad News About the Federal Budget," *Fortune*, November 1972, pp. 92–95, 190–196. It might go without saying that the interested reader should also look at current budget documents.

net result is that in 1973 federal revenues were $26 billion below the level they would have been if 1963 taxes had remained in force. If present taxes are not increased and current programs develop as expected, revenue will be insufficient to meet needs and a substantial deficit will exist. With present tax rates there will be little leeway for new programs during the next 5 years. Yet numbers of new programs are being considered in education, health, pollution control, and other fields. The political pressure for these programs is likely to make their passage all but inevitable. Of course some current programs may be cut to make room for new ones, but our political system does not make cutting easy. Yet tax increases are hardly popular. Perhaps the most likely prospect for the next few years is a modest tax increase combined with largely symbolic or inexpensive new programs. But no matter the outcome the continuing pressure on the budget is likely to yield continuing interest in analysis, evaluation, and experimentation. PPB will not be revived, but attention is certainly going to continue to be given to how budget choices are made and justified.

14 Evaluating Government Programs

A subject getting increasing attention in the bureaucracy and also attracting the attention of researchers and writers in the field of public policy and administration is evaluation.[1] In recent years more thought than ever has been given to the evaluation of government programs and policies. The growing interest and emphasis on evaluation can be viewed in part as growing out of the budget approaches represented by PPB and its more recent modifications. Partially the interest in evaluation may arise from our growing awareness of how bureaucracies function and our increasing sensitivity to the probability of gaps in their performance.[2] Partially the interest in evaluation may come from the view that programs can be likened to hypotheses or indeed plausible guesses or hunches. They may work, but they may not and in fact may make the problems worse; whether a program is

---

1. Consistent with the growing interest in evaluation, several books on the subject have been published recently. See Joseph Wholey *et al.*, *Federal Evaluation Policy* (Washington: The Urban Institute, 1970); Francis G. Caro, *Readings in Evaluation Research* (New York: Russell Sage Foundation, 1971); Carol H. Weiss, *Evaluating Action Programs: Readings in Social Action and Education* (Boston: Allyn and Bacon, 1972); Carol H. Weiss, *Evaluation Research* (Englewood Cliffs: Prentice-Hall, 1972); Peter H. Rossi and Walter Williams, *Evaluating Social Programs* (New York: Seminar Press, 1972).

2. For discussion of performance gaps see Anthony Downs, *Inside Bureaucracy* (Boston: Little, Brown & Co., 1966), pp. 191–193.

working as intended can only be determined by research. The current interest in evaluation may also arise in part from the desire of many social scientists to do something apparently useful or relevant. Evaluation research can be viewed as applied social science. And, finally, the growing federal budget together with apparently still growing problems (whether problems are really growing may depend on what one measures and how) has caused many observers to wonder whether what the government is doing in this area or that is working. For all these reasons and perhaps others there is substantial interest today in the evaluation of government programs and policies.[3]

This chapter begins with some consideration of evaluation and its objectives and moves on to consider the participants in evaluation and their relations with one another. The process of evaluation is discussed, and the chapter concludes with some consideration of the effects or impact of evaluation.

Evaluation and Its Objectives

What is evaluation? What does it mean? A long answer is implicit throughout this chapter, but a short answer is useful at the beginning. To start we can simply say that program evaluation means determining whether the goals of a program are actually being met, and how well. It is tempting also to say that evaluation involves research, but it need not. Citizens, journalists, congressmen, and executives commonly assess or judge or evaluate on the basis of intuition, guess, or hunch, with often little research in the background. Still, evaluation research is an increasingly heard term. Such research ideally involves the careful collection of information and its analysis and interpretation for the purpose of determining whether and how well a program is working. But, of course, evaluation research may be poorly planned, inappropriate or insufficient data can be collected, analysis can be limited and unimaginative, and erroneous conclusions can be drawn. Evaluation is a term that covers a multitude of activities.

The basic question of evaluation involves asking whether

3. There is at least a possibility that if social programs recede, at least temporarily, in the near future, interest in evaluation research will also slacken. But a case could be made that with resources apparently getting tighter and tighter it is more important than ever to know what works and what doesn't.

a program is doing what it is supposed to. Though this may sound like a straightforward task, it commonly is not. It may be difficult to discover what the goals of a program are; any program is likely to have many goals which persons in different positions (beneficiary, administrator, taxpayer, congressman) rate of different importance, and as evaluation is being carried out goals may shift. In addition to discovering whether goals are being met, evaluation may also be concerned with other questions. Are the goals of a program appropriate? Who is benefitting from a program and who is being disadvantaged? Is a program having unintended or unanticipated consequences and are these harmful or beneficial? How much is the program costing and who is paying? In short, what difference(s) does a program make?

Within this general framework a variety of activities may be labeled evaluation. To get some idea of the variety consider the grants that the Law Enforcement Assistance Administration makes through state and regional agencies to local police departments, courts, correctional institutions, and so on. Evaluation research might focus on the impact of LEAA funds in a single police department. What difference did the increased money make? (Obviously the reader can substitute for police departments, schools, welfare offices, libraries, or other organizations of interest to him.) An evaluator could look at several police departments and compare their performance. It might be possible to look at states either individually or comparatively to evaluate their systems for dispensing money, and the effectiveness of funded programs in reducing crime, recidivism, or whatever. An evaluation could look at strategies used in reducing street crime in different cities and try to assess their comparative effectiveness. (What effect do beat patrolmen have?) Or, much more globally, an evaluator (a whole team) could try to assess the performance of the Law Enforcement Assistance Administration. Clearly, evaluation can vary greatly in scale, breadth, and focus.

Evaluation can vary in other ways as well. Evaluation or assessment may be carried out by economists, sociologists, lawyers, journalists—or none of these. It may be carried out by bureaucrats, congressmen and their staffs, private companies, and university faculty working either under contract or on their own. The training, skills, values, and positions of evaluators may effect what is evaluated, how the evaluation is conducted, and what conclusions are reached. A lawyer might look at a program and find it sound—that is constitutional and in accord with existing legislation and regulations. An economist might look at it and think it terribly expensive. A sociologist might find both officials and clients delighted, and a political scientist might find wide public support. Another economist might discover that the problems the program was apparently intended to confront were getting no better. Put this way we see the multidimensional character of evaluation; we see also the many objectives a program may have, or at least the many criteria that it may have to satisfy. And we may also get the feeling that evaluation as a concept is not terribly new. Lawyers and journalists have been evaluating programs for a long time—as have citizens, congressmen, and bureaucrats. What is new in evaluation is the thought being given today to measuring and evaluating the results or consequences of programs in more or less precise quantitative terms.

Why assess consequences? Why try to find out what impact a program is having? Why evaluate? There are answers, and then there are answers. The obvious answer is that evaluation is conducted to get information that can lead to program modification and improvement, and to propose cancellation and the reallocation of resources. Put even more simply we evaluate as a first step to changing and improving. We evaluate the results of experiments to see what works. Perhaps all this can be summed up in Carol Weiss's sentence, "The purpose of evaluation research is to provide information for decision making about programs."[4]

As we shall see later the findings or conclusions of evaluation research rarely effect program decisions. (You may want to think now about why this would be so.) But right here it needs to be emphasized that evaluation, perhaps here we should say "evaluation," often is not motivated by a desire to improve programs. Instead it may have a number of other objectives. Carol Weiss has described these in detail: "Program decision makers may turn to evaluation to delay a decision; to justify and legitimate a decision already made; to extricate themselves from controversy about future directions by passing the buck; to vindicate the program in the eyes of its constituents, its funders, or the

---

4. Carol Weiss, *Evaluating Action Programs*, p. 14.

public; to satisfy conditions of a government or foundation grant through the ritual of evaluation."[5]

In a rather different way Edward Suchman has pointed to similar uses. His list of what he termed "misuses" of evaluation is worth quoting:[6]

> 1. *Eye-Wash:* an attempt to justify a weak or bad program by deliberately selecting for evaluation only those aspects that "look good" on the surface. Appearance replaces reality.
> 2. *White-wash:* an attempt to cover up program failure or error by avoiding any objective appraisal. Vindication replaces verification.
> 3. *Submarine:* an attempt to "torpedo" or destroy a program regardless of its effectiveness. Politics replaces science.
> 4. *Posture:* an attempt to use evaluation as a "gesture" of objectivity or professionalism. Ritual replaces research.
> 5. *Postponement:* an attempt to delay needed action by pretending to seek the "facts." Research replaces service.

To add a bit to the complexity it should be noted that no evaluation study is likely to be singly motivated. Rather the motivations behind any evaluation may be many and complex. Individuals themselves may have multiple motives (a desire to get useful information, but also interest in building political support), and many individuals are likely to participate in one way or another in even a single evaluation study. They all may have somewhat different motives and different interests. Given this complexity it is small wonder that "evaluation" is a term that can be applied to so many studies (different in quality, length, precision, utility), and it is small wonder that in the end evaluation studies often make little difference.

The Participants in Evaluation

Any program evaluation is likely to involve a number of different participants, each with a different role to play and with different interests. Some awareness of the participants, their

---

5. Carol Weiss, *Evaluating Action Programs*, p. 14.
6. See Edward A. Suchman, "Action for What? A Critique of Evaluative Research," in Weiss, *Evaluating Action Programs*, p. 81.

relationships with each other, and the consequences each may see in different outcomes or conclusions is essential if one intends to understand why evaluation research is carried on as it is and has the impact that it has.

Organizations and individuals responsible for carrying out programs are one large category of participants; they can be called the operators. This category or group of actors can of course be subdivided; some operators are likely to be simply carrying out routines while others may view themselves as actively engaged in solving or at least ameliorating problems. Operators in other words can be either drones or zealots, and doubtless there are many types in between. But for all the differences that may exist among them operators are likely to have some similarities. Commonly they do not evaluate what they are doing (except perhaps to develop evidence intended to show that they are doing a good job and what they are doing is working), and they may resist evaluation by others.[7] If evaluation is carried out operators may not cooperate with evaluators (or, under orders, do so only formally), and the conclusions of evaluators may be resisted and criticized.

Normally an organization responsible for a program will want to continue it and if possible expand it. Evaluative data will be interpreted by operating agencies in ways that will allow this. And if evaluators find some goals not being met operators may shift goals, so that they can continue. It is not normally in an organization's interest to cancel programs that it carries out. To do so may result in a reduced budget, laid-off employees, closed offices, hurt clients, and lost political support. Aside from all this it should be emphasized that many operators sincerely believe in what they are doing. Granted they may have little empirical evidence of effectiveness, they still believe, and are likely therefore to be critical of attempts to assess or measure program performance and are even more likely to reject conclusions that are critical. Indeed, operators committed to a program may not be able to conceive of a careful evaluation having negative results. In addition, operators (at least some of them) may understand that some programs have symbolic value (they express awareness and concern) even though they may not have precisely measurable output. People may believe they work,

---

7. See Aaron Wildavsky, "The Self-Evaluating Organization," *Public Administration Review*, Vol. 32, No. 5 (1972), pp. 509–520.

whether or not they can be shown to. And operators may be more sensitive to the value of this function, indeed willing to settle for it, than evaluators. One further point can be suggested; evaluation implies the possibility of change, and change may be resisted by both drones and zealots—drones because they cherish routines and by zealots because they know they are doing good.

In addition to operators another major set of participants in an evaluation are of course the evaluators. In principle the task of the evaluator is clear enough: find out the effects or consequences of a program. Is it working? Yet it may not be clear what is or was intended, and different spokesmen may articulate different goals. Obviously, if objectives are not clear or to all appearances unknown, it becomes difficult to tell whether a program is achieving them. Or a program may have multiple goals, some obvious and some not. Reaching any overall judgment is no easy matter, and the judgment reached may certainly be questioned. And throughout an evaluation an evaluator may confront data and measurement problems. What will show whether a program is working as intended?

Although the notion of research may suggest objectivity or neutrality, in fact evaluation is a political activity, it may have political consequences, and evaluators may be viewed as political actors. Evaluators, may, like operators, be committed to a program and anxious to show that it is working. Their choice of evidence, their interpretation of it, and indeed how and to whom they communicate results may all follow from a desire to reach a favorable conclusion. Alternatively, evaluators may be super-critics—out to prove that a program is not working, and should be abandoned. Their critical bias may affect their study design and their interpretation of data. In sum, there is no reason ever to assume that evaluators are simply neutral or that another set of evaluators would reach the same conclusion. Indeed it is important to remember that both supportive public relations and ideological opposition may be labeled evaluation.

Even without these complications different evaluators looking at the same program may reach different conclusions regarding its merits. The training, skill, and imagination of an evaluator may effect everything from his initial questions to the sophistication of his analysis and the framing of final conclusions. Evaluation may be carried out within an agency (for example by members of the research and analysis section), it may be contracted for (paid for by the agency, but carried out by outsiders), or it may be done completely by an outside agency. Who evaluates and the circumstances of the evaluation may effect analysis and conclusions.

Given the possible variety of evaluators and the various possible purposes of evaluation, what can be said of the relations that exist between evaluators and operators? It has already been suggested that operators are likely to resent evaluation. But now this must be qualified. If an evaluation is in effect forced on an agency and the agency has little control over the data collection or conclusions reached, there is certainly likely to be friction. But if an agency can select its own evaluators, perhaps members of its own staff, be involved in data collection and analysis, and have some voice in the preparation of final conclusions so that the evaluation and its conclusion serve agency ends, then relations between evaluators and operators are likely to be smooth.

It is worth noting that to forestall an evaluation by more or less uncontrollable outsiders an agency may decide to devote some of its own resources to funding its own evaluation. Here the point is that from an agency perspective evaluation involves both risk and possible gain. The problem for the agency is to minimize the one and increase the other. The solution may be no evaluation (if that is at all feasible) if the risk seems great and the need for gain small. If evaluation is unavoidable, an in-house evaluation (and thus more controllable) may be opted for. If evaluators are outsiders then an agency (and its supporters) may either try to educate them so that conclusions are not harmful, or they may begin to discredit the researchers while commenting on the difficulty if not impossibility or at least the untimeliness of the evaluation.

Two other points can be made about the operator-evaluator relationship. It has been indicated already that operators may not be able to imagine negative results. This being so operators may on occasion welcome an evaluation and see it as an opportunity to document and publicize their efforts and results. If and as it becomes apparent that negative conclusions are in the offing their relations with evaluators may rapidly deteriorate. Operators will grow uncooperative and balk at answering questions and providing data. A good beginning relationship may also deteriorate if the operator expects quick current data to aid him in his day-to-day decision-making while the evaluator wants to be careful, precise, methodical, and until the end reach no conclusion. The operator's failure to get quick information and assistance can lead over time to his giving an evaluation project low priority. Friction can also develop if during the course of a program an operator wants to modify or alter what he is doing and an evaluator wants a given procedure to be continued for a set length of time.

In addition to evaluators and operators there is another group of participants in the evaluation process. Perhaps the most appropriate term for this group is simply audience. The audience includes those who commissioned the evaluation; they will receive results and decide whether to act on them, ignore them, or call for more research. But there are numbers of others in the audience who must be taken into account once evaluation conclusions become public. (Think about it briefly and you will understand that agency officials may have strong incentives not to make public the results of evaluation—especially if they are negative and their intention is to ignore them.) Officials in other agencies may learn of a negative evaluation and conclude in public that their agency could do the job in question better. Critical congressmen may say that the data show that the program is not working. Benefitting interest groups may say that it shows nothing of the kind and the press may so oversimplify a report that readers who think they understand both the program and its evaluation will be wrong on both counts. Persons in the same professional field as the evaluators will comment on the research techniques, the quality of the data, and the appropriateness of the statistical tests that were used. Critics of a program will have an opportunity to say I told you so; it won't work. In the end audience reaction may determine how an evaluation is received, interpreted and used. The audience that is intended and anticipated may also effect how an evaluation is initially designed and carried out. But if it is intended for one audience but dealt with by another, its intended outcomes may never occur and wholly unanticipated ones take place instead.

The Evaluation Process

The evaluation process involves a number of stages and reviewing each of them may make the difficulties of evaluation research even clearer. At the start, an evaluation must be commissioned, agreed to, and supported. An immediate question concerns the circumstances under which evaluation is likely— an important question as many programs have never been evaluated in any systematic way. The converse question is also important—under what circumstances is evaluation not likely? Any reader should now be able to answer these questions plausibly, but some brief conclusions may be helpful. A number of years ago in their book *Organizations,* March and Simon asserted that satisfaction limits search.[8] Search in their context meant search or research for the causes of trouble, for changes in the environment, solutions to problems, new courses of action. Evaluation is a form of search activity; evaluators search for information that will tell them how well an organization is doing, or how well a program is working. And so we conclude that satisfaction limits evaluation. If things seem to be working, why spend money and manpower looking for trouble, why rock the boat? But, obviously, dissatisfaction—on the part of administrators, clients, or budget officials—may lead to evaluation. A crisis—rapidly rising workloads, a shortage of funds, deteriorating client relations or the erosion of political support—can lead to a decision to evaluate. A decision to evaluate may also be made with the intent of accomplishing one of the objectives mentioned in the first section—delay, whitewashing, or whatever. A decision to evaluate of course is made in a context of other considerations—the resources available, the possible risks, the press of time, the interests of outsiders. Given equivalent amounts of trouble in two programs, one set of administrators may decide they have money to conduct an evaluation and the possible gains outweigh the risks. Other administrators may, though faced with trouble in the program, decide not to evaluate but simply carry on and hope things turn out all right.

If evaluation is agreed to, then research must be designed. Before there can be any thought of measuring progress toward objectives they must be defined. Some objectives may not be public, and the staff involved may not agree on what the objectives of a program are. To emphasize the problem, consider a program providing federal funds to schools with large numbers of disadvantaged children. Clearly one objective may be to benefit the children and raise their performance to that of other children. (How might progress toward that objective be measured?) But one can imagine a number of other objectives. Easing the financial burdens of local school districts might be one

---

8. James G. March and Herbert Simon, *Organizations* (New York: John Wiley and Sons, 1958), pp. 173 ff.

objective and alleviating the high level of unemployment among teachers might be another. Reassuring (symbolic reassurance) parents and teachers that the administration (or a particular agency) is concerned may be another objective, and maintaining the good will of Congress may be another. Or consider a program of federal aid to local police departments. Possible goals include lowering the crime rate in general, lowering the incidence of some crimes in some areas, increasing the resources of police departments, getting more uniformity in police standards and practices across the country, testing the efficacy of different police practices, demonstrating a general concern with maintaining law and order, and freeing up local funds for expenditure on other problems. A program providing inexpensive milk in public schools may be intended to improve the nutrition and academic performance of children, lower family food costs a bit, and at the same time aid the dairy industry. An evaluation team setting out to do a study must decide what to focus on; it may also have to rank objectives in terms of importance. In the end, evaluators may find that goal x is not being met, but administrators may then say that x is really not very important and goal y which is very important is being met. So the program continues. The potential for friction and disagreement is clearly great.

If it is possible to reach agreement on objectives, evaluation can move to the development of measures, the design of research, and the collection of data. There are numerous difficulties associated with these steps. What questions should be asked? How large a sample should be used and how should it be composed? What time period should be studied? Will there be control groups? Careless or inappropriate answers to such questions may substantially reduce the value of any evaluation. In any case the answers are likely to be criticized. If an evaluation made during the first year of a program reaches negative conclusions, supporters of the program will say the program was not given a chance. (If five years elapse, the program may have so many supporters evaluation is pointless—and after five years a bad program may have done harm.) To determine the effect of a program it may make scientific sense to randomly provide program benefits to some while denying benefits to others and then see whether the benefits had the intended or hoped for effect. But such experimentation may be politically impossible and ethically troublesome. (Without control groups assessing the differences between alternative programs or between acting and not acting may be difficult.) It may also make sense to use a relatively small sample, but critics who do not understand probability will find fault with a sample apparently too small.

Aside from such points it is important to remember a basic fact of evaluation research: data collected is loaded with difficulties, some obvious and some more subtle. Collecting and analyzing information costs money, and when there is no money for data collection there can be no evaluation. A little money may bring insufficient data. Collecting information also takes time. This is especially true when the collection is not routine or the data not readily available and a study to collect the necessary data must be especially designed and carried out. Sometimes there may seem to be no time for study when a problem seems serious or a crisis atmosphere prevails. When an attitude of "do something now" prevails careful research is not likely. Collecting information also takes people with skill and imagination. The collection and analysis of information absorbs trained manpower resources, and their lack may be an obstacle to the collection of information.

Bureaucratic secrecy or just discretion may hinder or completely prevent the collection of necessary information. Officials may be hostile toward or at least not candid with the press, academics, and members of evaluation teams. Officials may be especially uncooperative and misleading if they fear the consequences of evaluation. Those who initially designed a program and those who have a stake in its continuation may be especially uncooperative. Respect for individual privacy may also hinder data collection, and potential respondents in a study or survey may themselves not want to answer questions. Another obstacle to data collection and evaluation is a lack of curiosity. Data collection for program evaluation starts with questions and perhaps with skepticism. But administrators charged with implementing a program are likely to be committed, to believe in a program's efficacy, to think positively—and if this is so evaluation is unlikely. Ideology and preconceptions are other factors that effect whether data is collected, what data is collected, and how it is collected.

After data are collected they must be analyzed, interpreted, given meaning. And of course there are problems, though only a few can be mentioned here. One problem concerns the difficulty of determining whether change, even change in the desired direction occurring after a program was instituted, happened because of the program. Consider the case of increasing the size of a police force, introducing foot patrols, and then finding a lower crime rate. One possiblity of course is that crime dropped because foot patrols were introduced. But there are numerous other possibilities. Perhaps crime went down because the area in question lost population; perhaps crime went down because of a seasonal change (there is less street crime in the winter); perhaps crime went down because of new probation and parole practices; perhaps the police simply altered their reporting practices (police can make crime rates appear to go down by how they classify and report crime). And of course one must also consider the location of crime and the length of time in question. Did crime go down or simply move from one area to another? Further, time series data, whether stock market movements or crime rates, fluctuate from day to day and month to month.[9] What looks like a drop if viewed between two points (whether from one month to the next or one year to the next) may simply be a normal fluctuation.

In any case the important question for the analyst of police practice and crime rates is—would crime rates have dropped anyway? Put in more general form, the question of whether the apparent effect would have occurred without the program is crucial for the analyst, and one seldom asked by the advocate. Individuals go through a training program and get jobs. Would they have gotten jobs anyway? Would at least some of them have gotten jobs anyway? Family planning clinics are opened up and the birth rate drops. Would it have dropped anyway? How much of the drop can be attributed to the family planning clinics?

In assessing programs and their effects there are other points to have in mind. There is a great deal of difference between a 6-year-old and a 16-year-old, and a dull-witted analyst might attribute the difference to 10 years of school. But of course this won't do. The 16-year-old has been exposed to family, peers, and a variety of experiences and is 10 years older. Trying to sort out what the school can be thanked or blamed for is obvi-

---

9. For a provocative discussion of the instability of time-series data see Donald T. Campbell, "Reforms as Experiments," in Weiss, *Evaluating Action Programs*, pp. 187–223. Campbell's article is also reprinted in Francis Caro, *Readings in Evaluation Research*.

ously a complex task, and the particular allocations may vary both among schools and individuals.

Two individuals have some nervousness and tension; a physican gives one a mild tranquilizer and the other a sugar pill. Both get better, and the effectiveness of placebos is illustrated. The placebo effect should also be considered in trying to assess social programs. Perhaps the equivalent of the placebo is the symbolic program. In any case, the essential notion, that if one thinks he is being helped he may be, should be kept in mind. (The evaluator might remember that the placebo works only when it is not recognized.) In the same vein the Hawthorne effect should be mentioned. It was discovered years ago when researchers in a factory altered various working conditions, hoping to determine the effect of the changes on work performance.[10] What they found was that no matter what the experimental conditions, productivity went up. The conclusion in the end was that selecting some employees to take part in a series of experiments affected their behavior. Work was positively affected because researchers and management were showing an interest in the workers.

In connection with evaluation research a Hawthorne effect might be looked for in at least two ways. First, social service programs may have an effect not because of their substance but because others (administrators, groups, workers, teachers, and so on) are showing an interest in beneficiaries. (A program delivering meals to shut-ins may be important nutritionally but also important socially.) Second, the presence of evaluators within an organization may effect both what is done and how well, and this may have important implications. Consider a number of health clinics supported with federal funds and located in many urban areas. An evaluation team might very well decide to look at the performance of only a sample, but if the evaluation itself has an effect on performance then it would be risky to assume that clinics not evaluated were performing like the ones to which evaluators had gone.

To all these difficulties can be added others. A major

10. For discussion of the Hawthorne effect see George C. Homans, "The Western Electric Researches," in Schuyler Dean Hoslett (ed.), *Human Factors in Management* (New York: Harper and Brothers, 1951), pp. 210–241.

problem may be a lack of standards or benchmarks or precedents with which to interpret data that is collected. Once one knows that 50 percent of the persons enrolled in a job training program got jobs after graduation, does this mean that the program is working poorly (90% should have), as well as can be expected (given the level of skill they are given and the job market), or really very well? (Problems mentioned already as well as others can be seen here: how many programs and trainees ought to be studied; would some have gotten jobs in the absence of a program; do they get jobs for which their training fitted them; how long did they stay on the job?) Data on organization performance can often if not always be interpreted in many ways. Agency heads, budget officials, congressmen, members of the press, and academic researchers may all look at the same body of data and draw different conclusions. It is a rather flexible and secure official who can conclude that his program is having no impact or that what his organization is doing is not working. Perhaps the word bias is too strong, but it is surely true that officials are likely to see in data what they want to see and what they are prepared to see; they are unlikely to find what they are not looking for or do not want to find.

Less obvious are problems associated with the perspective or breadth of an evaluation. If one remembers that a program is likely to have multiple goals, then it is clear that an evaluation in terms of only one is partial. Further, as it frequently may be impossible to obtain a full statement of program objectives, many if not most evaluation must be viewed as partial. Awareness of this may help explain why evaluation research is so frequently ignored. Evaluation research is likely to be partial in another sense as well. One can imagine analysts evaluating the effectiveness of a program to train computer programmers, but not assessing the market for computer programmers. The result may be a flood of well-trained graduates who cannot find positions. One can imagine a housing program that is found successful (the planned number of housing units are being built on schedule within the allowed cost), but because of the success more and more people are being attracted to the area with consequences ranging from rising welfare and crime rates to rising rents. The point is that no evaluation can deal with everything; there will inevitably be unassessed effects and unstudied consequences. These last examples also emphasize, however, that evaluation may properly assess not only progress in meeting objectives but also the appropriateness of the objectives themselves Yet to say this is to emphasize that evaluation may go beyond the scientific and empirical and get into questions of politics and judgment.

The Impact of Evaluation

Given all the problems, uncertainties, and conflicts that surround evaluation research it should come as no surprise to learn that it commonly has little impact on what does or doesn't happen. A number of observers have reached this conclusion. Peter Rossi, for example, has observed, "I do not know of any action program that has been put out of business by evaluation research."[11] Joseph Wholey has commented in a similar vein, "The recent literature is unanimous in announcing the general failure of evaluation to affect decision making in a significant way."[12]

There are a number of reasons for this. First, it is important to know that systematic evaluation of programs (as differentiated from more or less intuitive assessment) is by no means common, and evaluations with a claim to respectability for social scientists are less common. Sheldon and Freeman note, "The empirical situation, however, is that there have been but a handful of respectable evaluation studies of social action programs."[13] Wholey, after a careful study of evaluative activity in the federal government reached similar though more strongly stated conclusions.

> The most impressive finding about the evaluation of social programs in the federal government is that substantial work in this field has been almost non-existent. Few significant studies have been undertaken. Most of those carried out have been poorly conceived. Many small studies around the country have been carried out with such lack of uniformity of design and objectives that the results

11. Peter H. Rossi, "Evaluating Social Action Programs," in Francis Caro, *Readings in Evaluation Research*, p. 278.

12. Joseph Wholey, *Federal Evaluation Policy*, p. 46.

13. Eleanor Bernert Sheldon and Howard E. Freeman, "Notes on Social Indicators: Promises and Potential," in Weiss, *Evaluating Action Programs*, p. 170.

rarely are comparable or responsive to the questions facing policy makers.[14]

This chapter contains many explanations for this state of affairs. Any list would certainly include skepticism about the value of social science research in general and evaluation research in particular, hostility to evaluation and uncertainty with regard to consequences, satisfaction with the status quo, and lack of funds and staff.

Even if evaluation is carried out its results and conclusions will very likely be ignored or attacked. Some reasons for this have been brought up previously, and others can be added. The evaluation itself may be poorly designed or executed and yield more-or-less useless results. Or the data may lend themselves to multiple interpretations, or the evaluators may so bury their conclusions in statistics and jargon that if not invisible they are at least undecipherable. The timing of an evaluation or a final report of it may be awkward or impossible from a policy-maker's point of view. Taking action apparently indicated by an evaluation may itself be costly, in terms of either politics or economics. Evaluators may not weigh the political or symbolic costs of program evaluation, but policymakers do and may thus ignore evaluation. And after all, the evaluator may be wrong. To all these points may be added another—that frequently no thought is given as an evaluation is planned about what will be done with different sorts of results. There is no prior planning or commitment regarding appropriate courses of action, whether positive or negative results are found. Unpleasant or surprising results can thus be ignored. In effect, as Peter Rossi has colorfully expressed it, operators may simply welch on the bet.[15] (They bet on positive findings; when negative results occur they may simply act as though they hadn't happened.)

At this point it might be appropriate to speculate about the possibility of increasing the volume, quality, and impact of evaluation and strategies for doing so. Some answers may be implicit in this chapter, and to think about the problem might be a useful exercise. But it seems more useful simply to remember that a major topic throughout this chapter has been "the politics of evaluation." Anyone who would improve the state of

---

14. Joseph Wholey, *Federal Evaluation Policy*, p. 15.
15. Peter H. Rossi, "Boobytraps and Pitfalls in the Evaluation of Social Action Programs," in Weiss, *Evaluating Action Programs*, p. 229.

evaluation must recognize and work within political realities. Administrative reform comes hard and reformers are frequently disappointed. A common error is to think that efficiency, economy and rationality (however vaguely these may be defined) are values shared by all. This patently is not the case. To be sure in principle it may seem true, but there are lots of other values, different people interpret the same principles differently, and self-interest is important. And it is worth remembering that even improvements and reforms are not immune from unanticipated and on occasion unfortunate consequences.

15 Organization and Reorganization

The Importance of Organization Structure

The importance of the government (or an agency) budget is likely to be obvious—even to outsiders. Outsiders may not realize the significance of organizational questions, however. Questions about lines of authority and division of responsibility may be passed over as either trivial or technical and labeled mere box-shuffling. They may be. Nevertheless, the structure of an organization can be important. The formal allocation of power, of rights, and responsibilities, of authorizations and limitations, is affected by the structure of an organization. Indeed, to organize means to allocate power and responsibility and to reorganize means to change the existing pattern of allocation. Certainly, just who exercises power may have little to do with who has what powers on paper, even at the presidential level. Political history is full of references to strong Presidents and weak Presidents. But even though there have been weak or ineffective Presidents, no one would argue that the formal powers of the President are meaningless. Formal powers give the man who has them an advantage in seeking actual power. They provide stepping stones to actual power. Structure can be important.

There are other reasons that may be given for the importance of formal organization, though all of them may be related to the basic question of power allocation. A formal organization chart is obviously something of a communications diagram; it shows who communicates with whom, or more politically, who has access to whom. Few would argue that all the communication within an organization is shown on the organization chart, but what the chart shows may be important, if only for symbolic reasons. One group may want its favorite governmental organization given Cabinet status because that symbolizes access to the President and presidential interest; another group may want its particular organization located in the Executive Office of the President for the same reason. By the same token an organization or group may resist being moved, if it means being cut off from the President or the department secretary. Bureaus within a department may resist being included in an administration or other subdepartmental organization headed by an assistant secretary if it might result in their losing direct contact with the Secretary. As Harold Seidman, for several years Assistant Director for Management and Organization in the Bureau of the Budget, has noted:

> Organizational arrangements are not neutral. We do not organize in a vacuum. Organization is one way of expressing national commitment, influencing program direction, and ordering priorities. Organizational arrangements tend to give some interests, some perspectives, more effective access to those with decision-making authority, whether they be in Congress or the Executive Branch.[1]

Organization structure is important for other reasons. Who will be responsible is determined in some measure by the formal organization. This matter may be critical, because who is carrying out an activity may have an effect on what is done and how well. In other words, structure can effect program. Bringing pollution-control activities into one agency may bring different results than scattering those activities among numerous agencies. The formal structure of an organization determines not only which units will be responsible but also which individuals. By reorganizing, shuffling responsibilities, and in some cases moving someone to one side or "kicking him upstairs," the performance of an organization may be changed.

There is no need to dwell longer on the importance of organization structure. But it is worth emphasizing that or-

---

1. Harold Seidman, *Politics, Position, and Power,* (New York: Oxford University Press, 1970).

EXECUTIVE AGENCIES AND FUNCTIONS OF THE FEDERAL GOVERNMENT ABOLISHED,
TRANSFERRED, OR TERMINATED SUBSEQUENT TO JULY 1, 1971

(For Executive agencies and functions of the Federal Government abolished, transferred, or terminated subsequent to March 4, 1933 and prior to July 1, 1971, see the 1971-72 edition of the *United States Government Organization Manual* or contact the Office of the Federal Register, National Archives and Records Service, General Services Administration, Washington, D.C. 20408).

BUREAU OF EMPLOYEES COMPENSATION.— As part of the Department of Labor since 1950, the Bureau administered the Federal workmen's compensation laws. On Mar. 13, 1972, functions of the Bureau were absorbed by the Office of Wage and Compensation Programs (see text).

COMMITTEE ON PURCHASES OF BLIND-MADE PRODUCTS.—Established by act of June 25, 1938 (52 Stat. 1196; 41 U.S.C. 46). Name changed by act of June 23, 1971 (85 Stat. 77) to Committee for Purchase of Products and Services of the Blind and Other Severely Handicapped (see text).

CONSUMER AND MARKETING SERVICE.— Established by the Secretary of Agriculture on Feb. 2, 1965, to administer broad inspection, marketing, regulatory, and related programs. On Apr. 2, 1972, by Secretary's order, renamed Agricultural Marketing Service (see text), and certain functions transferred to the Animal and Plant Health Inspection Service (see text).

FEDERAL FIELD COMMITTEE FOR DEVELOP-MENT PLANNING IN ALASKA.— Established by EO 11182 of Oct. 2, 1964, as the principal instrumentality for developing coordinated plans for Federal programs which contribute to the economic and resources development in Alaska. Abolished by EO 11608 of July 19, 1971.

FOSTER GRANDPARENT PROGRAM (NEW)— Authorized by act of Sept. 17, 1969 (83 Stat. 112; 42 U.S.C. 3044—3044e), to provide opportunity for the elderly poor to assist needy children. Functions transferred to ACTION by Reorg. Plan 1 of 1971, effective July 1, 1971 (see text).

OFFICE OF BUSINESS ECONOMICS.— Established by the Secretary of Commerce on Dec. 1, 1953, to provide basic economic measures of the national economy, summarized by the gross national product. Renamed Office of Economic Analysis and on Jan. 1, 1972, became a part of the Social and Economic Statistics Administration (see text).

OIL IMPORT ADMINISTRATION (INTERIOR).— Established by Proc. 3279 of Mar. 10, 1959. On Oct. 22, 1971, the Administration was merged into the Office of Oil and Gas (see text).

OIL IMPORT APPEALS BOARD.— Established by the Secretary of Commerce on Mar. 13, 1959. On Dec. 23, 1971, the Board was made a part of the Office of Hearings and Appeals (see text).

OFFICE OF MINERALS AND SOLID FUELS (INTERIOR).— Established by the Secretary on Oct. 26, 1962. Abolished and its powers, functions, and responsibilities reassigned to the Deputy Assistant Secretary (Minerals and Energy Policy) in the Office of the Assistant Secretary—Mineral Resources, effective Oct. 22, 1971.

PEACE CORPS.— Established as an agency of the Department of State by EO 10924 of Mar. 1, 1961, and continued in existence under the Peace Corps Act (75 Stat. 612; 22 U.S.C. 2501 et seq.) pursuant to EO 11041 of Aug. 6, 1962. Functions, powers, and responsibilities transferred to ACTION (see text) by Reorg. Plan 1 of 1971, effective July 1, 1971.

PRESIDENT'S ADVISORY COMMITTEE ON MANAGEMENT POLICY.— Established by EO 10918 of Feb. 16, 1961, to study, and to advise and make recommendations to the President with respect to policies that may be followed by labor, management, or the public which will promote free and responsible collective bargaining, industrial peace, sound wage and price policies, higher standards of living, and increased productivity. Inactive.

VOLUNTEERS IN SERVICE TO AMERICA (VISTA).— Established by act of Nov. 8, 1966 (80 Stat. 1472; 42 U.S.C. 2991—2994e), provide volunteers to work in domestic poverty areas to help the poor break the poverty cycle and administered by the Office of Economic Opportunity. Functions transferred to ACTION (see text) by Reorg. Plan 1 of 1971, effective July 1, 1971.

Source: U.S. Government Organization Manual
        1972/73

ganization structure is often the subject of intense political conflict as differently affected parties struggle for advantage, struggle to preserve and enhance their positions. As Harvey Mansfield has observed, "Reorganizations have political objects and objections, and so, notoriously, involve conflicts of purpose and contests of strength unless the parties concerned share a common political indoctrination."[2] Whenever a new organization or reorganization is proposed an important question is: What will this do to the organizational or program balance of power? Who will gain power? Who will lose? With answers, we are on our way to knowing who will favor the reorganization and who will oppose it. It may pay to be skeptical of statements maintaining that power relationships will not be affected. Such is the argument of those who stand to gain.

Why Are Reorganizations Proposed?

Granted that organizational structure is important and that proposals to change it will often occasion intense conflict, we can go on to ask why change proposals are made. Many of the answers were suggested in the last section. Proposals for reorganization may come from those who wish to increase their power, their visiblity, their access to important decision-makers, or to alter the scope or emphasis of a particular program. Reorganization—or change in jurisdiction—may be used to strengthen a program or prevent its dilution. Those who want to strengthen the education-support activities of the federal government may call for the creation of a Cabinet-level Department of Education. On the other hand, reorganizations can be used to weaken or abolish a program. Programs taken out of the Office of Economic Opportunity and put elsewhere may gradually fade from view. And as the OEO loses programs it gets smaller and smaller and smaller until finally. . . .

There are other points to be made about the reasons for reorganization.[3] As an organization increases in size it may re-

---

2. Harvey C. Mansfield, "Federal Executive Reorganization: Thirty Years of Experience," *Public Administration Review*, Vol. 29, No. 4, (1969), p. 333.

3. The following discussion draws on an essay by Frederick C. Mosher, "Some Notes on Reorganizations in Public Agencies," in Roscoe C. Martin (ed.), *Public Administration and Democracy* (Syracuse: Syracuse University Press, 1965), pp. 129–150. See also Mosher's lengthy analysis in his *Governmental Reorganization: Cases and Commentary* (Indianapo-

organize; increasing size leads frequently to increasing specialization and increasing subdivision. As more and more people
are added to an organzation, more and more supervisory levels
may be created. When an organization takes on more responsibi-
ties, it must decide whether to give the new duties to an existing
unit or to create a new one. When Congress authorizes a new program, it must decide whether to give responsibility for it to an
existing organization or whether to create a new organization.

The growth of the executive branch testifies to the fact that
new organizations are often created to administer new programs.
The National Aeronautics and Space Administration did not
exist until the United States had a space program, and the
Environmental Protection Agency was created to administer a
new set of programs. Lest it be thought that the creation of such
organizations is "obvious" or natural, it would have been plausible
to give responsibility for space to the Defense Department and
responsibility for the environment to the Department of the Interior.

Related to changes in organization and program may be
changes in workload. As the workload of an organization increases, more employees may have to be hired; and the increasing number of employees make their reorganization advisable.
Alternatively, it may be possible to utilize an existing work force
differently (reorganize) and thus cope with increased workload
without takng on new employees. Workloads of course may decrease, and this too may affect organization structure.

Changes in work methods or technology may have an effect
on organization structure. The most obvious example is the computer; its introduction may have a substantial effect on formal
organization. Examples of the effects a computer can have
are several: a clerical force may be much reduced in size, a staff
of professional employees (programmers, mathematicians) may
have to be employed; and decisions in the hands of middle
management may be placed in the hands of top management.
The introduction of machinery to replace men, automation, can
have substantial effects on organization structure.

Demands for efficiency and economy may also lead to organization. One may well be skeptical here, because often there
may be very little substantial evidence that reorganization will
in fact lead to the claimed savings. The claim of efficiency and

---

lis: Bobbs Merrill Co., 1967), pp. 475–517, and the article by Mansfield
cited in footnote 2.

economy may be simply a rationalization for a reorganization intended to alter the distribution of power. Still one must admit that by centralizing purchasing, for example, it may be possible to buy at lower cost. Introducing machines and letting men go may lower production costs. Contracting jobs out instead of creating a government organization to do a job may keep costs lower. While efficiency and economy may be only surface goals of reorganization, they may also be the real goals.

Of course efficiency and economy are not the only covers for a politically motivated reorganization. All of the immediately foregoing justifications—changes in size, workload, program responsibilities, and technology—may be used to justify a proposed reorganization that is intended to reallocate power or shift access, because they may seem relatively apolitical, or neutral, or technical. A neutral justification may be used in the hope that it will win more widespread support for a reorganization than a political justification would.

It should be kept in mind, of course, that even if a reorganization proposal results solely from a change in technology or size it still may have an effect (real or imagined) on the distribution of power and access and thus may be opposed by those who think they will be adversely affected. This observation leads to the most important point: that reorganization proposals are likely to have both multiple causes and multiple effects, though different participants will usually emphasize one effect or another.

Some Current Problems

Today in the federal government there is considerable interest in or concern over questions of organization. There is concern about the apparent fragmentation of effort and responsibility in many program areas and worry that communication and coordination between agencies engaged in the same general field are not all that they should be. (Of course, what should be is by no means always clear.) This concern has been expressed by citizens and congressmen, and by the President. For example, in a message to Congress in 1971 President Nixon observed:

> Nine different Federal departments and 20 independent agencies are now involved in education matters. Seven departments and eight independent agencies are involved in health. In many major cities there are at least 20 or

30 separate manpower programs, funded by a variety of Federal offices. Three departments help develop our water resources and four agencies in two departments are involved in the management of public lands. Federal recreation areas are administered by six different agencies in three departments of the government. Seven agencies provide assistance for water and sewer systems. Six departments of the government collect similar economic information—often from the same sources—and at least seven departments are concerned with international trade.[4]

The reasons for such apparent fragmentation or duplication are obviously many, and it would surely be imprudent to defend this status quo as a matter of principle. Yet, put this way, without explanation or further detail, the problem may seem worse than it is. For example, in the health field a major agency is the Department of Defense; the military services all have medical personnel and facilities. Surely it would make little sense for battlefield medical care to be provided by a unit of HEW. And it would not make much sense for the Defense Department to fund community health care centers (this has been an OEO mission) or to fund major programs in medical research (a function of the National Institutes of Health). The point is that though numerous agencies are involved in health care they are not all doing the same thing; they are not working on the same problems or serving the same clienteles. Of course this is not always true, but it is true often enough to make sweeping statements about fragmentation risky.

This point aside, it is worth noting that consolidation can lead to inflexibility and slow response times while redundancy may not only increase flexibility but enhance the opportunities for innovation and invention. Especially may this be the case if there are several units working on the same problem. Further, redundancy (another word for duplication) may reduce the likelihood of failure and inaction. Numerous agencies engaged in the same problem may lead to competition, and from competition citizens may benefit. A lack of duplication may be interpreted as a monopolistic situation. To be sure, even when there are several agencies apparently competing, internal agree-

---

4. See the President's Message on Cabinet Reorganization (March 25, 1971), reprinted in *Papers Relating to the President's Departmental Reorganization Program*, a reference compilation (Washington: U.S.G.P.O., 1971), p. 6.

ments may lessen competition and make the bureaucratic environment more stable, more predictable. Numerous agencies in the same policy area may also provide more possible access points for interests wishing to be heard within the bureaucracy.[5] Valuable as duplication may be (at least on occasion) it remains to emphasize that the 1960's raised many questions about administrative structure, organizational coordination, the need for more efficiency, and similar topics. The questions, however, were clearer than the answers. Indeed, while many call for coordination few can define it and fewer still can say with certainty how to achieve it. And there is always the problem of what to coordinate with what. Should one coordinate health care for the poor with other poverty programs or with other health programs? It is no help to say with both. One must make choices; one must allocate effort and attention. In the end health care for the poor must be placed with health programs or with poverty programs—or it can be made independent. Any placement may have both benefits and costs.

In addition to the fragmentation problem the enlargement of government activity in the 1960's raised clearly two other organization problems. One pertains to field structure. With more and more service being delivered in the field by federal agencies, questions of supervision, communication, and control become increasingly important. How much discretion should local units have; how much nationwide uniformity should there be; and how can and should headquarters in Washington keep track of activities around the country? A related topic concerns the appropriate mechanisms for coordinating in the field the activities of different federal agencies. Should there be little White Houses in major cities across the country or field stations of the Office of Management and Budget or interagency councils of federal executives in major cities? Any one of these might be chosen and in the past some have been, but the promise of each must be considered in the light of the strong pressures for agency independence and autonomy.

A second major organization problem concerns the allocation of responsibilities between (and the relations between) federal agencies and state and local agencies. State and local au-

---

5. For a provocative discussion elaborating on these and other points see Martin Landau, "Redundancy, Rationality, and the Problem of Duplication and Overlap," *Public Administration Review,* Vol. 29, No. 4 (1969), pp. 346–358.

thorities are often confused if not hopelessly lost in what they regard as a chaotic collection of agencies and programs. Grim comments about Washington bureaucrats, red tape, and alphabet soup are common. Federal officials for their part may want to impose a particular form of organization on state and local agencies; they may have particular personnel, planning, and reporting requirements, and they are likely to be unhappy with the general quality of state and local administration. One solution to the problem, of course, is simply for the federal government to take over an activity in question. Another solution is to leave a problem entirely in state and/or local hands. But for a host of problems there is shared responsibility, frequent friction, and also frequent calls for reorganization or reallocation of responsibilities. A recent example is President Nixon's revenue sharing proposals.

The Sources of Reorganization Proposals

We have considered why reorganization proposals come up; we have not as yet considered the sources of reorganization proposals, but this subject is worth some attention as the source of a reorganization proposal may be related to its substance and its chances of success. We can begin by dividing the sources into two types—external and internal—and then look at each type more closely.

External sources are those outside the organization being reorganized, though not necessarily outside the government as a whole. There are a variety of such groups. Perhaps best known are the commissions and task forces appointed by the President to advise him either on general matters of government organization or on problems in a particular policy area, such as health, welfare, or defense. The two Hoover Commissions that inquired into the operations of the government in the late forties and early fifties are examples of this type of commission. The National Advisory Commission on Selective Service which made rather sweeping proposals for the reorganization of the Selective Service System is an example of a more specialized external body that makes recommendations.[6] In recent years a number of advisory commissions and task forces have been appointed—

6. See *In Pursuit of Equity: Who Serves When Not All Serve*, Report of the National Advisory Commission on Selective Service (Washington: U.S.G.P.O., 1967). The reorganization suggested in this report was not

both publicly and on a confidential basis—and they have recommended changes in organizations administering the programs or coping with the problems they were set up to consider. President Johnson appointed a Task Force on Government Organization headed by Ben W. Heineman, and even more recently President Nixon set up a Council on Government Organization headed by Roy Ash. (It is interesting to note that this Council, whose deliberations resulted in a major departmental reorganization proposal from the President, included no one from the academic field of public administration.)

Members of the White House staff may make proposals for reorganization, as may the Office of Management and Budget and other central service and control agencies. A Secretary's office may propose changes in the bureau structure within the department. When we come to this level, though, we come close to internal sources of reorganization. But external-internal may be more of a continuum than a dichotomy.

The external sources named so far have all been more or less official. Even though many task forces and advisory commissions are composed largely if not exclusively of private citizens, they exist with official sanction. Suggestions for reorganization can come from the particular groups affected. Housing and urban groups for a long time asked for a Department of Urban Affairs, and finally the Housing and Home Finance Agency became the Department of Housing and Urban Development. Organized labor was delighted when it finally succeeded early in the twentieth century in getting a Department of Labor. Other groups or individuals with special interests have asked that particular departments or agencies be created to serve their interests or that a unit be created within the Executive Office of the President to look after a particular problem. Particular congressmen or committees may also suggest new organizations or the reorganization of existing ones.

What about internal sources of reorganization? It has been said already that departments may suggest and carry out reor-

---

carried out. Another example of reorganization proposals coming from an outside commission is provided by the commission appointed to investigate the assassination of President Kennedy. According to the *New York Times*, a reorganization of the Secret Service carried out in 1965 was "the direct result of the Warren Commission's investigation of the assassination of President Kennedy. The commission found several deficiencies in the service. . . ." *New York Times*, November 11, 1965.

ganizations of their constituent bureaus. In addition, departments, agencies, and bureaus may initiate their own reorganizations, though in particular cases just who initiated what may not be clear. In 1966 the Department of the Navy reorganized itself, apparently on its own initiative.[7] After receiving a good deal of criticism the National Aeronautics and Space Administration began to examine carefully its own organization structure as well as its management processes, and it set up two new divisions.[8] In 1965 the Office of Education carried out a rather sweeping reorganization of itself.[9] And these are only three examples of what is a more or less constant phenomenon.

Principles, Proverbs, and Patterns

What forms are reorganization proposals likely to take? There is probably no branch or subject of administration where the supply of conventional wisdom is put to more use than in the field of organization design. And for good reason: there is very little sound research on the relationships between organization structure and organizational functioning. Usually, if not invariably, anything that might pass for data is lacking, and the proposers of reorganizations and new organizations rely on patterns and proverbs (often in the guise of principles), occasionally seasoned with a bit of imagination.[10]

---

7. See *The New York Times*, March 8, 1966, p. 1. "Secretary of the Navy Paul H. Nitze announced today a sweeping reorganization of the Navy's management structure. The principal changes will strengthen the authority of the Chief of Naval Operations and eliminate all but two of the traditional bureaus that once were virtually autonomous."

8. See the *New York Times*, April 5, 1967, p. 1. "With an eye to improving its operations, the National Aeronautics and Space Administration has begun a permanent, high-level review of its organization and management. . . . The operation began without fanfare last month with the creation of a new division to act as a sort of watchdog for the agency's headquarters in Washington and its 14 field centers, laboratories and launching bases. A new office for coordinating planning was also established."

9. See Stephen K. Bailey, "The Office of Education: The Politics of Rapid Growth," paper prepared for delivery at the 1966 Annual Meeting of the American Political Science Association, New York City.

10. A classic statement is Herbert Simon's "The Proverbs of Administration," *Public Administration Review* (Winter 1946), pp. 53–67.

Textbooks on public administration often mention purpose, process, area, and clientele and suggest that these words be borne in mind when considering the structure of an organization. Units with the same purpose should be grouped together, or units serving the same people, or units utilizing employees with the same skills. But what is not made clear is that it is usually impossible to say what is or ought to be the basis for any particular organization. For example, if the Veteran's Administration were to be reorganized should its functions be given to the Defense Department or to HEW? And if the latter, should housing loan programs be given to HUD? Conventional wisdom offers little assistance.

Conventional wisdom says that similar services should be grouped together (everything from secretarial pools to personnel recruiting to central purchasing to the government's education programs), but it is perfectly plain that in many circumstances the decentralization of services is more flexible (and perhaps no more costly) than the centralization of services. Span of control is another common phrase; it means that the President or a Secretary or other executive can control only a limited number of subordinates and consequently should have only a limited number reporting to him. Put this way, it is sensible but hardly helpful. Put more specifically—that an executive can control no more than 10 or 15 or 20 or whatever subordinates—it is at best arguable and at worst nonsense. Everything depends on the ability of the executive, the ability of the subordinates, whether subordinates have limited discretion or unlimited, whether close supervision is a goal to be achieved or behavior to be avoided (a wide span of control makes close supervision impossible), whether subordinates are all doing the same thing or all doing separate things, and so on.

In his 1971 proposal to reorganize several cabinet departments, President Nixon offered a variant of "purpose" as the rationale for the suggested changes.

> We must rebuild the executive branch according to a new understanding of how government can best be organized to perform effectively.
>
> The key to that new understanding is the concept that the executive branch of the government should be organized around basic goals. Instead of grouping activities by narrow subjects or by limited constituencies, we should or-

ganize them around the great purposes of government in modern society. For only when a department is set up to achieve a given set of purposes, can we effectively hold that department accountable for achieving them. Only when the responsibility for realizing basic objectives is clearly focused in a specific governmental unit, can we reasonably hope that those objectives will be realized.[11]

Despite the rhetoric the rationale seems hardly new, and a moment's reflection is enough to reveal several problems. What are the great purposes and the basic goals of modern society? At a minimum there is room here for debate and disagreement (not least from some of those limited constituencies—like farmers and organized labor), and in the absence of answers on which we are all likely to agree there is likely to be conflict over the specific form that a reorganization should take. In fact a reorganization proposed in March 1971 had gotten almost nowhere by the end of 1973. Moreover, goals that are articulated are likely to be so few and broad that one must still decide how to assign jurisdiction for hundreds of programs and scores of bureaus, divisions, offices, and administrations. More specifically, the President proposed the creation of a Department of Natural Resources, a Department of Community Development, a Department of Human Resources, and a Department of Economic Affairs. Even an outsider could see difficulty in dividing programs between community development, human resources, and economic development. The dividing lines are less than obvious. And a little thought may lead to doubts about the feasibility (at least the difficulty) of abandoning such client departments as the Department of Agriculture, the Department of Commerce, and the Department of Labor. Many people may agree that the present government structure lacks coordination, is inefficient, wasteful, and so on. Not nearly as many are likely to agree on a specific set of remedies. In a way the difficulty is similar to the classic budget problem. Citizens (and congressmen) may think that government in general is spending too much, but no one wants the programs that benefit him cut. No one wants to lose his organization. It is hard to imagine the House and Senate Agriculture Committees (to take just one policy area) watching

---

11. The President's message appears in *Papers Relating to the President's Departmental Reorganization Program* (Washington, D.C.: U.S.G.P.O., 1972), p. 11.

calmly as the Department of Agriculture is dismembered and merged away.

Clearly the common phrases, the proverbs, are little help. So patterns are commonly used. What does this mean? It means that organizational structures already in being are often copied when a new organization is created. And when existing structures are reorganized, they are reorganized along lines probably existing (and apparently working well) in another organization. In other words, the past experience of other organizations is copied. Now this does not mean that there is systematic study of past experience, and certainly there is no systematic analysis of the effect of structure on performance. Rather there is simply copying, with more or less modification based on personal experience, common sense, and conventional wisdom. In a particular case, attention may be paid to the Congressional committee structure (an organization put one place may be reviewed by one committee, another location may mean another committee, and committees vary in their sympathies), to the implications of different organizational types (a cabinet organization has status and visibility; a corporation has independence and sounds businesslike) and the personnel involved.

All this is not to deny the existence of invention. Surely, there is some, but there is more copying than inventing and in the absence of substantial knowledge this may make sense. Still, one is justified in being skeptical when a new organization or a reorganization is justified in terms of principle.

The Acceptance and Rejection of Reorganization Proposals

When are proposals for change likely to be made, and when are they likely to be accepted? A common time for changes to be proposed is when a new administration takes over, particularly when this involves a new party coming to power. Organization changes are likely to be part of the new program proposals of a new administration. If a new President presents a variety of new program proposals as did President Roosevelt, President Kennedy, and President Johnson, he is likely to present simultaneous proposals for new organizations to carry out his new programs or at least proposals for the restructuring of existing organizations. And even if he does not present many new programs he may suggest reorganization in order to enhance his control, in the hope of saving money, or simply as a way of indicating inexpensively that he is doing something.

Reorganization proposals are also likely when a particular program or existing structure becomes the subject of unusual criticism. In recent years, for example, such different organizations as the Post Office, the Secret Service, and the Selective Service System have come under criticism for varying reasons; and reorganization proposals have in each case come on the heels of the criticism. Reorganization and improvement in performance are closely associated in the minds of both managers and politicians. Reorganization proposals are also likely whenever a manager finds that he is not getting what he wants and thinks a reorganization would be at least a partial solution (what he wants may be anything from more economical operation to faster decisions, more information, or increased control), or when a manager is faced with new demands that his existing structure cannot meet.

If half the question is, "When are reorganization proposals likely?" the other half is, "When will they be accepted?" More accurately perhaps the question is, "Under what conditions will proposals be accepted and under what conditions will they be rejected?" No hard and fast rules are possible; yet it does seem possible to suggest some conditions that if present will mean acceptance and if absent will mean rejection. They can most clearly be presented in the form of a list. A reorganization will be accepted if it has:

1. The President's support (acquiescence).
2. The Office of Management and Budget's support (acquiescence).
3. The support of top management in the immediately affected organization.
4. Support or acquiescence from other executive branch agencies.
5. Support or acquiescence from relevant committees in Senate and House.
6. Support or acquiescence from relevant interest groups.

There is little question that a reorganization proposal will be accepted if it has the support of all these groups; and many lower-level reorganizations do get ready acquiescence and can be thought of as routine reorganizations. Because many reorganization proposals do not have anything like unanimous support, their sources of support, the amount of influence the supporters have and how intensely they feel as opposed to the influence and intensity of the opponents are important. Some examples may clarify these points. The proposal of the National Advisory Commission on Selective Service to reorganize the Selective Service System fell flat. Why? The proposal came from a Presidential Commission, but was turned over by the President to another task force for further study. In other words, he did not immediately accept it, and furthermore he appointed the director of the Selective Service System to the task force. The director, General Hershey, was openly and consistently hostile to any reorganization, and allied with him were the chairmen of the House and Senate Armed Services Committees. Clearly with this kind of opposition and with the President apparently unwilling to press hard, the reorganization was bound to fail. The creation of the Department of Transportation presents the other side. There was opposition, both from affected agencies and from groups concerned, but the President wanted a Department of Transportation and was willing to work to get it. He compromised, he bargained, he persuaded—and the Department of Transportation was created.[12] There is no question that presidential interest and influence were decisive. But it is also worth noting that the creation of the Department of Transportation had important symbols on its side. It was possible for supporters of the bill to point to the proposed new department and predict coordination, the elimination of waste and duplication, new efficiency and economy, and rational planning.[13] Whether all these would result and in what degree was of course open to question, but that these favorable symbols could be associated with the reorganization was a plus.

Though President Johnson was successful in getting a Department of Transportation, President Nixon has so far been

---

12. The *New York Times* (March 13, 1966) reported that the Administration was optimistic over passage of the bill to create the Department of Transportation. "One reason for the optimism is that a deliberate attempt has been made to keep the bill as non-controversial as possible. . . . A key part of this strategy was to drop an attempt to establish uniform standards for setting rates, fares, route awards, and subsidies in different areas of transportation."

13. See the testimony of administration officials in *Creating a Department of Transportation*, Hearings Before a Subcommittee of the Committee on Government Operations, House of Representatives, 89th Congress, 2nd Session (Washington: U.S.G.P.O., 1966).

unable to establish the Department of Community Development
that he has favored. A Department of Community Development
was one of the four new departments that President Nixon proposed in 1971 and the one to be taken most seriously. It was the
department with the best chance of reasonably prompt acceptance, yet it failed. It failed for a number of reasons, and some
consideration of them is instructive.[14]

The proposed Department of Community Development
would have involved renaming the Department of Housing and
Urban Development and bringing into it units of several other
departments. The Federal Highway Administration and the Urban Mass Transportation Administration from the Department of
Transportation and the Farmers Home Administration and Rural
Electrification Administration of the Department of Agriculture
would have been brought into the Department of Community
Development, as would units of other departments. Highway and
agricultural groups strongly opposed these transfers and lobbied
strenuously against the inclusion of organizations serving them
in the Department of Community Development. Congressmen
allied with agriculture also expressed their opposition in no uncertain terms.

In support of the reorganization there was not enough to
balance this opposition. Clearly reorganization was not a popular
issue; the man in the street probably could not have cared less
one way or the other if indeed he was even aware of the matter. Support from potentially supportive urban groups was not
strong, if only because other legislation pending at the same
time was attracting a major portion of their attention and effort.
Perhaps most important it was not clear that the administration
actively worked to achieve its proposed department. One observer
noted in October 1971 that the administration "had not begun
the necessary business of behind the scenes persuasion," and
Senator Ribicoff, a supporter of the reorganization, noted, "They
[the administration] are not systematically working with Congress and the interest groups."[15]

Despite this slow start it appeared at one point that the

---

14. The discussion below relies on several articles that have appeared
in the *National Journal.* See Vol. 3, No. 41, pp. 2030–2038; Vol. 4, No. 17,
pp. 701–704; and Vol. 4, No. 38, pp. 1459–1465.

15. For both these quotations see the *National Journal,* Vol. 3, No.
41, p. 2031.

Department of Community Development would in fact be created. But then it collapsed. The *National Journal* reported in the fall of 1972, "The Community Development Department reorganization has died in the House Rules Committee, after a successful attack by no fewer than seven chairmen of important House committees and subcommittees."[16] It may, to be sure, be brought up again in coming years but unless the White House pushes very hard it does not seem likely that major programs can be split out of existing departments and away from particular standing committees of the Congress and placed in a new department.

The Costs of Reorganization

So far in our discussion of organization and reorganization we have mentioned only goals and hoped-for results; we have not mentioned the costs of reorganization. But these exist and can be great; so important are they that in inquiring into the acceptability of reorganization proposals it is worthwhile to consider the costs. What are they?

Depending on the type and extent of the reorganization, individuals may lose status, money, the chance for promotion, perhaps even their jobs. They may be required to learn new jobs or may have to behave in different ways. They may have to work with different people. At the organizational level there are also costs. Some employees may resign.[17] Morale may deteriorate. Access to higher levels of authority may change, and a new congressional committee may assume jurisdiction. New standards of performance may be expected. If units themselves are transferred from the parent organization and no new ones take their place, the parent organization obviously shrinks in size and budget and may shrink in prestige as well.

Both individuals and organizations may resist reorganization. For anyone affected to support a reorganization the benefits must appear to him to be greater than the costs; if they appear otherwise, he may be passive or hostile. It would be simple to

---

16. See the *National Journal*, Vol. 4, No. 38, p. 1460.

17. The *New York Times* (April 24, 1966) reported, "An exodus of administrative, scientific, and technical personnel, resulting from a governmental reorganization, is threatening to slow down President Johnson's efforts to clean up the nation's water supplies."

say that for a change proposal to be accepted there must be more supporters than opposers, but this would be too simple. Intensity of feeling is important; a few intense individuals may be able to equal or overcome many men with relatively mild feelings. Political influence is also important. Many bureaucrats in opposition may not kill a proposal if the President favors it. Who opposes and supports is as important perhaps as how many support and oppose. But even here it is well to keep in mind the notion of cost-benefit. Even though he might have won the battle, the President perhaps did not fight for the Selective Service reorganization because it might have cost him support in the Armed Services Committees, support he needed for measures that he considered more important.

These sections, like the preceding ones, have emphasized the politics of reorganization, with good reason. Structure, along with budgets, personnel, and program, may be a subject of political contention; and what structure emerges from a conflict may have implications for the balance of political power as well as for program effectiveness and administrative economy and efficiency. Surely not all reorganizations are hotly disputed, but then neither are all budget decisions. The potential for conflict is still there.

Epilogue

Some Current Issues and Future Prospects

It is not uncommon in the last chapter of a text to look back and summarize what has gone before; this brief chapter differs. It tries instead to look ahead and consider future problems and possibilities. The goal is to build on what has gone before, rather than simply to shorten and repeat it.

We should begin by thinking of the current context of American government. Put succinctly the time is one of rapid change along multiple dimensions—technological, environmental, social, political, and economic.[1] Each of these categories could be subdivided again and again. Conditions are developing on every side that require (or at least might appear to) a government response, and even the solutions to some problems bring problems of their own.[2] The central cities of the country continue to decay while the rural areas of the country continue to

---

1. Nowhere is this point made with more force than in Alvin Toffler, *Future Shock* (New York: Random House, 1970).

2. There are numerous examples of this. One or two will suffice. Freeways built into cities to speed traffic flows have demolished housing, caused relocation problems, increased the demands for parking spaces, and brought in cars to further pollute the air. Housing projects intended to at least ameliorate the living conditions of poor people have themselves become human horrors; and subsidized single-family housing brought in its wake shoddy construction, disgruntled owners, enriched builders, and some official corruption. The program of Aid to Dependent Children is charged at a minimum with contributing to family instability. The list of programs that bring their own problems could be extended.

lose population. Population concentrates in the suburbs of the country and exacerbates already serious transportation problems. Crime rates go up, and both narcotics addiction and alcoholism are major medical (and social) problems. Depression is a national malady. Men and women are bored with their work, though substantial portions of the population are unemployed and a number unemployable. A significant portion of the population is poorly housed, poorly fed, and poorly educated. The country, despite its poor, is the richest in the world and consumes materials at an inordinate rate while in the process fouling air and water and creating tons of solid waste. Supplies of energy move dangerously low. The population itself is growing, though at a slowing rate (which may itself bring problems), and it is mobile. And of course this is but the briefest sampling. Other observers might comment on the high price of health care, the urban traffic jam, the myriad problems in the schools, or the ubiquitous problems associated with civil rights and civil liberties.

But these problems must themselves be put in context. Rich as the United States is, its resources are limited. At any particular time, the resources available limit the problems the government can attend to, how many problems it can attend to, and how much it can do. To be sure, as the economy grows more revenue becomes available, assuming taxes are not cut. But while some of this may be available for funding new programs and coping with new problems, or old problems in the past ignored, some of it must also be used to pay higher prices, higher salaries, and to cope with higher workloads.[3] To be sure, higher taxes can bring in more revenue, but tax increases are never popular, and currently they are highly unpopular. Within a more or less stable or slowly growing budget, funds can be reallocated, but this simply means that to apply more money to x less is applied to y. The political price of this can be high, and those who lose rarely submit quietly. In any case, it is unlikely that there will be money enough to cope or cope adequately with all apparent problems. There is no book that says problems and resources have to equal one another.

Though limited funds are certainly important, limits on

---

3. For a full discussion of such matters see Charles Schultze *et al.*, *Setting National Priorities: the 1973 Budget* (Washington: The Brookings Institution, 1972).

other resources are also important. Manpower resources are or may be limited, and this may prevent the accomplishment of some goals. Though manpower resources can be expanded—the supply of doctors, for example, can be enlarged—to do so takes both time and money, and in the meantime limits on health manpower restrain the kinds of programs that can be carried out. And of course it should not be forgotten that men attracted to medicine (or whatever other field) are attracted *from* another field, which in turn may turn up short.

Also important, and perhaps in social welfare and human resource areas most important, are the limits on knowledge (knowledge is a resource) that exist. Available knowledge bearing on a host of problems—everything from crime to poverty to alcoholism to narcotics addiction—is severely limited and so are the chances of successfully coping with such problems. In many fields policy results from common sense, intuition, conventional wisdom, and perhaps some research. The results, or their lack, are predictable. Of course more research might lead to answers, but research costs money and the supply of that is limited. And there might be neither money nor inclination to implement the findings of research.

Unlimited problems and limited resources is one interpretation that can be placed on current conditions. Can the government, can public administration, cope adequately with this situation? No one can answer this with much assurance, but success surely is not certain. In any case, it may be useful to consider some of the future implications of present policy-making structures and practices. A moment's thought is enough to call to mind a number of these; government is federal, pluralistic, elitist, fragmented or divided, and bureaucratic.

We might begin by thinking about the federal system. Currently states and localities are pressed for funds as never before to carry out programs and meet their growing obligations, while their legislative and administrative structures (with a very few exceptions) are the subject of substantial criticism and/or skepticism. What courses of action are available to the national government? To do nothing seems an option not open, though perhaps it is. In any event, several other alternatives are available. One possibility would be simply to continue on an expanded scale (expanded both in terms of problem coverage and in terms of dollars) the grant-in-aid programs of past years together with the general revenue-sharing program that was approved in 1972.

Another possibility would be for the federal government to abandon many of the narrow grant-in-aid programs while substantially enlarging the general revenue-sharing program (not likely, as Congress is reluctant to provide money without having some say in its use) or at least combining the many grant-in-aid programs into a few broad categories of aid. (This has been pressed by the Nixon Administration but so far not successfully.) Yet another possibility would be for the national government simply to take full responsibility for some programs now administered by the states with the assistance of federal funds. This has begun to happen in the welfare field. Yet another possibility is that the federal government will find relief for its own fiscal problems by cutting back some grant-in-aid programs and under cover of decentralization and self-reliance allow the states to cope with their own problems. This might be one interpretation of the federal budget proposed for 1974. No doubt there are other possibilities.

Each of these must be set against the fact that the federal government is itself under financial pressure, a fact which both militates against greatly increased generosity and encourages federal agencies to watch state and local agencies carefully. Close supervision and strict enforcement may yield conflict and a demand that the federal government either just take over or provide funds without strings. Neither of these is likely to prove at all popular, but in the end federal takeover seems more likely, though this may well depend on what sets of values are in power. If federal takeover occurs it need not be accompanied by a substantial expansion of the federal civil service. Service can be contracted out, and some major ends might be achieved (or at least their achievement might be attempted) through use of the tax system. Tax credits or deductions could be provided for one purpose or another. But in any event the federal budget would go up. It is possible also to imagine that in future years some services may be provided by some states for themselves, while others will contract with the federal government to provide them. Tax collection is the most obvious possibility, but other services might also be provided by the federal government on a reimbursable basis.

One obvious problem has not been raised—the simple existence of the states. There is no rationale today for the existence of 50 states, and if one were dividing the country today the subdivisions of the national government would certainly be fewer and larger than they now are. State borders today make little sense. But they do exist, and to talk of abolishing them and setting up 10 or a dozen regions is so much wasted breath. Their existence, however, will prove a source of continuing difficulty to be coped with over and over again as problems shift.

It is commonplace to speak of American government and politics as pluralistic, composed of many groups and interests. In the past it was commonly assumed that conflicts between the groups generally ended in widely acceptable compromises and generally happy results. ("That government is best which is" might have been the motto.) Surely today this is open to question. Outcomes may have been favorable to interests that had access to and influence with decision makers. Outcomes may have been favorable to those that controlled political resources, but what of those that didn't? Often of course they were passed over, ignored, or burdened. Increasingly, the passed-over and ignored demand a voice and evidence that they've been heard. This has consequences for administrative agencies. There are in effect more signals for the administrator to attend to—and there is more noise. With more interests wanting to participate, there is likely to be more conflict, the environment of the administrator is likely to be more turbulent, there will be more jobs that are labelled impossible. Administrators will face a variety of demands from outside and also demands from below and from above; yet responsiveness to any may offend others.

Several consequences seem possible. One consequence is that administrators will increasingly need to have well-honed political skills if they are to survive. Without political sensitivity other professional skills may go for naught. (Lawyers used to conflict and negotiation will be in high demand as administrators.) Another consequence is that administrators will be increasingly short-termed; if any decision makes enemies, then in fairly short order an accumulation of decisions can result in enemies enough to overwhelm any administrator. But a third and rather different possible consequence is that multiple and conflicting signals accompanied by much noise can simply result in administrative paralysis. When the right choice is not clear, no choice is likely. The problem this presents for coping adequately with a rapidly changing environment is obvious. In the worst of all possible worlds (but hardly an altogether improbable one) individuals will cope with discord and confusion and apparent chaos by withdrawing (paralysis), but the unplanned and unwanted consequence will be that agencies and government as a whole will decreasingly be able to cope successfully with problems and changes in their environment.

If it has been common to speak of American politics as pluralistic it seems to be becoming common to speak of it as elitist. The argument (and it is a varied and vague one) is that America and its locales are governed by and for the benefit of a few rather than by and for the many. Some observers may find a single and small elite while others find multiple but overlapping elites; but in any case the emphasis is on decision-making by a few. Within limits this surely is plausible, given the limited number of influential positions in American politics and the numbers of American citizens who take no active part in politics at all. Yet there can be substantial argument about the size of the elite (50 or 5,000 or 50,000), the basis of their influence, and what they personally gain—and avoid. We need not enter these arguments here. Rather it seems simplest to agree that major decisions in American politics are often made by just a few—the final details of a Social Security bill may be worked out by a small task force working in Ways and Means Committee rooms on Capitol Hill and major foreign policy decisions may be worked out by a small group working in the White House situation room. Myriads of other decisions are made by small groups (even twos and threes) and ratified by larger groups. A New York or Washington lawyer may meet with someone from the Department of Justice or a regulatory commission—and a decision is reached. A presidential Special Assistant working with only a few others decides to accept or ignore a Task Force Report—itself basically the work of not very many. Decisions are made and work is done not in large public meetings but privately (though not necessarily secretly) among groups. And this is likely to continue if any work is to be done at all.

But this point must be elaborated or qualified. Increasingly there may be an emphasis on knowledge, skill, merit—both in government and out. The bureaucracies may be (or be becoming) meritocracies.[4] And membership in the elite (and retention in it) may require merit. Of course that is not all that will be required. Good luck, appropriate personality attributes, and no doubt loyalty and proper values are all important too. But merit,

---

4. For a provocative discussion see Michael Young, *The Rise of the Meritocracy* (Harmondsworth: Penguin, 1961).

skills, and knowledge will be critical. And insofar as this is true, decision-making will be elitist. (The conflict here with openness and popular participation is worth reflecting on.)

Elitist policy-making has other dimensions that warrant consideration. If it is true that decision-making and control lie more and more within the hands of a few decision-makers in the White House, fewer and fewer are at least trying to be in charge—then surely it is accurate to say that decisions are made (or not) by an elite, though not by an elected elite. But having said this it must be remembered that important members of the governing elite may not now be officials and may never have been. Attorneys, publishers, scientists, and professors may all be members of the elite, if it is defined broadly enough. They may not be involved in final decision-making, but their advice may be both sought and listened to, and this is likely to continue. Commissions, committees, and task forces, to say nothing of less formal contacts, are useful ways of gathering information, eliciting probable reactions, and building support.

American politics and administration (not only American of course) is often said to be fragmented and divided, and this can be interpreted in many ways. The federal structure can be viewed as a form of fragmentation. There are fifty state governments, and so many local governments (thousands) that it is hard for revenue-sharing officials to keep track of them all. The separation of powers into three branches of government can be viewed as another dimension of the fragmentation, and the departmental and agency structure can be viewed as yet another form. Hundreds of agencies, with many frequently engaged in the same problems (at least apparently), either competing or cooperating with one another, often make policy-making difficult. The field structure of the federal government—units of this agency and that operating across the country and around the world—also contributes to the meaning of fragmentation. And if one includes in the policy-making machinery everything from trade associations to contractors, the fragmentation is multiplied manyfold. Within this fragmented structure some of the fragments, at least on paper, articulate with one another, but others are well nigh free-floating

What are and may be the consequences of this fragmentation, and what are the prospects for change? To answer the last question first, the chances for substantial reduction in the amount of fragmentation seem minimal. We may all in principle favor some tightening, but who will be the first to give up power and authority? It is possible indeed that we have a policy-making structure that we can not agree to improve, but one nevertheless which will increasingly be unable to work effectively. What more specifically of the consequences of fragmentation? The time it takes to respond to changing conditions and problems is likely to be great. As a chain may be no stronger than its weakest link, our system may be no faster than its slowest wit. By the time the last portion of the system understands the problem or the solution or simply gets the word it may be too late, whether the problem is environment pollution or population growth, or poor nutrition, or what.

There are other points to be made. Fragmentation may make it likely that the system will generate a lot of innovative ideas and new inventions, but the same fragmentation will greatly hinder their rapid and widespread adoption. Fragmentation increases the costs of communication, makes coordinated effort difficult, and indeed solutions to problems that require widespread well-coordinated and uniform administrative action may simply be impossible. The appearance of duplication may be encouraged. In a fragmented system it may be easier and cheaper to cope anew with a problem than to find out whether someone else has earlier experienced the same problem and solved it satisfactorily under similar conditions. Attempts at co-ordination and control, in a system used to discretion and independence, may generate resistance and conflict, and in any case require the commitment of substantial resources. In a dispersed and fragmented system it requires tons of paper to maintain even the semblance of an adequate command and control system. And after a while, if lots and lots of reports are required from lots and lots of units, no one in headquarters will be able to either read or assimilate them. They will simply come in while the units go on their way. On the other side of all this it might be said that fragmentation leads to flexibility. True. It brings also, however, its own kind of inflexibility, or at least inability.

Given the problems of fragmentation one should consider thoughtfully calls for decentralization, calls heard today in particular agencies and in the national government as a whole. Clearly such calls are a reaction to current failures, as well as a reflection of an ideological, almost cultural, bias against "big government." But decentralization has its own problems, and if it goes very far is likely to be followed with calls for recentralization. The answer to the question of whether the problems of fragmentation can be solved is no. But the answer needs quali-fication. The problems of fragmentation can be expected; and when programs demand responses that a fragmented system is unlikely to deliver, that can be pointed out.

American politics and policy-making is not only pluralistic and fragmented, it is bureaucratic. Surely much has been said on this point already. But the consequences of this fact deserve further attention. Consider just a few of the common character-istics of bureaucratic organizations—hierarchy, reliance on rules, standard operating procedures, reduction of action to routine, emphasis on career service—and it is easy to conclude that bureaucratic organizations are best adapted to coping with a fa-miliar and stable environment. Yet implicit in this conclusion is an important question about the ability of bureaucratic organiza-tions to cope with a rapidly changing environment. With sub-stantial oversimplification, we might say that policy making has been bureaucratized at a time when bureaucratic forms of or-ganization were becoming less and less appropriate. To add to the problem we have a form of organization that relies on rank and expertise and is prone to secrecy at a time when new groups are demanding the right to participate.

What of the future? One possibility of course is that the classic bureaucracy will simply become extinct and government will be made up of much more temporary and fluid organiza-tions. "Adhocracies" is Toffler's delightful term. But for this to happen would require the cooperation of a great many current bureaucrats who personally benefit from their positions. They have authority, responsibility, some hope of a future, and both financial and job security. They have powerful incentives to pre-serve the organizational status quo, and the increasing unioni-zation of government employees has to be reckoned with. In short the organizational (that is, the bureaucratic) structure of the government is not likely to change very much or very fast and thus may find itself increasingly unable to cope with change in the environment. This may be likened to the familiar eco-nomic and environmental problem which Garret Hardin once described as the tragedy of the commons. No one bureaucrat will favor giving up his position and perquisites. This surely is un-derstandable, but the result may be the retention of inappropriate and increasingly powerless government organizations and the increasingly rapid deterioration of the social and physical environment of each bureaucrat—not to speak of the citizenry at large.

If traditional bureaucracies continue more or less intact (as they are likely to) then there are likely to be continuing conflicts between their members and outsiders who do not have or understand the values of bureaucracies. Those outside may demand access, programs that benefit them, too, and jobs. Bureaucrats may respond in bureaucratic fashion. And in the end not much may change, while skirmishing continues. As important as the conflict between those who value (and likely benefit from) bureaucratic ways and those who demand participation rights and beneficial outcomes is the very real conflict that may exist between bureaucratic policy-making and the popular image of American democracy with its voting and elections. In simple language, bureaucrats are not elected; mostly they are not even known. We elect on the other hand men who may be not so much participants as observers, and perhaps often not even that. Perhaps it would be too much to say that American government has moved from democracy (many would say it never was that) to bureaucracy, but surely the rise of the huge bureaucracies (not only public but also private) has transformed American policy-making and over time (who knows) may paralyze it.

A Selected Bibliography

Allison, Graham T. *Essence of Decision.* Boston: Little, Brown and Co., 1971.

Anderson, Patrick. *The President's Men.* Garden City: Anchor Books, 1969.

Barnard, Chester I. *The Functions of the Executive.* Cambridge: Harvard University Press, 1938.

Bauer, Raymond A., ed. *Social Indicators.* Cambridge: M.I.T. Press, 1967.

Blau, Peter M. and W. Richard Scott. *Formal Organizations.* San Francisco: Chandler Publishing Co., 1962.

Blau, Peter M. *Exchange and Power in Social Life.* New York: John Wiley and Sons, 1964.

Caiden, Gerald E. *The Dynamics of Public Administration.* New York: Holt, Rinehart and Winston, Inc., 1971.

Caro, Francis G. *Readings in Evaluation Research.* New York: Russell Sage, 1971.

Corson, John J. and R. Shale Paul. *Men Near the Top.* Baltimore: The Johns Hopkins University Press, 1966.

Coser, Lewis. *The Functions of Social Conflict.* New York: The Free Press, 1964.

Cronin, Thomas E. and Sanford D. Greenberg. *The Presidential Advisory System.* New York: Harper and Row, 1969.

Cronin, Thomas E. "Everybody Believes in Democracy Until He Gets to the White House . . . An Examination of White House Department Relations," *Law and Contemporary Problems,* Vol. 35, No. 3, Summer 1970, pp. 573–625.

Davis, James W. Jr. and Randall Ripley. "The Bureau of the Budget and Executive Branch Agencies: Notes on Their Interaction," *Journal of Politics*, Vol. 29, 1967, pp. 749–769.

Davis, James W. Jr. and Kenneth Dolbeare. *Little Groups of Neighbors: The Selective Service System.* Chicago: Markham Publishing Co., 1968.

Davis, James W. Jr. *Politics, Programs, and Budgets: A Reader in Government Budgeting.* Englewood Cliffs: Prentice-Hall, 1969.

Downs, Anthony. *Inside Bureaucracy.* Boston: Little, Brown and Co., 1967.

Edelman, Murray. *The Symbolic Uses of Politics.* Urbana: University of Illinois Press, 1964.

Edelman, Murray. *Politics as Symbolic Action.* Chicago: Markham Publishing Co., 1971.

Etzioni, Amitai. *Modern Organization.* Englewood Cliffs: Prentice-Hall, 1964.

Fenno, Richard F. Jr. *The President's Cabinet.* Cambridge: Harvard University Press, 1959.

Fenno, Richard F. Jr. *The Power of the Purse: Appropriation Politics in Congress.* Boston: Little, Brown and Co., 1966.

Goffman, Erving. *The Presentation of Self in Everyday Life.* Garden City: Anchor Books, 1959.

Gross, Bertram M. *The Managing of Organizations.* New York: The Free Press, 1964.

Harris, Joseph P. *Congressional Control of Administration.* Washington, D.C.: The Brookings Institution, 1964.

Haveman, Robert and Julius Margolis, eds. *Public Expenditures and Policy Analysis.* Chicago: Markham Publishing Co., 1970.

Henderson, Thomas A. *Congressional Oversight of Executive Agencies: A Study of the House Committee on Government Operations.* Gainesville: University of Florida Press, 1970.

Hirschman, Albert O. *Exit, Voice and Loyalty.* Cambridge: Harvard University Press, 1970.

Hitch, Charles J. and Roland N. McKean. *The Economics of Defense in the Nuclear Age.* Cambridge: Harvard University Press, 1960.

Holtzman, Abraham. *Legislative Liaison: Executive Leadership in Congress.* Chicago: Rand McNally, 1970.

Homans, George C. *Social Behavior: Its Elementary Form.* New York: Harcourt, Brace and World, 1961.

Horn, Stephen. *Unused Power: The Work of the Senate Committee on Appropriations.* Washington, D.C.: The Brookings Institution, 1970.

James, Dorothy Buckton. *The Contemporary Presidency.* New York: Pegasus, 1969.

Katz, Daniel and Robert L. Kahn. *The Social Psychology of Organizations.* New York: John Wiley and Sons, 1966.

Kaufman, Herbert. "Emerging Conflicts in the Doctrine of Public Administration," *American Political Science Review,* Vol. 50, 1956, pp. 1057–1073.

Kaufman, Herbert. *The Forest Ranger.* Baltimore: The Johns Hopkins University Press, 1960.

Kaufman, Herbert. "Organization Theory and Political Theory," *American Political Science Review,* Vol. LVII, 1964, pp. 5–14.

Kaufman, Herbert. *Administrative Feedback: Monitoring Subordinates' Behavior.* Washington, D.C.: The Brookings Institution, 1973.

Kilpatrick, Franklin P., Milton C. Cummings, Jr. and M. Kent Jennings. *The Image of the Federal Service.* Washington, D.C.: The Brookings Institution, 1964.

Kirst, Michael. *Government Without Passing Laws.* Chapel Hill: University of North Carolina Press, 1969.

Krislov, Samuel. *The Negro in Federal Employment: The Quest for Equal Opportunity.* Minneapolis: University of Minnesota Press, 1967.

Landau, Martin. "Redundancy, Rationality, and the Problem of Duplication," *Public Administration Review,* Vol. 29, 1969, pp. 346–358.

Levine, Robert A. *Public Planning.* New York: Basic Books, 1972.

Lindblom, Charles E. "The Science of Muddling Through," *Public Administration Review,* Vol. 19, 1959, pp. 79–88.

Mann, Dean E. *The Assistant Secretaries.* Washington, D.C.: The Brookings Institution, 1965.

March, James G., ed. *Handbook of Organizations.* Chicago: Rand McNally, 1965.

March, James G. and Herbert Simon. *Organizations.* New York: John Wiley and Sons, 1958.

Martin, Roscoe C. *Public Administration and Democracy.* Syracuse: Syracuse University Press, 1965.

McConnell, Grant. *Private Power and American Democracy.* New York: Alfred A. Knopf, 1966.

Merewitz, Leonard and Stephen Sosnick. *The Budget's New Clothes.* Chicago: Markham Publishing Co., 1972.

Mosher, Frederick C. *Governmental Reorganization: Cases and Commentary.* Indianapolis: Bobbs-Merrill, 1967.

Neustadt, Richard E. *Presidential Power.* New York: John Wiley, 1964.

Niskanen, William A. *Bureaucracy and Representative Government.* Chicago: Aldine-Atherton, 1971.

Ott, David J. and Attiat F. Ott. *Federal Budget Policy.* Washington, D.C.: The Brookings Institution, 1969.

Presthus, Robert. *The Organizational Society*. New York: Alfred A. Knopf, 1962.

Rivlin, Alice. *Systematic Thinking and Social Action*. Washington, D.C.: The Brookings Institution, 1971.

Robinson, Marshall et al. *An Introduction to Economic Reasoning*. Garden City: Anchor Books, 1967.

Rossi, Peter H. and Walter Williams, eds. *Evaluating Social Programs*. New York: Seminar Press, 1972.

Rossiter, Clinton. *The American Presidency*. New York: Harcourt, Brace and World, 1960.

Rourke, Francis E. *Secrecy and Publicity*. Baltimore: The Johns Hopkins University Press, 1961.

Rourke, Francis E., ed. *Bureaucratic Power in National Politics*. Boston: Little, Brown and Co., 1972.

Sayre, Wallace S., ed. *The Federal Government Service*. Englewood Cliffs: Prentice-Hall, 1965.

Schein, Edgar H. *Organizational Psychology*. Englewood Cliffs: Prentice-Hall, 1965.

Schick, Allen. "The Budget Bureau That Was: Thoughts on the Rise, Decline, and Future of A Presidential Agency," *Law and Contemporary Problems*, Vol. XXV, 1970, pp. 519–539.

Schultze, Charles M. *et al*. *Setting National Priorities: The 1974 Budget*. Washington, D.C.: The Brookings Institution, 1973.

Seidman, Harold. *Politics, Position, and Power: The Dynamics of Federal Organization*. New York: Oxford University Press, 1970.

Shapiro, Martin. *The Supreme Court and Administrative Agencies*. New York: The Free Press, 1968.

Sheldon, Eleanor B. and Wilbert E. Moore, eds. *Indicators of Social Change: Concepts and Measurement*. New York: Russell Sage, 1968.

Stahl, O. Glenn. *Public Personnel Administration*. New York: Harper and Row, 1962.

Truman, David B. *The Governmental Process*. New York: Alfred A. Knopf, 1952.

Tullock, Gordon. *The Politics of Bureaucracy*. Washington, D.C.: Public Affairs Press, 1965.

Waldo, Dwight. *The Study of Public Administration*. New York: Doubleday, 1955.

Wallace, Robert Ash. *Congressional Control of Spending*. Detroit: Wayne State University Press, 1960.

Weiss, Carol H. *Evaluative Research*. Englewood Cliffs: Prentice-Hall, 1972.

Weiss, Carol H. *Evaluating Action Programs: Readings in Social Action and Education*. Boston: Allyn and Bacon, 1972.

Wholey, Joseph S. *et al. Federal Evaluation Policy.* Washington,
    D.C.: The Urban Institute, 1970.
Wildavksy, Aaron. *The Politics of the Budgetary Process.* Boston:
    Little, Brown and Co., 1964.
Wilensky, Harold L. *Organizational Intelligence.* New York: Basic
    Books, 1967.
Yarwood, Dean L. ed. *The National Administrative System.* New
    York: John Wiley and Sons, 1971.

INDEX